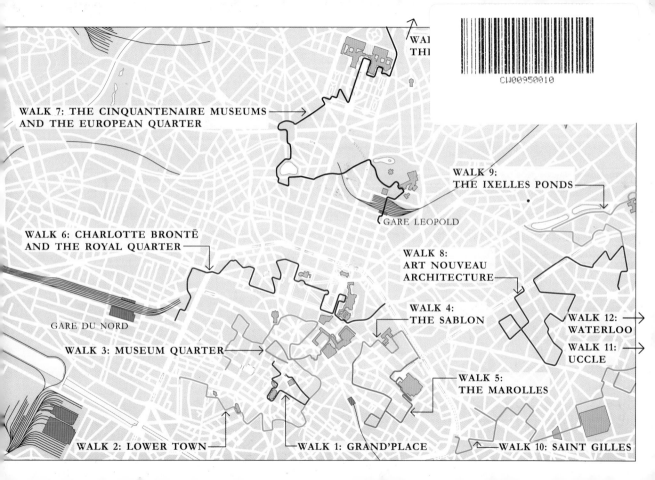

WALK...
THE...

WALK 7: THE CINQUANTENAIRE MUSEUMS
AND THE EUROPEAN QUARTER →

WALK 9:
THE IXELLES PONDS →

GARE LEOPOLD

WALK 6: CHARLOTTE BRONTË
AND THE ROYAL QUARTER →

WALK 8:
ART NOUVEAU
ARCHITECTURE →

GARE DU NORD

WALK 4:
THE SABLON

WALK 12:
WATERLOO →

WALK 11:
UCCLE →

WALK 3: MUSEUM QUARTER →

WALK 5:
THE MAROLLES

WALK 2: LOWER TOWN →

← WALK 1: GRAND'PLACE

← WALK 10: SAINT GILLES

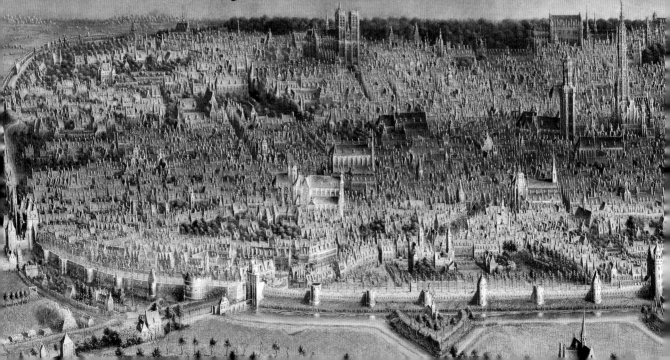

Derek Blyth BRUSSELS

FOR PLEASURE

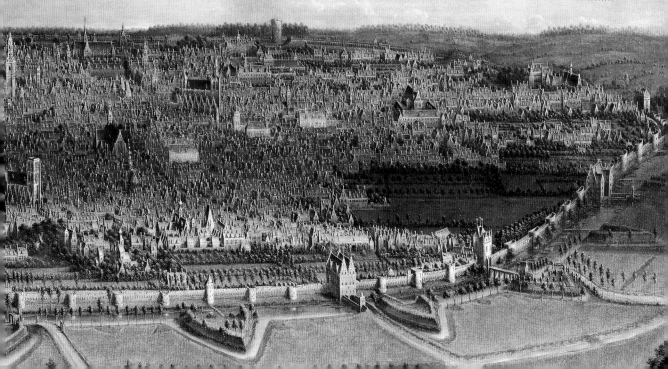

CONTENTS

Introduction

Years ago, when I first visited Brussels, I immediately fell for its curious, slightly dated charm. It was not very fashionable in those days to admire Brussels or indeed anything Belgian (apart perhaps from Bruges), so I gave no thought at the time to a guidebook on the city, and merely included it as one of the chapters in *Flemish Cities Explored*. Twenty years on, Brussels has become a much more popular destination, thanks partly to Eurostar but also aided by the city's recent efforts to improve a rather tarnished image. Many of the historic buildings have been restored, several of the great museums have been revamped, and neighbourhoods such as Place des Martyrs and Place Saint Géry have improved beyond recognition. Brussels now has high-speed trains to London and Paris, an impressive new European Parliament building,

its own Prime Minister and, somewhat more curiously, a Minister of Agriculture (with responsibility for the one farm that remains within the city limits). The city has introduced new trams, restored its 19th-century street lamps and rediscovered, after almost a century of neglect, an extraordinary Art Nouveau heritage. Yet, despite all these changes, Brussels still retains much of the charm that brought me here in the first place.

This book, like *Flemish Cities Explored*, was inspired by J. G. Links' *Venice for Pleasure*, which I found by chance in a Dutch secondhand bookshop. Links was erudite, humorous and unfailingly captivating, but perhaps he will be best remembered for suggesting that the first thing to do in Venice was to sit down and have some coffee. Let us, in his honour, do the same.

I. First impressions. We might begin in Le Cirio on the Rue de la Bourse, or perhaps the terrace of Mokafé in the Galeries Saint Hubert. These cafés retain the hint of faded grandeur that struck me when I first visited Brussels. It seemed a strangely romantic city, with yellow trams rattling along the boulevards, noisy brasseries offering enormous steaks drenched in butter, and elegant boulevard cafés where customers drank beers the colour of cough medicine. I enjoyed the odd, quirky details, such as the statues in the Parc de Bruxelles, the Surrealist art in the depths of the modern art gallery, and the forgotten medieval rooms of the Cinquantenaire Museum. I also took a liking to the people, especially the elderly ladies who tottered down to Cirio at eleven in the morning for a glass of half and half (white wine mixed with *Spumante*, for the record).

Some of the city's eccentric sights are well known, such as the statue of a little boy relieving himself in the street which has amused visitors since the middle ages, and the steel Atomium in the form of a giant iron molecule built for the

World Fair in 1958. Other quirky features take time to discover, like the Sudden Death Café, the Pigeon Monument, and the lugubrious Café Le Cercueil in Rue des Harengs where customers sit around polished wooden coffins. Sadly, Brussels has lost a few of its former delights, such as the Potato Museum, The Palace of Slippers and the Our Lady of the Snows quarter. At the time of writing, the Penguin Museum, which had recently taken to calling itself the *European* Penguin Museum, had also closed down, and the Museum of Underwear has recently gone quiet, but the Lift Museum in the Rue de la Source may yet satisfy a curiosity for eccentricity.

This modest and amiable city has grown over the last forty years into the capital of Europe, where issues affecting an entire continent are debated and decided. The people of Brussels have had to make painful adjustments to allow their city to pursue its European goal, and nobody can deny that some regrettable planning mistakes have been made, but anyone who takes the time to explore the city will find that much

of its unique character has survived.

The charm of Brussels often lies in the odd details that crop up unexpectedly on one's wanderings. Take the European Quarter, which looks at first glance like a grim office district, but slowly reveals appealing secrets such as the romantic Square Marie-Louise where Isherwood and Auden lived at No. 70, the extraordinary Musée Wiertz with its enormous paintings, and the curious temple in the Cinquantenaire Park which has remained locked for over a century because a sculpture inside was considered so shocking. Admittedly, the old centre can sometimes look quite run-down on a rainy day, yet on closer acquaintance it too turns out to have hidden charms, such as the grand cafés (we may be sitting in one), the 19th-century arcades and, in the dingiest street imaginable, the splendid cartoon museum.

For all its delights, Brussels is still seen as a boring city. It is certainly true that people here tend to dress soberly – though not if they buy their hats at Elvis Pompilio, a local hatter whose weird styles include a lime green felt top hat with floppy rabbit ears. Fans of Elvis, though, are something of an exception. Most people in Brussels lead quiet lives, retreating to suburban neighbourhoods that are deserted after dark. Even the great Brussels artists were rather retiring – Hergé drew Tintin cartoons in a bourgeois villa in Uccle, while Magritte, the great 20th-century subversive, lived much of his life in a suburban house in Jette.

It doesn't help that Brussels has become a bureaucratic city, where the governments of Brussels, Flanders and Belgium have their offices, together with the sprawling institutions of the European Union and Nato. The only time Brussels ever features in the foreign news is when European Union ministers meet to settle on a fishing quota or a new regulation to upset French farmers. Poor Brussels, for all its charms, doesn't stand much of a chance when newsreaders insist on announcing that *Brussels* has decided something, as if a clique of scheming Belgians was running Europe, whereas the decisions are in fact made by national governments and merely implemented by the 20,000 or so European civil servants based here.

As the capital of a country divided into a French-speaking south and a Dutch-speaking north, Brussels has been officially bilingual since 1932. Every administrative notice and street sign has to be in two languages, which is solved in the case of street names by a neat use of the fact that most French street names begin with *Rue* or *Avenue* whereas the Dutch street names tend to end with *straat* or *laan*. This permits addresses to be written as Rue Américainestraat or Avenue Molièrelaan.

Perhaps the language issue would not be a problem if the two sides lived in harmony, creating a city that was a hearty blend of Latin sophistication and Germanic order, but they are more like a bickering couple who fell out many years ago, and remain together merely for the sake of appearances. Each side has its ardent activists dedicated to promoting their language, sometimes through the furtive and strangely pedantic pursuit of blotting out road signs. Often, you will come upon a sign to, let us say, Mons/Bergen where *both* names have been obliterated, so that nobody has the faintest idea of the right direction to take. My favourite sign stands on the main road from Waterloo, where visitors were originally welcomed to Brussels in four languages. But Flemish activists have blotted out the word *Bienvenue*, French radicals have retaliated by obliterating *Welkom* and, finally, someone with a grudge against English speakers has blacked out *Welcome*. The result is that we are now greeted as we arrive in Brussels with a solitary German word, *Wilkommen*.

The sign on the Waterloo road may be discouraging, but it has to be said that visitors here are generally made to feel welcome. Waiters in restaurants can normally speak enough English to take an order for mussels and perhaps advise you not to drink the house wine, tram drivers are mostly helpful if you haven't a clue about the ticket system, and people in the streets can generally be counted on to point you in the direction of Grand'Place. Cinema usherettes may snap at you if you don't produce a fifty cent tip, and taxi drivers can be quite brusque if you fail to have the correct change, yet the general atmosphere remains fairly tolerant for a city of almost a million people.

So why are so many people disappointed by Brussels? Perhaps it is because it takes time to discover its hidden pleasures. Some people make the mistake of expecting Brussels to be a smaller version of Paris, while others are disappointed that it does not look more like medieval Bruges. The truth is that Brussels is a unique city with an astonishing range of cultures and styles that do not quite blend together. The pleasure of Brussels lies in seeking out the curious museums, flamboyant restaurants and stylish cafés that lie hidden in the most unexpected of places. It is almost a rule in Brussels to conceal treasures behind grubby façades. Perhaps this is a sensible precaution in a country that has been invaded so often. But it means that we never know quite what to expect. The shabby streets of the Marolles, doggedly resisting every attempt at gentrification, are dotted with wonderfully scruffy shops selling old tin toys, antique push-chairs and stuffed crocodiles. And then there are astonishing suburbs where we find endless examples of whimsical eclectic architecture.

We may shudder, sometimes, at the reckless driving, the funeral parlours tactlessly located opposite hospitals, and the general lack of civic pride. Yet we will probably find consolation in the gaudy baroque churches with trays of squat red candles flickering in the gloom, the little specialised shops, and the steaming Belgian frites served on market squares. Brussels can be baffling, annoying and chaotic, but never boring. A brief account of its history may help to explain how it came to be such a confusing place.

II. A brief history. The history of Brussels began with an early medieval settlement on the marshy banks of the River Senne. Its old name, Brucsella, derives from the medieval Dutch words *bruoc* (a marsh) and *sella* (a dwelling), revealing, incidentally, the fact that Brussels was originally a Dutch-speaking settlement. The 'dwelling on the marsh' became a more significant town in the 10th century after Charles, Duke of Lower Lorraine, built a castle

on one of the islands in the Senne. He later added a small chapel where the relics of St Gudule were kept. This encouraged administrators, craftsmen and traders to settle around the island. Slowly, as European trade grew, Brussels became the crossroads of two crucial land routes that connected Calais with Cologne, and Paris with Antwerp and the Dutch cities.

After Charles's son Otto died, the lands of Lower Lorraine passed to the Count of Leuven, Lambert I, who began work on a new castle on the Coudenberg hill to the south of the Senne valley, of which nothing now remains. His son, Lambert II, completed the castle and founded a church on the Molenberg hill. Dedicated to St Michael and St Gudule, this became the main church of Brussels. Even by this early date, we can see that Brussels was beginning to split into two different towns, with the shopkeepers and craftsmen concentrated in the Lower Town, and the nobles and administrators settling in the Upper Town.

By 1100 Brussels was surrounded by a fortified stone wall, fragments of which can still be found in unexpected locations – the Tour d'Anneessens next to a bowling alley on the Boulevard de l'Empereur; the Tour Noire looming over the Place Sainte Catherine and, most surprising of all, a rebuilt section of wall in the atrium of the SAS Hotel. By 1194, when Richard the Lionheart visited Brussels, the town could boast a cloth hall, several churches and a lepers' hospital.

The county of Leuven eventually passed to Henry I, Duke of Brabant, who granted Brussels a charter in 1229. The tumultuous 14th century began in Brussels with a rebellion in 1303 by the weavers and fullers. The rebels won an initial victory over the aristocracy, but were finally defeated by John II, Duke of Brabant, at the battle of Vilvoorde. Despite the troubles of the 14th century, Brussels continued to expand, so that a new wall had to be built, twice the length of the old one, with seven enormous gates. This sturdy fortification enclosed the city until the 19th century, when Brussels, following the lead of other continental cities, demolished its old walls to create a ring of boulevards. The

Porte de Hal was spared because it was being used as a jail at the time, but the rest was torn down in the name of progress.

After the Low Countries became part of Burgundy in the 15th century, the character of Brussels began to change. The cloth trade was in decline, and the city tried to revive the economy by persuading the Duke of Burgundy, as it would later persuade the European Union, to establish a court in Brussels. The bid was successful and Philip the Good moved the Burgundian court from Dijon to Brussels in 1430, though he also spent extended periods in the ducal palaces at Lille, Bruges and Arras (setting a precedent that would be repeated by the European Parliament in its endless travels between Brussels and Strasbourg). Many of the Burgundian nobles, unable to keep up several homes, chose to settle in Brussels, building magnificent gothic palaces on the Coudenberg. All traces of these have vanished apart from the solitary Hôtel Ravenstein, the Hôtel Lalaing-Hoogstraeten and the chapel of the Nassau palace.

It was during the Burgundian period, from 1384 to 1477, that Brussels began to develop into a bilingual city. The nobles and officials of the Burgundian court introduced French language and manners to the Upper Town, while the Lower Town, where the trade guilds were based, continued to speak Dutch. The language border between Latin and Germanic Europe thus ran more or less through the heart of Brussels, splitting the Germanic Lower Town from the Latin Upper Town. Even as late as the 17th century, the guild houses on Grand' Place bore Dutch names like De Vos (The Fox).

The economy of Brussels revived during the brief but spectacular period of Burgundian rule thanks to the ostentatious habits of the nobility, who ordered tapestries, paintings and enormous banquets. By 1402, the town was rich enough to begin work on a new town hall in the ornate Brabant gothic style (inspiring among others the 19th-century town halls of Munich and Vienna). The enormous wealth circulating in Brussels drew artists and sculptors here from all over the Low Countries, including Roger van der Weyden who painted numerous portraits of the nobility.

The Burgundian period came to a sudden end in 1482 in a wood near Bruges, when Mary of Burgundy died after a fall from her horse. The Low Countries passed to the Hapsburgs through Mary's husband, Maximilian of Austria. His son, Philip the Fair, married Joanna the Mad of Castile and Aragón, which meant that their son, Charles V, born in Ghent in 1500, inherited a vast empire that included the Low Countries, Spain, Naples, Sardinia, Sicily and, to round it off, the Holy Roman Empire. It was under Charles V, in 1521, that Brussels was declared the *Princelyke Hoofdstadt van 't Nederlandt*. Its role as Princely Capital of the Netherlands was boosted by François de Tassis, who began Europe's first postal service from his palace on the Sablon in 1516, providing a regular mail service throughout the Hapsburg Empire. The city also became an important inland port after the Willebroek canal was constructed under burgomaster Jean de Locquenghien. Something of Brussels' prosperity

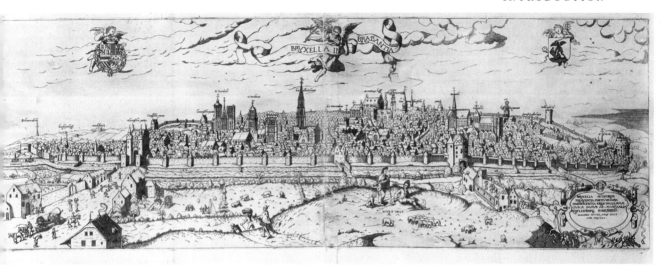

can be gauged from the print of 1579 above, which shows a hint of shipping to the left. The lower town is marked by the vast height of the town hall; the upper town has royal palaces and chapels crowding on the Coudenberg. Just 24 years before the print was made, the palace on Coudenberg, much expanded since the days of the Dukes of Brabant, provided the setting for Charles V's abdication in 1555. The sprawling empire passed to his son Philip II, an austere and devout Catholic, who set about ridding the Low Countries of Protestant heretics. After his retreat to the morbid Escorial in 1559, Philip left Margaret of Parma, his sister, to run the Low Countries. Urged on by her advisers Cardinal Granvelle and the Count of Berlaymont, Margaret dutifully continued her brother's policy of persecuting heretics. This led to the famous incident in Brussels in 1566 when several hundred nobles soured the wedding of her son Alexander Farnese with their protest demanding a more tolerant approach to religious dissenters. It was on this occasion that Count Berlaymont whispered in Margaret's ear that these nobles were nothing but *gueux* (beggars), a name the nobles later took in pride.

Disturbed by the growth of Protestantism, Philip sent the Duke of Alva to the Low Countries at the head of an army of ten thousand Spanish soldiers. Taking over as governor in 1568, he stationed troops in the main cities and set up the 'Council of Blood' to deal with heretics. Egmont and Hoorn, who were the mildest of radicals, were arrested that same year. Charged with 'religious crimes', they were beheaded on Grand'Place. Dozens of other nobles were imprisoned or executed in Brussels, but William of Orange managed to escape and raise an army, which succeeded in driving Alva's troops out of the city in 1577. Brussels remained in Dutch hands until 1585 when, after a long siege, it fell to the troops of Alexander Farnese, at whose wedding the troubles had begun almost two decades earlier. The Dutch army retreated north, abandoning Antwerp later that year, and settled in to defend the region beyond the great rivers.

A change of mood came over the city after Philip II, nearing death, entrusted the Spanish Netherlands to his daughter Isabella and her husband Albert of Austria. The couple, both bearing the title of Archduke, entered Brussels in triumph in 1599, riding two horses which, subsequently stuffed, are now preserved in the Army Museum. Initially fired with enthusiasm for Philip's cause, they laid siege to Ostend, which was still in the hands of the Dutch. Admiral Spinola finally captured the town in 1604, but that was as far as they reached. A twelve year truce was signed in 1609, allowing the

Archdukes to consolidate Catholicism in the southern Netherlands while the Dutch turned the northern Netherlands into a prosperous seaborne empire.

The view of Brussels by Jan Baptist Bonnecroy on pages 4-5 shows the city in about 1665 when it was enjoying the fruits of peace. The artist painted the view from a spot to the north of the city, not very far from where his predecessor had drawn the view we have just seen. They were both standing on a hill that has now been devoured by the industrial suburb of Molenbeek. Like the print, the painting, which hangs in the Musée des Beaux-Arts, shows the seven gates of the 14th-century wall, the churches clustered around the centre and the cathedral on the highest summit.

On 13 August 1695, seventy thousand French soldiers led by Marshal de Villeroi took up position on the hill where our artists had stood thirty and a hundred years earlier. Villeroi had been sent by Louis XIV to attack Brussels following an unsuccessful attempt to break the siege of Namur (which had left the French garri-son trapped there). Aiming his eighteen heavy cannons and thirty-three mortars at the spire of the town hall, Villeroi ordered a bombardment of the city that lasted three days. Some three thousand mortars and more than one thousand red-hot shot fell on the undefended city, setting fire to most of the churches and houses that had been lovingly painted by Bonnecroy. The results can be seen overleaf, in a watercolour by Augustin Coppens, and in the prints on pages 58 and 69. Coppens picked his way over the ruins shortly after the fires were extinguished; here he is looking from the Marché aux Herbes towards the town hall tower; unflatteringly for the reputation of the French artillery, this was the one building that stayed standing throughout the bombardment. A century later, Napoleon judged the attack by his fellow Frenchmen to have been 'as barbaric as it was pointless'.

The cities of the Spanish Netherlands immediately came to the aid of the devastated capital. Bakers from Mechelen sent bread, street pavers flocked to the city to lay down new cobblestones and wealthy Antwerp merchants

helped to finance the reconstruction. Most of the city was rebuilt within a few years, as we know from the year stones on the guild houses on Grand'Place, which are mostly carved with dates ranging from 1696 to 1699. The exuberance of these buildings is conveyed by the drawings overleaf and on page 60, by F. J. De Rons, of the east and north sides of the square. Yet not all the damage could be repaired; some of the gothic spires were replaced by the then fashionable baroque bell towers, such as the one we will see on the Eglise Notre-Dame de la Chapelle.

The period of Spanish rule finally ended when Charles II, the sickly King of Spain who gave his name to the Roi d'Espagne café on Grand'Place, died in 1700 without an heir. The War of Spanish Succession broke out two years later after France's claim to the Spanish Netherlands was opposed by England and Holland. The Duke of Marlborough attacked from the south, taking most of the southern towns, and finally forced the French to renounce their claim under the Treaty of Utrecht of 1713. The duke

was given Blenheim Palace (named after a victory on the Danube) as a reward for victory, and the Catholic Netherlands passed back to the Austrian Hapsburgs. But the new governor, Charles VI, soon became unpopular with the guilds of Brussels when he tried to abolish privileges that went back to the middle ages. A rebellion broke out in 1719, led by Frans Anneessens, master of the guild of chair-makers. He was imprisoned in a medieval tower that now bears his name and was later – like Egmont and Hoorn – beheaded on Grand'Place.

A new era of content began in 1744 when Charles, Duke of Lorraine, was appointed governor by his sister-in-law, the Empress Maria Theresa. He embarked on an ambitious plan to turn Brussels into a Vienna of the north, which has left the city with some splendid neoclassical public spaces, such as the Place des Martyrs in the Lower Town, the Place Royale on the site of the old ducal palace, and the Parc de Bruxelles on part of the ducal hunting estate.

The Austrian interlude ended in 1793 when Belgium was annexed by France. Many people

al de huijsen van a
den hoeck van de
heerinck straet, tot
aen den hoeck van
keijserstraedt, op
groote meet,

16 97

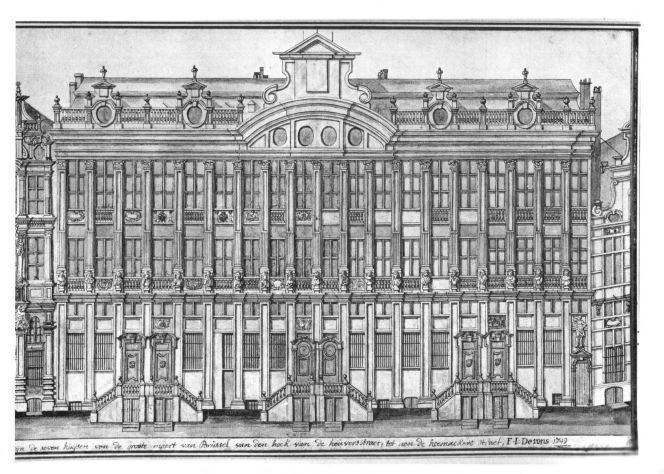

zijn De seven huijsen van de groote maert van Brüssel, aan den hoeck van de heüvers straet, tot aen de hoemaeckers straet, F. I. De vons 1749

welcomed the French Republicans as liberators; a 'Liberty Tree' was planted on Place Royale on the site of the statue of Charles of Lorraine. But others saw it as a disaster, particularly after the French began to tear down the great abbeys and cathedrals. The French were driven out of Brussels in 1814, but Napoleon was back again the following year. He came within twelve miles of the city walls before being finally defeated by the combined forces of Wellington and Blücher at Waterloo. Under the terms of the treaties of Vienna and London, the former Austrian Netherlands were joined to the Dutch Republic to form the Kingdom of the Netherlands under King William I.

The union might have looked good on paper, since it effectively reunited the medieval Low Countries, but the two regions had been going their separate ways since 1568. The north had become a Dutch-speaking Calvinist country, whereas the south was mainly French-speaking and strongly Catholic. It might have seemed inevitable that the two would one day split, but who could have predicted that the rift would be sparked off by an opera? The uprising began in 1830 during a performance of Auber's *La Muette de Portici* in the Monnaie theatre. As the leading singers began to sing a duet titled *Amour sacré de la Patrie*, several members of the audience rose to their feet and rushed out into the streets declaring that the revolution had begun. It was a curious start to 'that little Biedermeier slapstick war,' as the Dutch writer Jeroen Brouwers described the Belgian revolution.

The following year, the London Conference recognised Belgium as an independent state and, after much searching around the aristocratic families of Europe, a suitable king was found among the Saxe-Coburg family of Germany. The chosen monarch was Prince Léopold, an uncle of Queen Victoria, who had already turned down the throne of Greece in 1830. Belgium was clearly more to his taste, and he settled into his new palace early in 1831. The Dutch were still stubbornly holding on to Antwerp at this stage, but they were eventually ousted by the French navy. Even then, William I refused to recognise Belgium until 1839 when the Treaty of London enshrining Belgian independence was signed by Britain, France, Russia, Austria and Prussia.

The Belgian constitution was one of the most progressive in the world, guaranteeing freedom of speech and limiting the powers of the monarch. Léopold I's Belgium became a cultured, prosperous country largely modelled on the Britain of his niece. When the first railway line on mainland Europe was opened between Brussels and Mechelen in 1835, the British engineer George Stephenson, inventor of the steam locomotive, was one of the invited guests.

Léopold's Brussels strongly appealed to the British, who flocked to the city after Waterloo. A character in Thackeray's *Vanity Fair* praises Brussels as 'one of the gayest and most brilliant little capitals in Europe', though Charlotte Brontë was of a rather different opinion. She and Emily had been sent in 1842 to one of the *pensionnats* in the city to be taught French and good manners. Charlotte subsequently based two novels on her miserable time in Brussels,

providing an invaluable insight into the city she tellingly called 'Villette' – the small town.

Though Charlotte disguised Belgium in her novel as the kingdom of Labassecour (the farm yard), Léopold I had grand ideas of colonial expansion at the time, as we can see on an astonishing map in the Dynastic Museum which marks the colonies that Belgium hoped to acquire by force or treaty. Léopold never lived to see his planned colonies in America and Australia, but Léopold II pursued his father's dream with ruthless determination and ended up with a private African colony that was eighty times the size of Belgium.

Before becoming King, the young Léopold, then Duke of Brabant, seems to have made an unpromising impression, judging from Madame de Metternich's waspish description of his marriage to Maria-Henrietta of Austria as the union of 'a stable boy and a nun, and by nun I mean the Duke of Brabant'. The print overleaf shows the young Duke of Brabant in 1848, looking relaxed for an aristocrat in the year of revolutions. He is posing with his brother

Philippe and his sister Charlotte, who later became Empress of Mexico.

By the time Léopold II was crowned in 1865, he had shaken off any resemblance to a nun. Obsessed with the notion of a Belgian colony, he established an International Association of the Congo in 1878. The following year he employed the Welsh journalist Henry Morton Stanley, famous for finding David Livingstone, to set up trading posts deep in the heart of central Africa. The Congo Free State was recognised by the Berlin Conference of 1884 and Léopold II was accepted as its sovereign the following year.

Léopold had the good fortune to acquire large rubber plantations in the Congo at roughly the same time that John Dunlop patented the pneumatic tyre for bicycles. The sharp increase in demand for rubber in the 1890's brought Léopold enormous private wealth, much of which he used to rebuild Brussels and Ostend on a heroic scale. The great picture galleries and museums of Brussels, the broad boulevards and arcades, the Palais de Justice and the Parc du

Cinquantenaire, were all built during his 44-year-long reign, largely with wealth accumulated from the Congo. But there was a price to be paid for this grandeur. Countless atrocities were perpetrated in the search for rubber and ivory, though perhaps not on the scale that Léopold's critics (such as the caricaturist here) suggested. He was clearly upset when the cruelty came to light. 'If there are abuses in the Congo, we must stop them,' he wrote to Edmond van Eetvelde. 'I will not be splattered with blood.'

Most of Léopold's grand projects benefited the Upper Town, the aristocratic French quarter of the city, while the medieval Lower Town was largely sacrificed in pursuit of Léopold's dream of creating a city of Parisian boulevards. Victor Hugo, for one, was not impressed. Returning to Brussels after a long absence, he was saddened by the destruction of old neighbourhoods and picturesque corners he had known. Hugo particularly lamented the conversion of local cafés into American bars, and the disappearance of dogcarts, such as the one we see on page 102. The locals, too, were upset by

Léopold's grand plans. When an entire district of the Marolles was levelled to build the Palais de Justice, Léopold's architect Joseph Poelaert was denounced as a 'skieven architek' (dirty

35

architect). It seems quite likely that the old Flemish quarters of Brussels would have vanished altogether during Léopold's reign had not Burgomaster Charles Buls campaigned strenuously for their preservation.

Not all the French in Brussels were as bitter as Hugo. Brussels had become an attractive refuge for exiled French writers, who could find a consoling hint of Paris in the boulevards, cafés and glass-roofed arcades. Many French writers in Brussels were political refugees from Napoleon III, including Hugo himself and the proto-communist Pierre Joseph Proud'hon ('all property is theft'). They were carrying on a tradition that had been initiated by the revolutionaries exiled after 1815 by the Bourbon restoration, the most famous being the painter Jacques-Louis David, who died in Brussels, and whose famous painting of Marat murdered in his bath, though painted in Paris, now hangs in the Musée des Beaux-Arts. Others fled here from France for less honourable reasons, such as Alexandre Dumas, who simply used Brussels as a convenient bolt hole from his creditors, and Charles Baudelaire, who was looking for a publisher willing to print his scandalous poems. The poets Rimbaud and Verlaine came to Brussels on a bohemian urge, but argued constantly until the former ended up in hospital with a bullet wound and the latter was sent to prison in Mons for two years.

By the end of the 19th century, Léopold had succeeded in transforming Brussels into one of the most scintillating capitals in Europe. It was here, in 1893, that the Art Nouveau architectural style was launched by Paul Hankar and Victor Horta. Over the next ten years, daring new buildings using iron and glass were built for progressive socialist patrons in the old centre and the southern suburbs of Ixelles, Saint Gilles and Etterbeek. (The photograph opposite shows a typical example, the rooftop decoration of the Old England department store.) Revenue from the Congo helped to fund some of the more extravagant constructions, private as well as public, such as the Van Eetvelde mansion, built for the Congo administrator mentioned above. The Congo also supplied much of the

exotic wood used in staircases and furniture, and may even have been the inspiration behind some of Art Nouveau's more exotic motifs. Those who dubbed the new architecture 'the Congo style' obviously saw a connection.

The buoyant mood of the late 19th century led to a series of exhibitions in Brussels which drew thousands of visitors to the capital. The first, in 1880, was held to mark the fiftieth anniversary of Belgian independence. Two enormous exhibition halls of iron and glass were put up in the Parc du Cinquantenaire, one of which is now occupied by the Army Museum and the other by the Museum of Decorative Arts. Another exhibition was organised in 1897, again in the Cinquantenaire Park, this time to promote the products of the Congo. Léopold took the opportunity to build a splendid Africa Museum in the village of Tervuren. He also funded the construction of the Avenue de Tervuren to take visitors out to his museum by tram. A third Exhibition, the Universal, was held in 1910 on a site in the suburb of Ixelles where the university now stands. Like its

predecessors, this exhibition featured a reconstructed old Belgian town which, as we can see
from the old postcard here, offered visitors the
comforting illusion of strolling through a corner
of Bruges. Though the exhibition was devoted
to industrial progress, the visitors could not
resist the old-fashioned houses and rustic restaurants in the Old Belgium quarter.

Brussels' golden age came to a sad and sudden
end on 4 August, 1914, when the German army
crossed into Belgium, violating the neutrality
guaranteed by the treaty of 1839. The German
generals were happy to dismiss the treaty, though
signed by Prussia, as a mere 'scrap of paper'.
Britain saw matters differently, and rushed to the
defence of 'plucky little Belgium'. By 20 August,
some 320,000 German soldiers had entered
Brussels. The German flag was hoisted over
the town hall and the city's clocks were adjusted
to Berlin time; 'francs-tireurs', or snipers,
resisted, to the fury of the Germans who
denounced their actions as being entirely
contrary to the laws of war, and carried out
furious reprisals. Meanwhile, the remnants of

the Belgian army retreated to a line behind
the IJzer canal, where they were led by King
Albert I, seen here poring over a map in a room
that seems to have a false painted background.

Edith Cavell, a prim British nurse, was
running three hospitals in Brussels when the
Germans marched into the city. She had moved
to Brussels in 1906, originally, like Charlotte
Brontë, to learn French, but later staying on to
work as a nurse. With typical Edwardian zeal,
she set about improving the antiquated Brussels

hospitals, earning the admiration of the Belgian Queen Elisabeth. After war broke out, she became involved in an underground operation that helped British soldiers stranded behind the German lines to escape to the neutral Netherlands. The network was eventually exposed by a German spy and Cavell, despite protests from Britain and America, was shot at dawn on 12 October, 1915. The firing range where she was executed became a popular tourist sight immediately after the war, though few people ever find their way to it these days.

Brussels rapidly recovered its cosmopolitan allure in the 1920's, when new apartment blocks in Art Deco style were built on the grand avenues. The most impressive was the Résidence Palace at Rue de la Loi 155, a luxury apartment complex built in 1926, complete with a restaurant, swimming pool and theatre. Once again, the mood of optimism was expressed in a World Exhibition, this one held in 1935 on the Heysel plateau to the north of the city. A strange building known as the Palace of the Catholic Life was constructed which, judging from the old postcard opposite, attracted long queues of visitors. The building has vanished, but the magnificent exhibition halls built in 1935 are still standing. Decorated with massive stone statues representing industrial workers, these Art Deco masterpieces are now used for major trade fairs.

The city authorities tried in 1958 to revitalise the economy by organising yet another exhibition on the same site as in 1935. They created a network of fast highways that circled the old town and ran down the broad boulevards, destroying at a stroke the leafy ambience of Avenue Louise and the quiet trails through the Bois de la Cambre. The exhibition site itself was dominated by the Atomium, a bizarre symbol of modernity modelled on the nine atoms of an iron molecule magnified several billion times. Yet alongside this uncompromising symbol of progress, they built yet another nostalgic mock Belgian town, suggesting a lingering reluctance to embrace the brave new world of highways and atomic power.

It turned out that Brussels needed more than an exhibition to revive its ailing economy. The

city finally found the solution to its woes in the European Community, an organisation set up in 1957 by the fusion of the European Economic Community, the European Coal and Steel Community and the European Atomic Energy Community. The bureaucracy was persuaded to put down its roots in Brussels, which gradually became seen as the capital of Europe. The presence of the EC, now the European Union, has turned Brussels into one of the world's most important political capitals, attracting thousands of journalists, translators, lobbyists and political groups. The new Europeans who have settled in Brussels have added greatly to its cosmopolitan flavour, bringing restaurants, bookshops, specialised food shops and cultural institutes.

Perhaps this European period will turn out to be a passing phase. It sometimes seems as if the locals consider the Europeans as simply another hostile occupying force, lording it over the Lower Town from their palaces in the Upper Town. Yet even if the Europeans quit Brussels one day, they will leave behind traces of their presence, like the Austrians and the Spanish before them, adding to the patchwork of cultures that makes Brussels quite unlike anywhere else.

III. The buildings of Brussels. Any hope of finding a gothic quarter, like that of Bruges or Ghent, vanishes as soon as we begin to explore the old city. An odd fragment of the first city wall may turn up unexpectedly, but most of the old city has disappeared. All that remains are a few scattered landmarks built in the flamboyant 15th-century Brabant gothic style, such as the town hall on Grand'Place, the twin-towered cathedral on the escarpment to the south, and the Eglise de la Chapelle where Bruegel is buried.

One of the joys of Brussels is that there are no two buildings the same. Even when the same architect builds on adjoining plots, the two houses will be quite different. This architectural individualism sometimes leads to urban chaos, with skyscrapers towering above 19th-century houses and medieval towers stranded in the middle of wasteland. The past forty years have seen some spectacular planning blunders in Brussels, particularly in the 1960's and 1970's when the city authorities were spellbound by the allure of the motor car and the office block. The presence of old buildings left to rot and gap sites surrounded by billboards has led to the term *Bruxellisation* entering the French language as a label for chronic urban blight. Much of the blame rests with the shabby politics and unseemly greed of those decades, though as the saga of the Palais de Justice shows, Brussels has a long tradition of wholesale demolition.

The destruction of Brussels in fact began in 1695, when most of the medieval town was reduced to smouldering ruins by the French artillery. The city was rapidly rebuilt in an Italian-Flemish baroque style, giving us the extraordinary guild houses on Grand'Place with their voluptuous female figures, gilt swags and pediments cluttered with statues. This elaborate baroque style spread to the gothic churches, which were often embellished with helmet-shaped towers or curious new portals.

The Upper Town, where the aristocracy lived, survived the 1695 bombardment, leaving the southern heights bristling with gothic turrets and gables. This district eventually, however, lost its medieval character in the 1760's when Charles of Lorraine demolished the former Palais de Nassau to build a neoclassical palace on the site. Charles then turned his attention to the gutted ruins of the ducal palace, which had been ravaged by fire in 1731 and then been left sprouting weeds for decades. The French architects Barnabé Guimard and Nicolas Barré drew up a plan to create a neoclassical square on the cleared site. This square, which has survived intact, was modelled on Place Royale (now called Place Stanislas) in Nancy, which had been built in 1752 by Stanislas Leczinski, the former King of Poland, as a grand setting for a statue of Louis XV. Charles of Lorraine, being rather more self-possessed, had a statue of himself placed in the centre of the Brussels square. The architectural details of Place Royale were copied almost exactly from the square in Nancy, with eight pavilions linked by arches to

43

create a harmonious neoclassical ensemble. The strict obedience to classical rules is all the more astonishing when we discover that the project was financed not by one absolute ruler but a loose consortium that included several abbeys, a hotel owner and the imperial lottery.

The creation of the Belgian state in 1830 led to a prolonged period of construction in Brussels under the Léopolds. The architect Cluysenaar looked to Paris when he built the enormous glass-roofed Galeries Saint Hubert in 1847, which was not only the first arcade in Brussels but the first project that involved the total destruction of a neighbourhood. Lengthy local protests cut no ice, and the prim neoclassical arcade became one of the great attractions of Brussels. Such was its success that several other arcades were built in the Lower Town, including the Galerie Bortier and the Passage du Nord.

Yet it was Léopold II whose grand plans changed the character of Brussels for ever. Having declared his ambition 'to make Belgium greater, stronger and more beautiful', the King embarked on a series of projects to embellish the capital, culminating in the colossal dimensions of Joseph Poelaert's Palais de Justice, the largest building constructed on the Continent in the 19th century. Other Léopoldian achievements include, as we have seen, the magnificent sweep of the Cinquantenaire Museums, completed by Gédéon Bordiau in 1880, and Charles Girault's Africa Museum in Tervuren, which was modelled on the Petit Palais he had built for the 1900 Paris Exhibition. The Paris Exhibition was also the inspiration for Léopold's Japanese Pagoda and Chinese Pavilion in the northern suburb of Laeken.

The southern suburbs of Ixelles, Saint Gilles and Etterbeek were largely created during the late 19th century, when Léopold's Congo was generating unprecedented wealth. Most of the houses dating from this period are narrow and tall, with three rooms in a row on each floor. The façades of the 1880's were built in robust eclectic styles, with examples of Bruges gothic, Flemish renaissance, French neoclassicism, and the occasional Venetian *palazzo* adding to the merry confusion. The most flamboyant are to be found in the streets bordering parks such as Josaphat in Schaerbeek and Duden in Forest, or overlooking the Ixelles ponds near Avenue Louise. Exploring these districts, we will find an astonishing wealth of architectural detail, including elaborate iron bell-pulls that probably no longer work, post boxes like this one that maybe never did, romantic turrets and fanciful balconies. We may also observe the slightly absurd sight of cold-water taps attached to the outside of the houses, originally designed to allow servants to slosh down the streets.

The interiors are often equally splendid, as we sometimes discover when we visit restaurants in these neighbourhoods. The fashion of the time was for high stucco ceilings, massive marble fireplaces and elaborate wood and glass partitions between the rooms. These stuffy rooms can be seen in some of the early paintings of Fernand Khnopff, such as his *Listening to Schumann*, (reproduced on p. 153), painted in 1883 in a town house in the Léopold Quarter.

A new style began to appear in these eclectic streets in 1893, when Victor Horta built the

Hôtel Tassel in Rue Paul-Emile Janson and Paul Hankar designed a house for himself in Rue Defacqz. These architects introduced a flamboyant style of bourgeois architecture involving the use of iron and glass. This was not altogether new, since iron and glass had been employed for decades in railway stations, exhibition halls and greenhouses. But they had never before featured in the design of private homes. For want of a better word, critics simply called it the modern style, or the Congo Style (after the Congo Exhibition when Hankar and other architects designed several interiors). The name Art Nouveau was coined after a shop with that name opened in Paris selling decorative art in the new style.

On our walks in Brussels, we will sometimes spot Art Nouveau buildings with the architect's name and date of completion chiselled into the masonry. Some architects signed their names in sober Roman capitals, but other adopted a flourishing calligraphy, like Ernest Blérot's signature on page 258. One of the pleasures of Brussels is to hunt out these elusive architect's signatures, which are sometimes buried by clematis or hidden under a tangle of electrical wiring. These signed buildings allow us to study the evolution of an architect's style while wandering through the streets where he worked. We can, for example, follow Ernest Delune's development during a brief stroll through the streets off Avenue Louise, beginning on the Chaussée de Vleurgat, where he signed two ornate neo-renaissance houses at Nos. 110 and 112. We can then look at Rue du Lac 52 and 54, built in 1897 in a fanciful blend of gothic and renaissance, and finally compare the row at Rue de la Vallée 44 to 54 where the occasional hint of the Vienna Secession has crept into Delune's repertoire.

These signed buildings demonstrate that Brussels architects were versatile in a range of styles. They could design a house based on the rules of neoclassical architecture, or concoct a fanciful neo-gothic mansion bristling with gargoyles and pinacles if that was their client's wish. By the middle of the 1890's, many traditional architects had begun to copy Art Nouveau motifs on house façades, but they dropped that style in favour of the Vienna Secession by the turn of the century. Even Horta (seen oppposite in about 1905) abandoned Art Nouveau in the 1920's to take up the new Art Deco style. He sold his astonishing Art Nouveau house in 1918 and eventually moved into a modern apartment on Avenue Louise.

The First World War brought an abrupt end to the golden age of Brussels architecture, for there was neither money nor skilled craftsmen to build such grandeur in the 1920's. In any case, Belgians had by then taken up the austere Modernist style that was being developed in France and the Netherlands. The wealthy families began to live in sophisticated apartments on the broad boulevards of the 19th-century ring, leaving their old *maisons de maître* to be divided into apartments or left to rot.

Apart from the Atomium, designed by an engineer and surely one of the most eccentric buildings ever constructed in Europe, little of interest was built between the late 1950's and 1980's, but the new European Parliament building on the edge of the Léopold Park is a

promising example of good modern architecture. The great glass and steel arch recalls Cluysenaar's glass-roofed arcades and Bordiau's exhibition halls, but it also harmonises with the quaint station clock on the front of the former Gare Léopold.

We are now seeing Brussels enter a more thoughtful period, when the city authorities, finally stung by constant criticism, have begun to repair the damage done over the past four decades. The government of the Brussels Region is now dedicated to protecting the urban environment from further destruction. For the first time since the days of Charles Buls, the city is taking a certain pride in its heritage. We find encouraging signs everywhere, such as the restoration of the Place des Martyrs, the rebuilding of the Saint Géry quarter and the conversion of the Old England department store into a museum of musical instruments. We will also find, despite our initial despair, that large areas of Brussels have been preserved intact, particularly in the 19th-century suburbs of Ixelles and Saint Gilles. These districts, south of the old town, boast an astonishing diversity of architectural styles ranging from the robust neo-baroque favoured by traditional Catholics to the exuberant Art Nouveau adopted by the fin-de-siècle idealists. It is in these neighbourhoods that we find some of the most extraordinary architecture. But let us begin with the baroque guild houses on Grand'Place.

WALK I

Grand'Place and its neighbourhood
FROM GRAND'PLACE TO THE ILOT SACRÉ

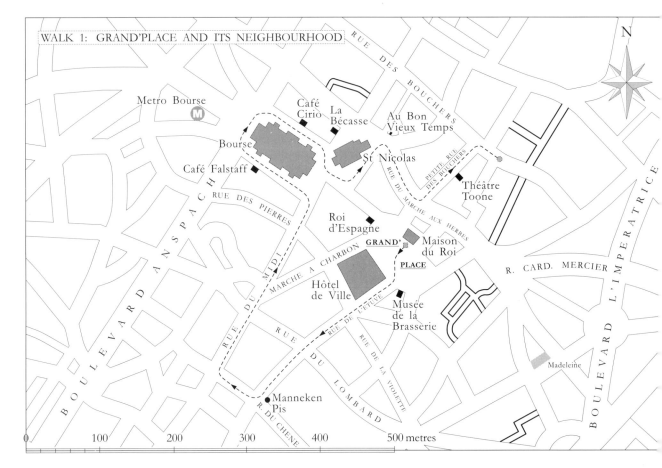

WALK 1: GRAND'PLACE AND ITS NEIGHBOURHOOD

N

RUE DES BOUCHERS

Metro Bourse
M

Café Cirio

La Bécasse

Au Bon Vieux Temps

Bourse

Café Falstaff

St Nicolas

PETITE RUE DES BOUCHERS

RUE DU MARCHÉ AUX HERBES

Théâtre Toone

RUE DES PIERRES

Roi d'Espagne

RUE DU MIDI

MARCHE A CHARBON

GRAND'
PLACE

Maison du Roi

R. CARD. MERCIER

BOULEVARD L'IMPERATRICE

Hôtel de Ville

RUE DE L'ÉTUVE

RUE

Musée de la Brasserie

BOULEVARD ANSPACH

RUE DE LA VIOLETTE

Madeleine

BOULEVARD

Manneken Pis

R. DU CHENE

RUE DU LOMBARD

0   100   200   300   400   500 metres

Grand'Place and its neighbourhood

On our first walk we explore the Grand'Place or Grote Markt, the old market square of Brussels, where, according to John Motley, 'so many tragedies, so many scenes of violence have been played out'. The 19th-century American historian of the Dutch Revolt was presumably thinking of the execution of Counts Egmont and Hoorn in 1568, the bombardment of 1695 and perhaps the fighting with Dutch troops in 1830. Yet Grand'Place has also provided the setting for countless pageants, concerts and markets. It is a scintillating square, changing its character at different hours and in different seasons. It looks particularly attractive at twilight on a crisp winter's evening, when the setting sun glints on gilded details, and cafés tempt us inside with their blazing fires, gleaming brass fittings and rich red *kriek* beers.

We are not going to do much on this walk apart from stroll around the square, drink some coffee and visit one museum. We should never try to rush things in Brussels, for we are likely to miss a great deal if we do; not least, on this occasion, the wonderful theatrical effect of entering Grand'Place. If we enter by the Rue Chair et Pain, next to the tourist office at Rue Marché aux Herbes 61, we get a thrilling view of the medieval spire of the town hall framed by the tall buildings on the Rue Chair et Pain. If we come by the Rue au Beurre instead, we have an intriguing glimpse of the statues on the roof of the Maison du Roi.

Once we are in the square, the best thing to do is to sit down in one of the cafés to read about the buildings around us. I am particularly fond of La Brouette at No. 3, with its browned Brussels posters and elegant lamps. The ideal place to choose, if we can, is one of the small tables next to the window, where we can watch the flower sellers from rural Flanders setting out boxes of marigolds and geraniums. As an alternative, we might choose La Chaloupe d'Or at Nos. 24-25, sitting again at a window to admire the row of houses pictured on page 63. Another possibility is the Roi d'Espagne, a convivial and cluttered café on three floors, with a blazing fire, solid wooden tables and a moth-eaten stuffed horse. This café is a favourite with Brussels students and, indeed, almost everyone. The best tables are on the mezzanine level, where we can enjoy a splendid view of Grand'Place through the tiny barred windows.

Or we might want to investigate the intriguing modern interior of the Jacqmotte Coffee House at No. 37. This café is run by a descendant of Henri Jacqmotte, who founded a coffee roasting firm in the Marolles in 1828. The deep, narrow interior is furnished with a tangle of bent metal tubes and overhead spotlights. We can perch at a tiny round aluminium table downstairs, or settle into a plump armchair on the first floor. The menu lists a tempting selection of thirty coffees, inviting us to savour the 'woody scent' of a Brazil Sul de Minas, the 'spicy aroma of fresh tobacco' found in the Guatemala Antigua, or the 'hint of flowers' in the Ethiopia Sidamo.

I. Grand'Place. We are now on the oldest market square in Brussels, founded in the 14th century soon after the city was granted a charter. If we are here on a Sunday morning, when the weekly bird market is held, we will find the square filled with the unexpected sounds of cocks crowing and geese cackling. Locals and tourists wander around the cages hoping perhaps to pick up a green parrot or even a pet swan. The man to look out for deals in Harz canaries, which are (or so he claims) the only birds in the world that can sing without opening their beaks. These maestros, bright yellow in colour, are

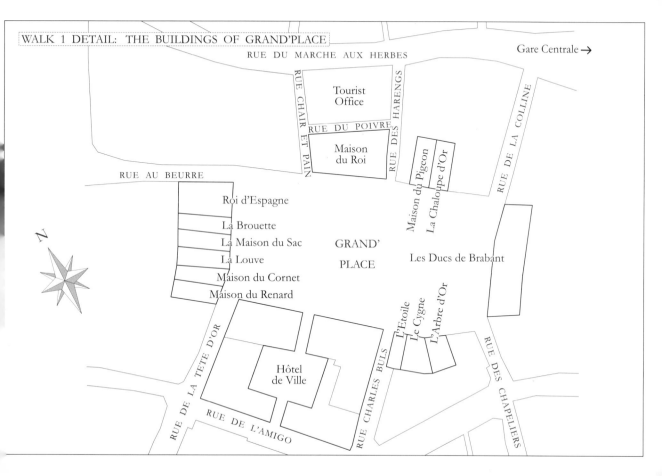

WALK 1 DETAIL: THE BUILDINGS OF GRAND'PLACE

Gare Centrale →

RUE DU MARCHE AUX HERBES

RUE CHAIR ET PAIN

RUE DES HARENGS

RUE DE LA COLLINE

Tourist Office

RUE DU POIVRE

Maison du Roi

Maison du Pigeon

La Chaloupe d'Or

RUE AU BEURRE

Roi d'Espagne

La Brouette

La Maison du Sac

La Louve

Maison du Cornet

Maison du Renard

GRAND'

PLACE

Les Ducs de Brabant

N

RUE DE LA TETE D'OR

L'Etoile

Le Cygne

L'Arbre d'Or

RUE DES CHAPELIERS

Hôtel de Ville

RUE CHARLES BULS

RUE DE L'AMIGO

descended from the 17th-century singing canaries of Nuremberg. Each bird is sold complete with a detailed report card listing its accomplishments in nine different skills, such as whistling, trilling, warbling and general deportment. The higher the bird scores, the more it is worth. A virtuoso warbler might cost as much as 25 euros, which would buy you an entire box of quails, though you do not get much of a song out of a quail.

Grand'Place is often the setting for concerts and parades. One day the local police will be seen marching in formation across the cobblestones; another time we might come upon a classical concert being performed under floodlights. The most outstanding event is the annual Ommegang procession which began as a religious ceremony in the 14th century, staged to celebrate the story of Béatrice Soetkens, the poor daughter of a draper who heard a voice telling her to go to Antwerp and bring a miraculous statue of the Virgin to the church of Notre-Dame du Sablon in Brussels. By the 16th century, the procession had become little more than a convenient excuse for the local aristocrats to parade in their finery.

The most spectacular Ommegang was staged in 1549 to entertain Charles V and his morose son Philip. Sixty-six years later, Philip's daughter Isabella impressed the crowds at the Ommegang of 1615 by shooting a wooden parrot from the spire of the Sablon church with a crossbow. To ensure that this achievement was properly remembered, Isabella commissioned the court painter Denijs van Alsloot to produce a series of six paintings of the Ommegang. We will have to wait until we visit the Musées des Beaux-Arts to see the one of Isabella shooting down the wooden bird (reproduced on page 145), but we will see the Procession of the Guilds (reproduced opposite and on pages 12-13) when we visit the Musée Communale in about half an hour. The six paintings originally hung in Tervuren Castle, but were moved to the Escorial in Madrid in the 1630's.

The Ommegang was revived in 1930 by the Royal Society of Archers of Saint George. The procession we see today is not the one depicted by van Alsloot, but the 1549 Ommegang staged for Charles V. A local historian sifted through old documents, paintings of the Ommegang and even a set of engravings published by Plantin in Antwerp to get the details exactly right. If we are in Brussels in late June or early July, we might be fortunate enough to catch a glimpse of this spectacular parade which features genuine Belgian aristocrats, peasants in Bruegelian costumes, and even the odd person playing Flemish bagpipes. A few improvements have been made to the original script, so that we now have a chess board painted on the cobblestones, a parade of giants and a spectacular battle on stilts that is fought to the last man.

II. The Hôtel de Ville. The oldest building on Grand'Place is the town hall, opposite us if we are in Jacqmotte's or the Chaloupe d'Or, but almost hidden from view if we have chosen La Brouette. Duke Wenceslas of Luxembourg laid the first stone of the original building in 1402. This wing, to the left of the spire, was built by Jacob van Thienen and Jan Bornoy in

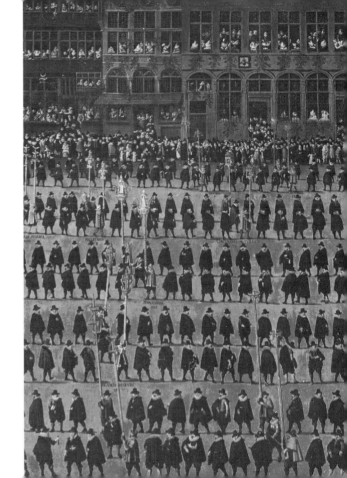

Hôtel de Ville.
BRUXELLES.

an ornate Brabant gothic style. In 1444 Charles the Bold, Duke of Burgundy, laid the foundation stone of the right wing, which was completed a mere four years later. The original architects had not envisaged a right wing, and the site proved too restricted to achieve symmetry, but the end result is still enormously pleasing, particularly now that the elegant sandstone spire, added in 1455 by Jan van Ruysbroeck, has been cleaned and the gilt statue on top of Saint Michael slaying the dragon glints like new in the sun.

It is time for us to leave our café and look more closely at the details on the town hall. The addition of the right wing called for the demolition of three wooden houses known as De Scupstoel, Papenkelder and De Moor. The names of these vanished houses inspired the three curious capitals we see in the arcade, one of which illustrates De Scupstoel (literally the shovel chair) by showing several men shovelling chairs. The Metropolitan Museum of Art in New York owns a drawing of this capital, which they attribute to Roger van der Weyden or his workshop. If we examine the other two capitals, we will find The Pope's Cellar and The Moor treated to a similar gentle mockery.

The other carved figures on the front of the town hall are neither as old nor as witty as these capitals. The niches on the town hall remained empty until well into the 19th century. They were gradually filled by minor Belgian sculptors, although two of the figures were carved by Constantin Meunier. The rows of figures we see represent medieval rulers, aristocrats, artists and intellectuals. The statues on the crowded left wing, some of which have vanished, mostly depict obscure counts and their wives. The names are carved on the consoles, though many are now illegible. We might spot Mary of Burgundy who died after falling from her horse, and now occupies a niche above the tourist office next to her husband Maximilian of Austria. Their son, Philip the Fair, appears in the next niche on the right, followed by Joanna the Mad, Margaret of Austria and Charles V, the last easily identified by his orb and sceptre.

We now go through the gate under the tower to look inside the courtyard. When not full of official cars, this is a seductive spot with splashing fountains and the scent of blossom. The two splendid fountains we see were carved in 1715 by Jean-André Anneessens, son of the guild leader executed on Grand'Place by the Austrians. The old man reclining on an urn (on the left) symbolises the River Meuse while the figure on the right represents the Scheldt. We can go through a door on the right to find out about guided tours of the town hall, though we may be disappointed to discover that none of the original medieval interiors survived the 1695 bombardment. The main features to see inside are the glittering 17th-century baroque of the Council Room, the nostalgic paintings of the River Senne in the Burgomaster's Room and the gaudy neo-gothic wood-panelling in the Marriage Room.

The town hall came close to being destroyed by the German army in September 1944. As the British army approached the city, a group of soldiers began to pour petrol onto the books and papers in the town hall's library, intending

to set the building alight. They were disturbed by Jack Trefusis, a British officer who had been smuggled into the town hall by the resistance. He ordered the sixty German soldiers to surrender, which, rather surprisingly, they did. Brussels was liberated soon afterwards, and Trefusis appeared on the balcony of the town hall with the mayor, Mons van der Meulebroek, and his dog Rip.

III. The Guild Houses. We now return to Grand'Place to begin our tour of the guild houses, most of which were built, as we can see from the dates on the façades, during the final five years of the 17th century. Villeroi's bombardment in the summer of 1695 had reduced most of the medieval square to rubble. The French had used the town hall spire as their target, but although they destroyed 3,830 houses and 16 churches, and set the town hall roof on fire, the spire itself survived.

The painter and engraver Augustin Coppens went down to the square soon after the bombardment to record the devastation in a series of engravings, including the one reproduced opposite (as well as the drawing on p. 28 and the print on p. 69) in which the skeletal stone ruins resemble photographs of Berlin in 1945. Despite the devastation, the entire square was totally rebuilt within a few years. The architects who worked on the guild houses gave Brussels an Italo-Flemish baroque style reminiscent of the buildings designed in Antwerp by Pieter Paul Rubens. Laden with statues, pinnacles and gilt details, these guild houses look as if they might be intended as the backdrop for a lusty opera.

It is worth strolling around the square to look at the details, beginning with the Roi d'Espagne at Nos. 1-2 and ending at the Maison du Roi where the Museum of the City of Brussels is located. We are fortunate to have a series of drawings by F. J. De Rons that show the guild houses in 1737 when they were still fairly new. The De Rons drawing overleaf illustrating the six guild houses at Nos. 1-7, shows how little has changed in the meantime. The Maison du Roi d'Espagne (House of the King of Spain) on the far right of the drawing was rebuilt by Jan

59

Cosyns in 1697. Named Het Beckers Huijs on the drawing, this palatial building was originally owned by the guild of bakers. The figure of Fame is perched on a cupola, while the baroque statues on the balustrade represent Energy, Grain, Wind, Fire, Water and Prudence, all essential to the baker's trade. The bust above the main door is St Aubert, the patron saint of bakers. Above him the King of Spain, Charles II, appears in a relief, flanked by Turkish flags and chained prisoners.

The house at No. 3 is called La Brouette, named after the wooden wheelbarrow we see above the entrance. Like the Roi d'Espagne, it was built by Jan Cosyns in 1697 after the original building was reduced to rubble. This was once the guild house of the tallow merchants, who traded in candles and oil. Their patron saint, St Giles, stands in a niche at the top.

The Maison du Sac (House of the Sack) at No. 4 was originally built in 1644. Named on the De Rons drawing as Het Timmermanshuijs, it belonged to the guild of carpenters and coopers. The lower floors survived the bombardment, so this is the first we see of the original guild architecture, but the top was redesigned by Antoon Pastorana, himself a carpenter, in the form of an elaborate baroque wardrobe. The house takes its name from the bas relief above the door showing a man rummaging through a sack.

The Maison de la Louve (House of the She-Wolf) at No. 5 belonged to the guild of archers. Its name comes from the relief above the door showing the infancy of Romulus and Remus. The four baroque caryatids on the second floor represent the paired opposites of Truth and Falsehood, Peace and Disorder. The bird on the pediment is a phoenix, put there in 1691 after the house had been twice destroyed by fire. The third reconstruction, carried out by Pieter Herbosch in 1691, proved sufficiently robust to withstand the French artillery bombardment four years later, as we can see from Coppens' engraving on page 58.

Antoon Pastorana took time off from cabinet-making to draw the plans for the eccentric Maison du Cornet (House of the Horn) at No. 6. Not much of the old building remained in 1695, as we can see from the Coppens view, apart from a stone carved with a horn above the entrance. The guild of boatmen employed Pastorana to design them a new building in 1697. If we turn to the De Rons drawing, we can see that Pastorana created a curious upper tier modelled on the stern of a 17th-century galleon. The bust in the medallion represents the sickly King Charles II of Spain, whose features we have already seen on the Roi d'Espagne. Here the king is flanked by the four winds and two sailors. Sea horses and lions add to the splendour of this building.

The Maison du Renard (House of the Fox) at No. 7 was designed in 1699 for the haberdashers' guild. Their patron, St Nicolas, is perched on top of the baroque gable. The trading activities of this guild are amusingly illustrated by the four bas reliefs on the ground floor, showing plump cherubs engaged in haberdashers' occupations – selling trimmings, working in a fabric shop, running a dye works and firing earthenware pots. The five statues above represent Justice and the four Continents where the haberdashers travelled in search of precious metals and spices. We can see the figure of Africa carrying ebony and ivory, while Asia is bearing incense and ivory, America is laden with gold, and Europe carries a cornucopia overflowing with riches. Australia had been discovered by then, but the haberdashers obviously saw little to interest them there.

Augustin Coppens stood in the rubble at the end of the Rue Tête d'Or to draw the view on p. 58 in 1695 showing the remains of the houses at Nos. 5 to 7. Some people on the left are sifting through the debris in front of The Fox at No. 7 – perhaps they were haberdashers searching for their precious metal and rare spices. A wooden bench outside the building has miraculously survived, as have the four bas reliefs decorated with cherubs. The Horn next door still has its panels decorated with cherubs and a stone carved with a horn. Yet the most astonishing sight is the façade of the She-Wolf at No. 5, which has somehow survived the heavy bombardment intact. We can clearly see the four caryatids decorating the third floor of the guild house, though the phoenix has been toppled from its perch.

Now let us look at the row of houses on the side of the square to the left of the town hall. We may think we recognise the narrow house known as L'Etoile at No. 8 from the De Rons drawing opposite, yet in the photograph on page 64 it seems to have disappeared even more completely than the man we see in the foreground consulting

van den hoeck van de
koeijmaeckers straede tot
aen den hoeck van de
Stoofstreet op de groote
meert 1729

his watch. The house was in fact demolished in 1852 to relieve congestion in the narrow Rue de l'Etuve, but Burgomaster Charles Buls ordered it rebuilt in 1897. The only concession he allowed was the insertion of an open arcade on the ground floor, and there is a monument to him there. The art nouveau plaque was carved by Victor Rousseau; the female figure on the left, holding a compass and a rolled-up plan, represents architecture, while the young boy holding a lamp symbolises immortality. We can see the Maison du Roi in the background, and underneath a list of Brabant architects connected with Grand' Place, though the inventive Antoon Pastorana is omitted, perhaps because he was a mere cabinet-maker.

The arcade also contains an elaborate bronze monument to Everard 't Serclaes designed in 1902 by Julien Dillens. The three bas reliefs illustrate an event that occurred during the Brabant War of Succession in 1356. The top tablet shows Everard and his men scaling the old city walls to expel Louis de Male, a count of Flanders who had staked his claim to the Duchy of Brabant and installed himself in L'Etoile. The second scene shows the citizens of Brussels welcoming Duke Wenceslas of Luxembourg as the rightful Duke of Brabant, while the bottom tablet illustrates the destruction of Gaasbeek castle after Everard was murdered by mercenaries in the pay of the lord of Gaasbeek. More than six centuries have passed since Everard died in a house on this spot in 1388, yet he is still revered as a martyr. According to a local legend, it brings good luck to touch the right arm of his recumbent figure, which explains its highly polished lustre. Not everyone, apparently, follows this tradition to the letter, for we can also see a very shiny dog, a gleaming cherub and even a glowing mouse concealed in a garland.

The house at No. 9 known as the Maison du Cygne (House of the Swan) was the guild house of the butchers at the time De Rons made his drawing. The Swan was built in 1698 as a private house in the French baroque style, but was bought in 1720 by the butchers who added the bulbous, almost Parisian, mansard roof above the pediment. This appears to be crowned with a balustrade in the De Rons drawing, though this (and the window bars) had disappeared by the time the Café du Cygne came to occupy the building. The old photograph on page 64, taken at about 10.45 am, shows the building when it contained a brasserie and billiard hall. Karl Marx was a regular visitor to this tavern during his three years of exile in Brussels. Expelled from Paris in 1845, he often sat here with Friedrich Engels working on Communist tracts. The rooms where they once discussed revolution are now, to the delight of locals, occupied by rich capitalists eating expensive lunches.

The name Maison des Brasseurs is boldly emblazoned on the frieze of No. 10, which continues to be occupied by the brewers' guild and contains a small museum of brewing. Designed by Willem de Bruyn, this portly pile is a masterpiece of baroque gusto, crowned with a staggering weight of ornamentation, including an equestrian statue of Charles of Lorraine hoisted up in 1752. If we look closely at the De Rons drawing, which was made fifteen years earlier, we can see that the building was then surmounted by a different equestrian figure, wearing what looks like a Roman centurion's helmet and surrounded by flags. This was Maximilian Emanuel II of Bavaria, who was Governor of the Spanish Netherlands during the 1695 bombardment. Besides making a brave stand against the French, Maximilian Emanuel contributed to the diaspora of Flemish art by acquiring many of Rubens' greatest paintings, which were sent back to Bavaria and now hang in Munich's Alte Pinakothek. Almost as soon as the original stone statue of Maximilian was installed, large pieces began to fall into the street, and the sculptor was forced to produce a bronze replacement, which is the version De Rons drew. The brewers replaced this with the statue of Charles to show their support of the popular Austrian governor.

The south-east side of Grand'Place is dominated by the Maison des Ducs de Brabant (House of the Dukes of Brabant), seen on p. 30 and rather more romantically opposite. Designed by Willem de Bruyn in 1695, it is named after the nineteen busts decorating the

long façade. De Bruyn created an unusual sense of baroque grandeur here by concealing six separate houses, each three bays wide, behind a palatial frontage. If we look closely, we can see the six different doors, in pairs, leading into Nos. 14 to 19. Tucked away in a corner, a tiny building at No. 13 is identified by a gilded figure of Fame blowing on a trumpet.

Standing now at the end of the Rue du Colline, we can see the buildings whose ruins Augustin Coppens recorded in another of his 1695 engravings, opposite. The town hall is on the left and the three floors of the resilient She-Wolf can be seen behind the four people in the middle of the square. In the foreground, we can see fragments of a frieze on which the words PICTORIBUS and ATQUE are legible. These might have come from Nos. 26-27, Le Pigeon, which was the guild house of the painters at the time of the bombardment. The façade was built in 1510 in an early Flemish renaissance style, though there is no evidence of any such inscription, so perhaps Coppens added it himself. But who are the people we see digging in the rubble of a renaissance guild house? Were they perhaps painters and sculptors searching for their works in the ruins of The Pigeon? The artists' guild was too poor in 1695 to reconstruct the destroyed building, so the land was sold to the architect Pierre Simon, who built the present house at No. 26-27 in late renaissance style. Victor Hugo rented two upstairs rooms of this building, now a lace shop, in 1852, as we can tell from no fewer than three memorials – two plaques (in Dutch and French) and a gilt inscription carved above the first floor windows. Looking out of his window, Hugo could admire the spire of the town hall opposite, which he had praised on a previous visit in 1837 as 'a jewel comparable to the spire of Chartres'. Le Pigeon was at the time of Hugo's stay owned by a fiery French woman called Madame Sébert who sold tobacco in the downstairs shop.

IV. The Maison du Roi. This side of Grand' Place is dominated by a building known in Dutch as the Broodhuis (Bread House), but in French by the grander title of the Maison du Roi (King's

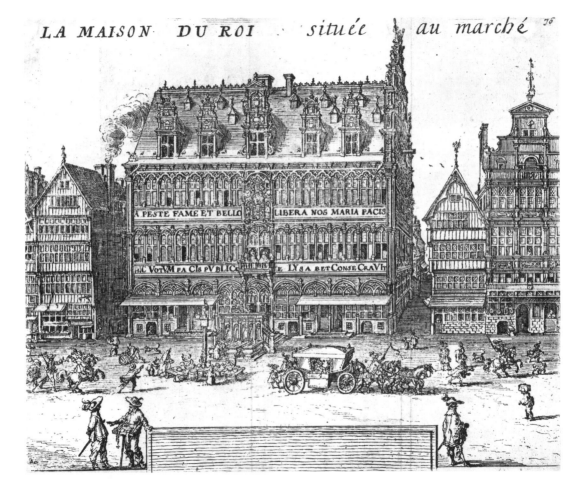

A PESTE FAME ET BELLO LIBERA NOS MARIA PACIS

IIC VOTVM FA CIS PVBLICA MIIIIIILIB LYSA BET CONSE CRAVI

House). The Dutch name is the more accurate, as this site was once occupied by the guild house of the bakers, whereas it was never a royal residence. Early in the reign of Charles V, the old Broodhuis was rebuilt in late gothic style.

In the summer of 1568, Egmont and Hoorn were imprisoned here before being executed on Grand'Place. Egmont spent his last night writing the painful letter to his wife that was to inspire Goethe's play *Egmont* and Beethoven's *Egmont* overture. Egmont had saved the country from a French invasion in 1557 by leading a heroic cavalry charge at Saint-Quentin. He protested against the Spanish tyranny and was arrested and condemned for treason by his enemy, the Duke of Alva. Egmont and Hoorn were beheaded the next morning on a scaffold outside the Maison du Roi, surrounded by hundreds of Spanish soldiers armed with long pikes. A large monument to Egmont and Hoorn, designed by Charles-Auguste Fraikin, was placed outside the building in 1864. The photograph on page 171 shows the statue in its original location, though it was moved after fifteen years to the Sablon after people protested that it was too large for Grand'Place.

The engraving opposite shows the Maison du Roi in 1627, two years after it had been rebuilt by Archduchess Isabella. A Latin scholar composed the elaborate chronogram we see on the lower frieze, which conceals the Roman date in enlarged letters. The inscription on the upper frieze says: *A Peste Fame Et Bello Libera Nos Maria Pacis.* This request to Mary of Peace for deliverance from plague, famine and war did not quite succeed – burning French cannonballs smashed through the roof in 1695, leaving the ruins we saw in the Coppens engravings. The Maison du Roi was rebuilt by Jan Cosyns, one of the team of architects involved in the reconstruction of Grand'Place. He was a baroque architect, with the result that the Maison du Roi became a curious mixture of gothic, renaissance and baroque features, bearing little resemblance to the building that Egmont and Hoorn had briefly known.

By 1860, when the city acquired the Maison du Roi, the building had fallen into utter ruin.

Burgomaster Charles Buls entrusted the restoration to Pierre-Victor Jamaer, an ardent disciple of Eugène-Emanuel Viollet-le-Duc, the French architect who had restored the medieval town of Carcassonne. After the various shopkeepers were evicted from the ground floor, work began on a reconstruction that would drag on from 1873 to 1896. Jamaer pored over old plans and documents, and even visited the Flemish town of Oudenaarde to inspect the gothic town hall which had been built there by Hendrik van Pede (one of the original architects of the Maison du Roi). But he added his own touches, such as the ornate tower and the gothic galleries, not to mention the little turrets which are nowhere to be seen on the 1627 engraving. The statues on the dormer windows, too, were his invention. We can see the final result in this photograph of about 1900, taken when the building was more or less brand new. By that date, the statue of Egmont and Hoorn had already been carted off to the Sablon.

At the time of the photograph we see here, the Maison du Roi was already occupied by the city museum, which had opened in 1887. The original collection consisted of twenty-six old Dutch and Flemish masters donated in 1878 by the British art collector John Waterloo Wilson. It now contains an engaging collection of Brussels paintings, tapestries, altarpieces, sculpture, furniture and porcelain, which we should visit at some time in our stay.

After buying our ticket we turn right into a room containing a 1567 painting, the *Wedding Procession*, attributed to Pieter Bruegel the Elder and showing a group of guests attending a country wedding, with an ashen-faced father at the head of the procession glancing back ruefully at his plumpish beaming daughter.

The *Saluzzo Retable* in the next room was carved in Brussels in 1505-10, possibly by Pasquier Borman. It depicts the Nativity and Childhood of Our Lord, and includes some amusing details such as a shepherd playing the bagpipes, a flock of sheep on a hillside and a miniature painting depicting the sacrifice of Abraham (the Old Testament forerunner of the sacrifice of Christ). After the altarpiece was finished, it would have been taken to the painters' guild house which we saw in ruins in the Coppens engraving. Once the work had been approved, it was branded with the word *Bruesel* as proof of its origin. If we look closely, we can see the branded name on each of the wooden frames.

The next room contains several large tapestries woven in Brussels in the 15th, 16th and 17th centuries. The colours have faded over the years, yet we can still appreciate the *Funeral Ceremony of Decius Mus* woven in the workshop of Jacob Geubels the Younger using a cartoon drawn by Rubens. The tapestry hanging opposite is one of four woven in 1516-18 to illustrate the *Legend of Notre-Dame du Sablon*. Or that at least is its title. We can indeed see some people taking the miraculous statue of the Virgin by boat from Antwerp to Brussels, but who are the other figures in the middle and right sections who appear to be passing around letters? All is explained by the kneeling figure. He is François de la Tour et Tassis, who commissioned the tapestry to hang in the family chapel in the Sablon church. De la

Tour et Tassis had recently established the world's first postal service in Brussels in 1516, organising mail delivery throughout the Holy Roman Empire of Charles V, and so, like any good businessman, had this achievement recorded in the tapestry. And so we see François de la Tour et Tassis in the company of Maximilian of Austria and Frederick III, while the Virgin is relegated to a supporting role in the background. She is entirely forgotten by the third panel, which is nothing more than an advertisement for the Tour et Tassis postal service.

Among the cabinets of porcelain in the next room, we find a few pieces produced in the factory established by Charles of Lorraine in about 1765 near Tervuren Castle. Charles no doubt hoped that Tervuren ware would become as famous as Dresden and Meissen, but the great plan failed when he died. Charlotte Brontë may have walked past the two stone caryatids carved by François Rude in this room, which once stood in front of a mansion in Rue Royale, near the boarding school where she stayed.

We now cross the entrance hall to look at the collection of weathered medieval sculptures from the town hall, including the original version of the *Scupstoel*, barely recognisable as the capital we saw earlier. We also see a sketch of Grand'Place made by Wenceslas Hollar in the mid-17th century, showing the wooden houses that would eventually be set alight by burning cannon in 1695. The next room contains a *Panorama of Brussels* painted by Theodore van Heil a few years before the Bonnecroy view on pages 4-5. Van Heil went further out of the city than Bonnecroy, chosing his vantage point on the Koekelberg (where Léopold II later founded a basilica). A few years after the Van Heyl painting, Marshal Villeroi lined up his mortars on the summit behind the large oak tree on the right to bombard the city below.

Returning to the entrance hall, we find several statues squeezed into a dark corner beside the stairs. The figure of *Adonis wounded by a boar* came from the Parc de Bruxelles, where Charlotte Brontë wandered during her stay in Brussels. A baroque door frame at the bottom of the stairs once led into a mansion numbered

23, presumably one of the many buildings torn down in the past century. Up the stairs is a fascinating collection of scale models, maps, topographical paintings and old photographs of Brussels, which enable us to grasp the tumultuous history that has led to houses like No. 23 being demolished. The collection is not always on display, but we should find a dramatic painting that shows burning shot landing in Grand'Place during the 1695 bombardment. We can see people running for cover as flames rise from the attic of the Maison du Roi. A painting of the ducal palace fire of 1731 shows people dashing through the palace gardens with buckets and ladders while others gawp at the flames. Here also are the now-familiar drawings by F. J. de Rons (worth admiring in their original colour) that show the new houses built on Grand'Place after the rubble was cleared away. Yet the city did not have the funds to reconstruct all the damaged buildings. We saw that the painters' guild house was never rebuilt, and a large wooden model in this room shows the classical tower that was planned but never built on St Nicolas Church.

The reign of Léopold II brought enormous changes to the old city, as we discover from the collection of watercolour paintings that show the River Senne winding through picturesque quarters reminiscent of Bruges. This old district was torn down, and the river bricked over, to create a line of broad boulevards inspired by Haussmann's Paris. Other paintings show old streets with quaint names that have vanished from the map, such as the Rue Jour et Nuit and the Notre-Dame aux Neiges quarter. A series of satirical sketches from *Charivari* magazine ridicule some of Léopold's more grandiose schemes, like the delightfully irreverent drawing which represents the Palais des Beaux-Arts by a group of artists performing in an empty space. Some of the projects were truly too far-fetched to be realised, including the colossal folly of an aerial arcade proposed in 1899 to connect Boulevard Anspach and Rue Royale, and the funicular planned in 1890 to take visitors from a lower station near Grand'Place to an upper station at the park.

An anonymous artist set up his easel in about 1790 near the round pond in the Parc de

Bruxelles to paint the romantic scene we see hanging on the far wall. The stone statues of a dog and a lion placed in front of this painting used to stand in the park, though not in the part shown in the painting. We still have one last floor to visit, where we discover Van Alsloot's painting of the Ommegang of 1615. He must have stood at one of the upper windows of the town hall to draw the scene, which shows the building we are in now, looking much as it does in the engraving on page 70, but with red cloth hung over the Latin inscription and banners fluttering from all the balconies. The painting shows the procession of the military guilds, including soldiers firing muskets in the air and two crossbowmen carrying their weapons on their shoulders. If we look closely, we can see a woman pulling a dragon on a lead, followed by St George on horseback, and a giant surrounded by figures in exotic costumes. The original version of this painting hangs in the Victoria and Albert Museum, but it is not so well preserved as the copy here. A previous owner of the London painting, George Jerningham, had the wooden frame sawn in half and the edges trimmed so that it would fit snugly in one of the rooms of Stafford Castle.

A side room on this floor contains a selection of the costumes worn by the Manneken Pis. The famous bronze statue of a urinating boy has amused visitors since the middle ages, though it was not until 1698 that anyone thought of squeezing the plump chap into a costume. The first suit of clothing was presented by Maximilian Emanuel of Bavaria, whose statue once stood on top of the Maison des Brasseurs. This ancient velvet suit is now in tatters, but the costume presented by Louis XV of France in 1747 is still in good condition. The custom of presenting the Manneken with a suit of clothes has grown into a mad cult, and the poor fellow has been dressed as Maurice Chevalier, Elvis Presley, Mickey Mouse and a Knight of the Order of the Dead Rat. At the time of writing, his wardrobe contained six hundred and twenty-nine costumes, but the number is bound to have increased since then. As for the statue itself, Baedeker's 1905 guide warned travellers that it was 'a great favourite with the lower classes', but conceded that 'the figure is not without considerable artistic excellence'. Let us see if we agree with Baedeker's opinion.

V. The Manneken Pis. We now cross Grand'-Place and head down the Rue de l'Etuve, pausing to stroke Everard's hand if we think it will do any good. Most people heading down this street are interested only in the Manneken, but a few literary pilgrims come this way in search of the spot where Paul Verlaine shot Arthur Rimbaud in the summer of 1873. A lace shop at Rue des Brasseurs 1, opposite the Hôtel Amigo, stands on the site of the hotel where the crime took place. Having abandoned his wife and son in Paris earlier that year, Verlaine had set off with the seventeen-year-old Rimbaud on a bohemian tour of northern Europe. After visiting Brussels they travelled to London, quarreling almost continually. Verlaine stormed off in a huff after Rimbaud accused him of bourgeoise pretensions, and returned to Brussels where he took a room in the Hôtel A la Ville de Courtrai.

Rimbaud arrived shortly afterwards to find his bohemian friend staying here with, oddly enough, his mother. Early on the morning of 10 July, Verlaine walked to the Galeries Saint-Hubert and bought a revolver and six bullets. He went back to the hotel room to show Rimbaud the weapon, telling him: 'This is for you, for me, for everyone.' Rimbaud prudently decided to pack his bags and leave on the next train to Paris. At this point, Verlaine lost his temper and fired two shots. Rimbaud was wounded in the wrist, though it was only a graze. Verlaine and his mother took the bleeding poet to Saint-Jean Hospital, near the botanical gardens, where the wound was dressed. Rimbaud then set off once again for the station, this time accompanied by both Verlaine and his mother.

They were nearing Place Rouppe, where the Gare du Midi used to stand, when Verlaine flew into a rage. Fearing for his life, Rimbaud summoned a policeman for help. Verlaine was dragged off to a cell in the Amigo jail, which stood on the site directly opposite us (where the Hôtel Amigo is now). He was sentenced to two years in prison, spending some of the time in a gloomy prison on the Rue des Petits Carmes before being transferred to Mons jail. Rimbaud based *A Season in Hell* on his experiences in Brussels, while Verlaine wrote *Romance sans Paroles* and converted to Catholicism. A plaque marking the hotel where Rimbaud was wounded was attached to the wall of the lace shop in 1991, exactly one hundred years after Rimbaud's death.

We now continue to Rue du Lombard where the corner building on our left at No. 30 has been drastically altered on the lower two floors, but retains splendid Art Nouveau features above. We may have to cross the street to appreciate the details of this building designed by Paul Vizzavona. A French architect, Vizzavona worked for a time in Horta's studio and went on to design curious buildings like this one in which Horta's Art Nouveau is combined with classical French themes. The roof is typically French, but the wrought iron balconies could only have come from a Horta disciple.

The next stretch of the Rue de l'Etuve has the

well-trodden look of a pilgrimage route. The shops along this street have long ago given up selling sensible items like bread or cheese, and now dedicate themselves with single-minded zeal to the sale of Manneken corkscrews, Manneken beer-dispensers and the like. By the time we have reached the statue, we may have seen more than enough of the Manneken, yet it is worth pausing a while, if only to read the notice listing his forthcoming engagements. The statue we see here was cast in 1619 by Jérôme Duquesnoy, though the Manneken was mentioned as far back as 1452. If we are here at the right time, we might catch a glimpse of the curious ritual surrounding the dressing of the Manneken, when an official of the Order of the Manneken Pis marches down the street in full regalia. A solemn speech is made, after which the official takes out a ladder stored behind the statue and climbs it to turn on the tap.

We now turn right down Rue des Grands Carmes and right along Rue du Midi. This brings us to the rear of the Bourse, where, if we turn left, we will find Café Falstaff at Rue Henri Maus 17-19. This splendid establishment which opened in 1903 has large Art Nouveau windows and wood furnishings designed by the joiner E. Houbion. Following a spectacular bankruptcy in 1999, it has been turned into a salsa bar, leaving its regulars stricken.

While we are in front of Falstaff, we should pause a moment longer to look at the side wall of the Bourse facing us (seen in an old photograph overleaf). This grand neoclassical exchange was built by Léon Suys in 1871-73, though the large arched section in front of us was a later modification by Jules Brunfaut. It was in this building that Henry Morton Stanley made a rousing speech in 1890 in praise of Léopold II's development of the Congo. That same year, Joseph Conrad travelled up the River Congo on the *Roi des Belges*, a decrepit two-deck steamer with iron roofs propped up on rickety wooden posts. He ended up with a far bleaker view of Léopold's Congo, which he described in an essay as 'the vilest scramble for loot that ever disfigured the history of human conscience and geographical exploration.'

The building is laden with symbolic sculpture representing commerce, industry and other virtues admired by stockbrokers. The decoration is indeed excessive, but it did at least provide employment for dozens of sculptors, including the young Auguste Rodin. He is said to have worked on the frieze we see above us, which is decorated with industrious cherubs, and the two groups of three figures – Asia on the left and Africa on the right – on top of the smaller arches at either end of this side.

We now walk round to the front of the Bourse, where the sculptor Jean-Joseph Jacquet was given the honour of carving the female figure in the tympanum representing Belgium, flanked on one side by Navigation (on the left) and on the other by Industry. He carved another figure of Belgium to stand on top of the arch that rises, in defiance of strict classical decorum, above the tympanum. This time, Belgium is flanked by Commerce and Industry.

We now turn right up the Rue de la Bourse, past an underground archaeological museum, Bruxella 1238, whose glass roof allows us to look down on the foundations of a 13th-century monastery. We have to take a guided tour to see anything more, such as the tomb of John I, Duke of Brabant, who died in 1294. Our aim now, though, is to visit Café Cirio at No. 18, which opened its doors in 1886 and has hardly changed since. The interior recalls Georges Simenon's description of a Brussels café: 'It was as restful as a warm bath, this huge room hazy with smoke, full of the fumes of coffee and beer, where the chink of plates and glasses blended with the languorous strains of a Viennese waltz.' My favourite corner is in the middle room, with its gleaming brass fittings and ancient cabinets filled with silverware. The best time to come here is in the afternoon, when elderly ladies sit on the striped benches drinking Cirio's concoction of Italian white wine and Spumante, while the waiters try not to stumble over their tiny pet dogs. The only possible complaint one might have is that the antiquated eau-de-cologne dispensers in the men's toilets have long ago ceased to function.

VI. The Ilot Sacré. The tangle of medieval lanes around Grand'Place was designated the Quartier de l'Ilot Sacré in 1960. This district is now exclusively devoted to eating and drinking, as the medieval street names seem to suggest. We will find a Butter Street, a Herring Street, a Butchers' Street, and a Meat and Bread Street. Many of the restaurants and taverns in this district are traditional Brussels establishments where simple and hearty dishes are served in dark wood-lined interiors. The restaurants in Brussels have long been famous for their generous portions; in 1905 Baedeker warned travellers that: 'A single portion of soup or beefsteak is enough for two persons, and a single portion of any of the other dishes is enough for three.' The portions have been reduced since then, but we can still feast on huge slabs of steak accompanied by large bowls of *frites* or enormous black pots of mussels. The atmosphere in many restaurants is particularly romantic in winter, when blazing fires are lit.

Our appetite whetted, we leave the old ladies in Cirio and turn left to reach St Nicolas. The first church here collapsed as long ago as 1367, its successor (which we can see to the left of the town hall spire in the painting on pages 4-5) was brought down in the 1695 bombardment, and a third toppled in 1714. There was a plan to construct a splendid neoclassical tower to replace number three, but it got no farther than the model we saw in the city museum. This was once the church of the merchants, who chose St Nicolas, the original Father Christmas, as their patron saint. The interior is mysterious and dark, with flickering candles and shadowy baroque confessionals.

We turn left on leaving the church, by a small Bruegel fountain, one of several in Brussels, this one decorated with three bronze figures copied from *The Blind leading the Blind*. We now go down the Petite Rue au Beurre which runs next to the church. Gérard de Nerval stayed for a while in 1840 in the Hôtel de la Ville de Francfort at No. 2. Nerval had acquired a certain reputation for eccentricity in Paris from his habit of walking a lobster on a lead, but he seems to have left it at home when he made his first trip to

Brussels in July 1836, accompanied by Théophile Gautier. His trip four years later marked the beginning of his mental breakdown. He had gone to see the Belgian première of his opera *Piquillo* at the Théâtre de la Monnaie, where a former flame called Jenny Colon was singing the lead. Nerval was tortured by thoughts of his lost love, who was by then married to a flautist. He wrote of her despairingly as if he were Dante and she Beatrice, and in one telling account described his Brussels trip as the beginning of his *vita nuova*.

One of his complaints about Brussels had been the absence of a river. 'What sort of capital is it where you cannot drown yourself?' he complained. This interest in suicide was more than academic, for in 1855 he finally killed himself, a few days after Nadar took this haunting photograph.

There are some interesting taverns down the cul-de-sacs in this corner of Brussels, such as Au Bon Vieux Temps at 12 Rue du Marché aux Herbes, A l'Imaige Nostre Dame at No. 6 in the same street, and La Bécasse, dating from

1877, at Rue de Tabora 11, where a brass wood-cock set in the pavement guides us to the inn. Any one of these taverns is worth a visit.

Our route now goes up the winding Rue du Marché aux Herbes, following a medieval trading route that once ran from the Rhine to the North Sea. We pass the handsome 19th-century front of the Follet porcelain shop at No. 39, still with its original gilt lettering and ornate lamps, and the Belgian tourist office at No. 61. We then turn left into the Petite Rue des Bouchers, which takes us into the heart of the restaurant district. The cobbled Impasse Schuddeveld, off Petite Rue des Bouchers, leads to the Toone puppet theatre, where marionettes perform traditional plays in a thick Brussels dialect (performances are sometimes staged in English or French for the benefit of those unaccustomed to *Vloms*). At the end of this street, we turn right up the Rue des Bouchers, a crowded lane where chefs create glistening displays of shellfish in the street to tempt people inside the restaurants (though we should resist, as the best restaurants do not need to lure customers). Among the reliable addresses are Aux Armes de Bruxelles at No. 13, an elegant and reliable old Brussels restaurant, and Chez Léon, at No. 18, where enormous potfuls of steaming mussels have been served with *frites* and beer since Léon Vanlancker opened his establishment in 1905.

Around the corner, Chez Vincent at Rue des Dominicains 8 is another reliable old Belgian restaurant with giant slabs of butter piled in the window. We enter through the kitchen, squeezing past waitresses hollering orders for steaks and mussels. Not far away, there is another tight squeeze opposite Rue des Bouchers 28: the Rue d'une Personne is so called for the obvious reason that no more than one person can walk down it at a time. Indeed, after a hearty meal at Vincent's, even one person might find the Rue d'une Personne hard going.

WALK 2

The Lower Town
FROM PLACE DE BROUCKÈRE TO PLACE SAINTE CATHERINE

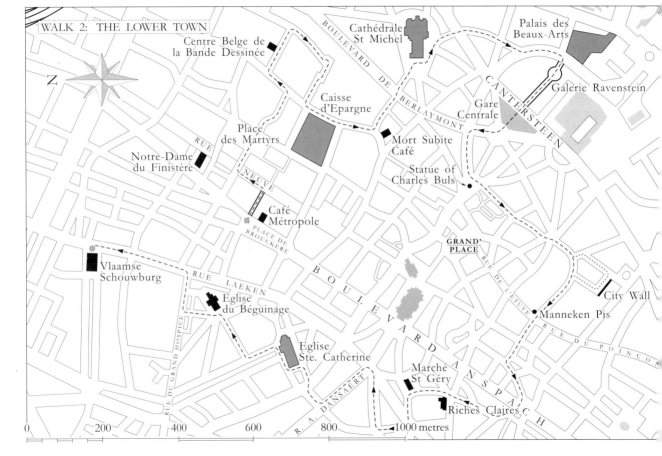

WALK 2: THE LOWER TOWN

Centre Belge de
la Bande Dessinée

Cathédrale
St Michel

Palais des
Beaux-Arts

BOULEVARD DE BERLAYMONT

Galerie Ravenstein

Caisse
d'Epargne

Place
des Martyrs

CANTERSTEEN

Gare
Centrale

Notre-Dame
du Finistère

RUE

Mort Subite
Café

Statue of
Charles Buls

NEUVE

Café
Métropole

PLACE DE
BROUCKERE

GRAND'
PLACE

RUE DE L'ETUVE

Vlaamse
Schouwburg

BOULEVARD

City Wall

RUE

LAEKEN

Eglise
du Béguinage

Manneken Pis

RUE DU POINÇON

Eglise
Ste. Catherine

RUE DU GRAND HOSPICE

ANSPACH

Marché
St Géry

R. A. DANSAERT

Riches
Claires

0   200   400   600   800   1000 metres

WALK 2

The Lower Town

FROM *PLACE DE BROUCKÈRE TO PLACE SAINTE CATHERINE*

On our second walk in Brussels we venture into the old Flemish quarter of the city, following streets that W. H. Auden described as 'tangled like old string'. This interesting area is visited only by the more inquisitive tourists, but contains a rich diversity of architectural styles bearing witness to the complex evolution of Brussels. Nowhere else in Brussels do we receive such a vivid impression of the many conflicting forces that have shaped and often shaken this city, from the 16th-century Spanish grandees to 20th-century American and Dutch corporations. Admittedly, this clash of cultures can be jarring, but it is the essence of Brussels.

I. The Métropole Hotel. We might begin the day in the Café Métropole at Place de Brouck-ère 31, sitting on a plump leather sofa inside the café, or at one of the round marble tables on the pavement terrace. The café, like the hotel of the same name, has seen better days, and the radio tends to play loud French pop music throughout the day. Yet we can perhaps still enjoy the brown coffered ceiling, plastic ferns and enormous chandelier laden with mermaids and wrought iron clematis. Framed pages from the visitors' book hang on the marble columns, hinting at the hotel's glorious past. On one page, we see Caruso's self-portrait of 1910 while another bears Sarah Bernhardt's enigmatic 1919 scribble: 'the last shall be the first.'

One year after Caruso stayed here, Ernest

WALK 2: THE LOWER TOWN

Solvay chose the Métropole as the setting for the first Solvay Physics Conference. This photograph shows the twenty-four eminent scientists gathered in one of the hotel's grand rooms. We can see Albert Einstein, second from the right, Max Planck, second from the left in the back row, and Marie Curie bending over some papers with Henri Poincaré. Easily recognised by his thick white beard, Ernest Solvay is sitting at the head of the table under the chandelier. Yet if we look closely at the photograph, we can see that he was in fact added later. He failed to make the meeting, but insisted on being included in the group photograph. He had, after all, paid the bill.

The day after the conference ended, a Paris newspaper ran a front-page story alleging that Marie Curie was having an affair with the man standing on the far right of the photograph, Paul Langevin. Curie, then a widow, was accused of destroying Langevin's marriage. He responded by challenging the journalist to a duel, though in the event neither man fired a shot. Einstein is said to have defended Curie, though not quite as gallantly as she might have hoped, observing that she was not attractive enough to have an affair. But the story was true, and she was devastated when it ended.

On leaving the Métropole, turn right and cross the road for a better view of the richly decorated Flemish renaissance building in the photograph overleaf. The curious name – *Hier is 't In Den Kater en de Kat* (This is the house of the tomcat and the cat) – can be read below the Flemish gable. Henri Beyaert designed the house in 1874 – the date is at the top – and added two cats on the roof to illustrate the house name. The white neoclassical building to the right still bears the name Musée du Nord, but we are here too late to enjoy this odd museum, which once contained a Hall of Modern Inventions, a Hall of Curiosities and Antiquities, and, most intriguing of all, a Hall of Fantasies of Nature. It had closed down by the time Einstein came here.

The Passage du Nord, though, has survived. It was designed in 1882 by H. Rieck and opened in 1885. We can wander down the glass-roofed gallery, admiring the odd little shops selling oysters and kitchen knives. The thirty-two

caryatids were designed by Joseph Bertheux and all seem to be based on the same doleful model. She appears in various guises – carrying a palette to symbolise art or a compass to represent architecture.

On reaching Rue Neuve, we should turn left. Rue Neuve is a crowded, unattractive modern shopping street now, but when it was genuinely *neuve*, in the 17th century, it was full of mansions. It was already becoming more commercial when Karl Marx briefly stayed here in the Hôtel de Saxe after being expelled from France. Arriving on a winter day in 1845 with his wife and daughter, he signed the hotel register: 'Charles Marx, doctor of philosophy'.

We are now bound for the Place des Martyrs, which is reached down the first street on our right, but we might want to continue a short distance down Rue Neuve to look at an 18th-century church called Notre-Dame de Finistère. The sober interior is decorated with a stucco ceiling, 19th-century paintings and carved confessionals. A small chapel on the right contains a gothic statue of Notre-Dame de Bon

WALK 2: THE LOWER TOWN

Succès which was shipped here from Aberdeen in 1625, though the most astonishing feature in the church is the carved pulpit decorated with cherubs struggling to secure a canopy using a complicated system of ropes and pulleys.

Now for the Place des Martyrs. This ghostly square was created in 1775 by Claude Fisco in the cool, white neoclassical style imposed on Brussels by the Austrian Hapsburgs. It is made more melancholy still by the subterranean mausoleum commemorating the four hundred and forty-five men who died in the Belgian Revolution of 1830. A female statue representing Patria – the mother land – stands on a huge pedestal flanked by four beautiful angels. Patria is inscribing the four dates in September when the revolution was fought. Four large panels on the base of the monument illustrate episodes in the revolution, including the famous attack on the Parc de Bruxelles. The sculptures on either side of the square celebrate two heroes of the Belgian Revolution. The neoclassical column on the left commemorates Hippolyte Jenneval, the author of the Belgian national anthem, and the Art

Nouveau statue on the right was carved by Pierre Dubois in memory of Count Frédéric de Mérode, who died of his wounds near Antwerp in 1830. It stands on a superb base designed by Henry van de Velde.

Years ago, when I first crossed these bumpy cobblestones, the buildings around lay derelict and empty, and weeds grew in the gutters, but the government of Flanders finally decided a few years ago that this notorious eyesore in the heart of its capital had to be repaired. Some of the buildings are now Flemish government offices, others have become luxury apartments and an attractive art and architecture bookshop has opened at No. 14. Following the Flemish initiative, the government of Wallonia, the less prosperous French-speaking region of Belgium, has been shamed into restoring a building on the north side of the square. But much still remains to be done. Lack of funds, as so often in Brussels, has slowed down the work.

We now go down Rue de Persil, a medieval lane that winds between modern office buildings. Turning left along Rue du Marais, we soon come to Rue des Sables on the right. An odd ceremony takes place in this run-down street every year on August 9 when the Meiboom (or Meyboom) is planted. One of the oldest ceremonies in Brussels, it dates back to 1213 when a group of local men saved the city from attack and were given the right to plant a tree every year. A hefty tree trunk is lugged from the Grand'Place to the corner of Rue des Sables and Rue du Marais, where it is placed upright amid grunts and cheers. This run-down quarter then briefly takes on a Bruegelian air as dancing and revelry goes on deep into the night.

We now climb Rue des Sables, a dilapidated street where we find one of the most remarkable museums in Brussels. It occupies the building at No. 20, originally an Art Nouveau department store designed in 1903 by Victor Horta. If we glance in the carriage entrance on the right, we will see an old marble sign salvaged from the Waucquez department store and advertising men's fabrics and the latest in women's fashions. Long threatened with demolition, the building was finally saved by the dogged deter-mination of a group of cartoon fans who proposed a museum that no Belgian – whether Flemish or Walloon – could easily resist. The building was lovingly restored to its original state and reopened as the Belgian Centre for Comic Books. A large model of Tintin's gleaming red and white space rocket provides a suitably nostalgic centrepiece in the entrance hall. Anyone with a soft spot for Lucky Luke or Tintin will enjoy the whimsical memorabilia displayed on the upper floors, which includes a full-scale wooden model of a saloon bar copied from Lucky Luke cartoons. Even if we decide to give the museum a miss, we should go inside the lofty entrance hall to look at the small exhibition devoted to Horta's vanished architecture. The museum shop sells cartoon books and Tintin souvenirs, and the lively Horta brasserie is full of Belgian and French tourists who have come to the museum to rediscover forgotten child-hood pleasures.

The building opposite was once the printing works of the Socialist newspaper *Le Peuple*. This bold Modernist edifice was designed by Fernand

and Maxime Brunfaut in 1932. We now turn right along the Rue Saint Laurent, past the front of *Le Peuple*, then right again into the Rue des Comédiens. At the end of this street, we turn left along the Rue Montagne aux Herbes Potagères, which takes us past the impressive copper-plated curve of the Caisse Générale d'Epargne et de Retraite, built by Alfred Chambon in 1946 and decorated with magnificent flag poles, a copper cupola and (around the corner) two long friezes by Oscar Jespers. The cupola is faintly echoed in the Radisson SAS Hotel opposite, which has a fragment of the first city wall preserved in the atrium. We continue straight ahead past (or perhaps into) the Café à la Mort Subite at No. 7. This magnificent café was designed in 1910 by Paul Hamesse, who departed from his usual Art Nouveau style to create a neoclassical interior filled with marble columns, tall mirrors and flower paintings. Owned by the same family since the 1920's, it sells its own Mort Subite brews. These traditional ales come from the Pajottenland, west of Brussels, where Bruegel went in search of peasant weddings and village feasts. Though the beers are labelled Mort Subite, the name has nothing to do with customers dropping dead on the spot, but recalls a dice game once played by regulars involving reckless drinking bouts.

II. The Cathédrale Saint Michel et Sainte Gudule. If we were tempted by Mort Subite, we now have to go back a short distance and turn up Rue d'Assaut to reach the cathedral. This street has changed considerably since a photographer took the melancholy view overleaf in the late 19th century. The antique shops on the left were torn down during the construction of the rail tunnel, leaving a bleak expanse in front of the cathedral. We can climb up to the west front, which is flanked by twin towers in Brabant late gothic style, completed in 1451 and 1475. After toiling up this slope in 1840, the depressive Gérard de Nerval wrote to a friend: 'The street ascends in a straight line, making it impossible for vehicles to negotiate and tiring in the extreme for those on foot. The slope is such that a staircase of thirty-three steps has had to be

installed, beginning on a sort of terrace in front of the beautiful church of St Gudule, which stands half-way up the hill, with the portal of the nave at street level.' Once he had recovered his breath, de Nerval had the grace to concede that the cathedral resembled 'a kneeling woman on the edge of the sea lifting her hands to God.'

We can go up the steps (thirty-four by my count), to enter the church by the main portal. We can now sit down to read the history of this ancient church, which was originally named Sainte Gudule after a 6th-century Flemish girl called Goedele who experienced a minor miracle. One dark night she was walking through the streets of Brussels on her way to church when a gust of wind blew out her candle. The young girl, terrified, fell to her knees and prayed, whereupon the candle was relit. This modest miracle gave Brussels its only saint, who was buried in a little chapel on the slopes we have just climbed. This became the Eglise Saint Michel et Sainte Gudule (St Michael being the patron saint of Brussels), though it was popularly known as Sainte Gudule and marked on old maps as such. An anonymous 16th-century artist who often included views of the church in his paintings is known as the Master of the View of Sainte Gudule (his best work is in the Louvre). Despite this ancient tradition, the church authorities resolved to drop Gudule in 1961 when the church was elevated to a cathedral within the new Archdiocese of Mechelen and Brussels. Maps and guidebooks have now taken to referring to it as Saint Michael's Cathedral, and all that remains of the pious Flemish girl is a splendid statue of 1900 next to the altar. This shows Gudule holding a lantern in one hand as a guardian angel replaces the candle, while her other hand holds an open book with a model of the twin towers of the cathedral on top.

The present cathedral was begun in 1226 on a site that had been occupied by a church since Gudule's relics were buried here. Nothing remains of the original building, though the foundations of a later, now vanished, 11th-century romanesque church have been laid bare in the crypt. Several paving stones in the nave have been replaced by glass panels, allowing us to glimpse intriguing spotlit details of this vanished building, such as the first four steps of a winding staircase and two leg bones unearthed during excavations. We can visit the crypt to discover more about this early church, which had a fortified west end, almost like a castle, defended by two solid towers. The round foundations of the towers can be seen, as can several scratched drawings on the outer wall representing a woman's face, a horseman and a bird.

The choir, begun in the early 13th century, is the oldest part of the cathedral above ground. The nave and transepts, probably the work of Jacob van Thienen, were added in the 14th century. The twin towers had not yet been built when Philip the Good organised a meeting here in 1435 of the knights of the Order of the Golden Fleece, a chivalric order founded on the myth of Jason. The knights wore chains around their necks with dangling fleeces, as we see in the Van der Weyden portrait on page 131.

The columns in the nave are decorated with

large statues of the twelve Apostles carved in about 1645 by several of the best Flemish baroque sculptors of the day, including Lucas Faydherbe (who did the figures of St James the Great and St Simon). The pulpit we see on the right-hand side of the nave was carved by Henri Verbruggen in 1699 for the Jesuit church in Leuven and moved to Brussels in 1776 after the church was closed by the Empress Maria Theresa. It is worth looking closely to see the figures of Adam and Eve being expelled from Paradise by an angel. The staircase is decorated with animals added in 1708.

We need to turn around to appreciate the stained glass window of the Last Judgement at the west end of the church. This splendid renaissance work was designed in 1528 (according to the date on the glass) by an unknown Antwerp artist. It shows Christ sitting in judgement as angels blow into trumpets and the dead rise out of their graves. We should also look at the two glowing stained glass windows in the transepts, which were designed by Bernard van Orley in the 1530's. The window in the north transept, to the left of where we are sitting, shows Charles V and his wife, Isabelle of Portugal. The opposite window shows Margaret of Hungary and her husband, Louis of Hungary.

Among the tombs we come across are those of Duke John II of Brabant and his wife Margaret of York, the daughter of Edward I of England (not to be confused with the later Margaret of York who married Charles the Bold). They are buried in the mausoleum of the dukes of Brabant behind the high altar. A florid late gothic chapel attached to the north side of the choir has the tombs of Archduke Albert, his wife Archduchess Isabella, and Charles of Lorraine. Roger van der Weyden, city painter during the 15th century, is said to be buried somewhere in the church, but the spot is not known. A mildewed reproduction of his *Saint Luke Painting the Virgin* used to hang in the choir, but this was removed during the most recent restoration, along with some wonderful antique lamps and various dusty statues of minor saints.

A beautiful late gothic chapel appended to the north side of the choir celebrates an ugly incident in the 14th century when a consecrated Host allegedly stolen by a Jew began miraculously to spurt blood after being stabbed by the congregation in a synagogue. This anti-Semitic story inspired the church authorities to build the Chapelle du Saint Sacrement in 1534-9.

When Charlotte Brontë visited the cathedral in 1843, she was so racked by loneliness and guilt that she entered a confessional and told the priest of her woes. This, from the daughter of a strict Yorkshire minister, was quite remarkable. She later used the scene in *Villette*, but moved the setting to a country church.

On leaving the cathedral, we go straight ahead up Rue de la Chancellerie and the minuscule Rue des Douze Apôtres, where a curious white stone sculpture sits in a triangular garden on the right. Victor Rousseau carved this work, called *Maturity*, in 1922. The man in the middle, who looks like King Léopold II, represents old age, while the amorous females on either side symbolise youth.

We now go up Rue Ravenstein until we come to the Galerie Ravenstein, a modern arcade built opposite the Palais des Beaux-Arts in 1954. It is worth crossing over and going inside this impressive institution, which was designed by Victor Horta soon after he returned from the United States at the end of the First World War. Brimming with new ideas, and eager to begin working again, Horta proposed the idea of a Palace of Fine Arts to the government. The building was finally completed in 1928 as we can read (if our Latin is up to it) on a plaque in the foyer. Horta had abandoned Art Nouveau by then, convinced that the future lay in the more sober Art Deco style. Yet there is perhaps a lingering hint of Horta's early flair in the Rotunda and the oval concert hall. If we go into the foyer and turn left, we enter a large gallery with a glass roof where sculptures were originally displayed. Brontë readers should note that this stands on the site of the garden of the Pensionnat Heger where Charlotte spent two years. An art bookshop in a side room sells Klimt mousepads, Monet playing cards and any number of books about Horta, but no copies of *Villette*, despite the fact that the shop stands on the very spot where the great Victorian romance was set.

We now go back across the road and into the Galerie Ravenstein. The circular basin we see at the bottom of the steps stands on the site of a 15th-century well (now in the Parc d'Egmont). At the end of the arcade, a flight of stairs leads into the booking hall of Gare Centrale. This station was designed by Victor Horta in 1937 in an Art Deco style and completed after his death by his student Maxime Brunfaut. We will see a large plaque near the entrance celebrating the completion of the railway tunnel linking the Gare du Nord and Gare du Midi in the 1950's, though not everyone hailed this project as a triumph. It required the destruction of a large part of the old town, including the hotel where Charlotte Brontë spent her first night in Brussels and many of the streets she would have known. As we leave the station, we can see, to the left and right of the entrance, carved reliefs that show some of the vanished hotels, taverns and shops, including Victor Frites, the Hôtel Saint Laurent and the Impasse de l'Enfer, though not the Hôtel de Hollande where Charlotte and Emily stayed in 1842.

If we now cross the road in front of the station and turn right, we will come to a gate leading to some steps that take us down to the Place d'Espagne. This new square is decorated with an impressive and unexplained statue of Don Quixote and Sancho Panza, copied from one in Madrid. We leave the Place by a lower gate, coming on a small square where, we may remember from the city museum, a funicular station was to have been built. Instead, we find a modern statue of Burgomaster Charles Buls with his dog pulling affectionately at his sleeve. Buls is holding a book titled *De Laudibus Dementiæ* while the fountain behind him is carved with reliefs of various Brussels buildings which he saved from ruin, including the town hall and a stretch of medieval wall we will see in a few minutes.

We now turn out of the square on the far side next to Le Gaufre de Bruxelles, past several baroque houses built after the 1695 bombardment (No. 111 is dated 1696). Turning down Rue des Eperonniers, we find a shop selling dolls'

WALK 2: THE LOWER TOWN

houses (No. 12), a postcard shop (No. 50) and a former antiquarian bookshop, now a restaurant, with an unusual mural of a girl trailing a garland on the side wall (No. 60). We are now at the Place Saint-Jean, where a statue commemorates Gabrielle Petit, a woman from Tournai who helped Belgian soldiers escape to the Netherlands during the First World War. She was known for her fearlessness, once entering a German barracks disguised as a soldier. Petit was arrested in 1916 and executed at the same firing range as Edith Cavell on April 1. Her last words were 'I will show them that a Belgian woman knows how to die.'

If we cross the square and continue down Place de la Vieille Halle aux Blés we come to a quiet square with a Bruegel fountain inspired by the *Wheat Harvest* of 1565. The Fondation Jacques Brel at No. 11 contains mementoes of a Belgian singer who made his name in the 1960's with songs such as *Ne me quitte pas*. Brel was born at No. 138 Rue du Diamant in Schaerbeek in 1933. He became famous in France in the 1960's, singing dark, melancholy folk songs in smoky

cafés and halls. Brel also made several not very successful films. His daughters set up the foundation after his death in 1978.

This square was reduced to rubble during the 1695 bombardment, as we can guess from the baroque house at No. 31, which is dated one year after the attack. We might make a brief detour here to look at a stretch of the first city wall, passing some attractive new apartment buildings along the way; we continue straight ahead along Rue de Dinant, then right again at a pink baroque house. A cobbled lane, the Rue de Villers, leads to the stretch of medieval wall saved by Buls, now looking in need of another burgomaster's affection. This is one of the last surviving fragments of the first city wall of 1267. It was the one scaled by Everard 't Serclaes and his troops in 1356 in order to eject the Count of Flanders. The wall was replaced the following year by a much sturdier structure. Nothing remains of this second wall apart from the Porte de Hal, though odd bits of 13th-century masonry still crop up in unexpected locations – a tower near Place Sainte Catherine saved once again by

Charles Buls and another tower near here next to the bowling alley at the bottom end of the Rue de Rollebeek.

We now go back to the pink house and, if we are curious to see one of Magritte's haunts, turn right into Rue des Alexiens. The café La Fleur en Papier Doré at No. 55 was where Magritte and other Surrealists sometimes met. The café's dark interior is crammed with worthless old paintings, scraps of paper with scribbled poems, enormous antique lamps and a cast-iron stove. Our detour ends here. We continue from Place de la Vieille Halle aux Blés down the Rue du Chêne. This leads to the famous Manneken Pis (described on p. 79). Squeezing past the crowds in front of the fountain, we go left down Rue des Grands Carmes, cross Rue du Midi and turn left along Rue du Marché au Charbon, a winding street where picturesque old shops are currently being turned into fashionable cafés. A good example is Au Soleil at No. 86, a former clothes shop which still has its 19th-century wooden front advertising *Vêtements pour hommes*. The interior, though, has been converted into a lively café

that spills out into the cobbled street on summer evenings. Just beyond Au Soleil, we come to the façade of Notre-Dame du Bon Secours, a baroque church built to replace one of the sixteen churches destroyed in the 1695 bombardment. The front was designed by Willem de Bruyn, the architect of the Chaloupe d'Or and the Maison des Brasseurs on Grand'Place, while the interior was entrusted to Jan Cortvriendt. It is built in a remarkable clover leaf plan, full of unexpected angles, to make the church on this very small site look a lot bigger.

III. The Saint Géry district. On reaching Place Fontainas, we cross Boulevard Anspach and turn right down the narrow Rue de la Grande Ile. Romantic though it sounds, we will find no trace of the Great Island that once stood here. It vanished when the insalubrious River Senne was turned into an underground canal in the 19th century and a line of grand boulevards built along its course. This ambitious town planning project was intended to give Brussels something of the grandeur of Haussman's Paris.

At the opening ceremony in 1871, Burgomaster Anspach boasted that he had 'replaced the dangerous and dreary river with the most important and arguably most beautiful boulevards in our city.' This did not impress Baudelaire, who grumbled about 'the sadness of a city without a river.' But then he would.

Rue de la Grande Ile takes us from here past the impressive Anneessens Technical Institute, built in the 1920's by Eugène Dhuicque in an impressive Art Deco style. The canopy above the entrance is decorated with squirrels hiding in branches and the coats of arms of six cities. We continue down the right side of the building to reach the Eglise Notre-Dame aux Riches Claires, designed by the Mechelen architect Lucas Faydherbe in 1665 and badly damaged thirty years later in the French bombardment. The choir of the convent church is an unusual composition with numerous tiny apses surmounted by scrolled gables and picturesque turrets. Not far beyond, we arrive at the 19th-century meat hall on Place Saint Géry, once the heart of the Grand Ile. It was on this site,

according to legend, that Saint Géry, Bishop of Cambrai, established a 6th-century church which has now vanished. The print overleaf shows Place Saint Géry as it was in the early 19th century, when teams of dogs were still being used to draw carriages. This curious form of transport was noticed by John Evelyn when he visited the Spanish Netherlands in 1641. Travelling from Brussels to Ghent, he saw 'divers little wagons prettily contrived and full of pedling merchandises, drawne by mastive-dogs, harnessed compleately like so many coach-horses, in some 4, in others 6, as in Brussels itselfe I had observed.'

The print also shows a large 18th-century obelisk that once stood in the middle of the square. It was originally a fountain in the grounds of Grimbergen Abbey, but was moved here in 1802 and saved when the Marché Saint Géry was built around it in 1881. It can still be seen inside the market hall. If the door is open, that is, for the revival of the disused market has not gone as well as had been hoped. Some years ago, the city council voted to tear down the

building but retain the obelisk, which would have restored the square to its appearance in the 19th-century print, but the market was finally saved in the hope that it might be restored like Covent Garden in London. After several false starts, the former meat market is now being used as a town planning centre, café and exhibition space. A row of old Flemish brick houses opposite the market has been restored and, to the delight of local historians, a short stretch of the River Senne can now be seen in a back courtyard (reached through the gateway at Place St Géry 23). This neighbourhood is gradually becoming fashionable, as old shops that sold a hundred types of string are replaced by fashionable cafés such as Zebra at No. 35 and Mappa Mundi opposite at No. 2 Rue du Pont de la Carpe.

We now turn down Rue Plétinckx, which runs to the right of the courtyard we have just visited. After crossing the busy Rue Van Artevelde, we turn right down Rue Saint Christophe where a handsome 19th-century corner building called A Saint Christophe has been converted into apartments. Until a few years ago, this was a run-down district, but old buildings are now being restored and fashionable design shops edging into the neighbourhood. If we were to turn left down Rue des Chartreux, we would reach the Place du Jardin aux Fleurs where a rustic building from 1762 is occupied by the legendary In het Spinnekopje (In the Spider's Web) restaurant. We might go here for a traditional Belgian lunch (it is closed on Saturday and Sunday), but otherwise our route goes in the opposite direction, turning right along Rue des Chartreux. If the clockmaker's shop at No. 42 is open, we should be able to spot in the entrance hall an intriguing fragment of a medieval stone turret which has survived from the city wall we met in the Rue de Villers. A museum of advertising called Album at No. 25 occupies a recently restored 17th-century house with ancient creaking stairs and exposed roof beams. Further along the street, we pass an art gallery at No. 26 that can be counted on to organise provocative exhibitions, and a shop filled with curious antique clocks at No. 3. This street also contains one of the most appealing cafés in the city. It may look slightly run-down, but Le Greenwich is a wonderful 19th-century establishment with Empire-style woodwork, gilded coat hooks and rows of square mirrors, not to mention the 19th-century Victorian ceramic fittings and wrought iron partitions in the men's toilets. This was once a fashionable café where Magritte tried without much success to sell his paintings, but its main claim to fame nowadays is as a chess café.

On leaving the Greenwich, we continue to the end of the street and turn left along the fashionable Rue Antoine Dansaert, past L'Archiduc at No. 6, an Art Deco bar where jazz musicans have played since the 1920's. We can buy Antwerp fashions in the Rue Blanche boutique at No. 9, roast chickens in a poultry shop at No. 14, or rye loaves dusted with flour in the Pain Quotidien bakery at No. 16. We might even be tempted to eat in the noisy brasserie atmosphere of Bonsoir Clara or the oriental interior of Kasbah (both described in the restaurant section).

IV. The Sainte Catherine district. We now turn right into the Rue du Vieux Marché aux Grains, but before turning down this street we ought to pause on the corner to admire the gleaming tile pictures of orange and banana trees on the upper floors of the Art Deco corner building at No. 11, constructed in 1928 by a firm that imported exotic fruit. We might also look further down the street at the unusual apartment building at Nos. 91-99, with its undulating façade and seven tiny beaver-tail roofs.

But we turn right on the corner to enter a strangely provincial square with an old dairy shop at No. 4 and a few café tables under the trees belonging to the Paon Royal tavern at No. 6. If time permits, we can take a detour here by turning left down the Rue de Flandre. Otherwise, we go straight ahead to the Place Sainte Catherine, described on page 107. Our detour brings us to a building which lies hidden from sight down a narrow passage at No. 46. Overlooking a secret courtyard, the spectacular Maison de la Bellone was designed in Flemish baroque style by Jan Cosyns in 1697. The architect gave this house a

similar look to the guild house he designed for the bakers on Grand'Place, but added four heads of Roman emperors and various military trophies. The inscription celebrates the Battle of Zenta, fought in 1697, when the Elector of Saxony defeated a Turkish army. A curious sculpture in the pediment shows an old man holding a book while a vase burns beside him, and a young man who is measuring a globe with a compass. The building, with its courtyard now covered by a glass roof, is used by the Maison de Spectacle for plays and exhibitions on French theatre in Brussels (open Tuesday to Friday, from 10 am to 6 pm).

The Rue de Flandre is an enjoyable old Brussels street for idle strolling. If we turn left on leaving La Bellone, we pass a lane with the quaint name of Ruelle du Nom de Jésus, then a taxidermist at No. 73, complete with stuffed toy dog, and finally an umbrella shop at No. 94. We turn right at the end of the street into Rue du Marché aux Porcs, no longer the scene of a pig market but now occupied by the touching *Pigeon Soldat* monument on the left, which commemorates carrier pigeons killed during the First World War. We then come to the impressive Monument Anspach at the end of the Quai aux Briques. This ornate fountain commemorates the burgomaster responsible for covering over the River Senne to create the grand boulevards. Designed by Emile Janlet in 1897, the monument is laden with symbolic sculpture, including twisted pumas, crocodiles and a marble relief showing a naked woman crouching under an arch, which symbolises the Senne tunnel. The fountain originally stood on the Place de Brouckère opposite the Café Metropole, but was moved to this forgotten corner when the metro was built.

We now carry on down the Quai au Bois-à-Brûler, trying to picture this busy quayside when the harbour was here. It was drained and covered over in 1909, leaving just the names of the quays as a reminder of the flourishing port. The modern port of Brussels is located to the north of here along the Canal de Charleroi. This industrial area is slowly being transformed into a docklands-development with art galleries and warehouse apartments. Interesting boat tours of the harbour now leave from a modern quay off Place Sainctlette. Our route brings us to Place Sainte Catherine, formerly the site of the fish market and still the best place in town for seafood. We can usually find a stall in the square where locals stop for a dish of mussels or perhaps oysters, washed down with a glass of Muscadet. The weather-beaten Eglise Sainte-Catherine looks as if it has been looming over the old fish market for several centuries, but in fact was not yet built when Charlotte Brontë passed this way. The church was designed in 1854 by Joseph Poelaert, the architect of the Palais de Justice, to replace a church of which all that now survives is the mysterious baroque tower we see on the south side of the square. The 19th-century church is now in a sorry state, but has so far survived repeated demands for its demolition. An old stone tower nearby, the Tour Noire, has also weathered various threats to demolish it. This ivy-covered relic of the first city wall is now enclosed on three sides by the new Novotel Hotel, behind the church.

We now walk back down the Quai aux Bois-à-Brûler, then turn right down Rue du Peuplier. This brings us to the beautiful, forgotten Eglise du Béguinage, a baroque church with a billowy façade divided into three bays, each topped with a curlicued Flemish scroll gable. This church once belonged to the order of Béguines, whose walled religious community formed a town within a town. Their peace was shattered in 1579, when a Protestant mob burst into the church and plundered the religious treasures. The Béguinage, or Begijnhof, was dealt a further blow in the 19th century when most of the sixty or so houses around the church were demolished.

Wandering in the garden of the Pensionnat Heger, Lucy Snowe could hear the bells of the Béguinage chime 'a sweet, soft, exalted sound'. This church is the setting for a strange episode in *Villette* when Lucy Snowe collapses in the arms of a priest. We can read above the entrance that the church was restored in 1856, so this is not quite the building that Charlotte Brontë knew. Yet the ornate Flemish baroque pulpit

THE LAMP REVEALED THE PRIEST'S FEATURES CLEARLY.

and the cherubs' heads at the base of the vaulting would have been seen by Charlotte; so, too, would the strange polished confessionals decorated with female caryatids.

We might end our walk here and return to Place Sainte Catherine to eat. Or we can continue for another half hour to discover a neglected 19th-century quarter. On leaving the church, we turn right to reach the Rue de l'Infirmerie, a grand street flanked by identical neoclassical buildings with green shutters. This leads to a strange, forgotten square shaded by trees. With its sandy gravel paths and wooden benches, this corner has the feel of a sleepy French provincial town. All that is missing is the click of boules and the smell of baking bread. We find a Bruegel fountain here, decorated with figures copied from one of his paintings. The large building straight ahead at No. 7 is the Hospice Pachéco, an old people's home founded during the Spanish period, when Isabelle Des Marez, the widow of governor Don Antoine Pachéco, left funds for the care of elderly women. The original hospice was established in 1713 on a site near the Jardin Botanique; the building we see here was completed in 1824 and must have seemed new in Charlotte's day.

We now turn right along the Rue du Grand Hospice, catching a glimpse of the very old belfry of the Béguinage (from which Lucy Snowe's bells were heard). We continue straight ahead, then turn left onto the Rue de Laeken, a run-down 19th-century street that still retains hints of its former grandeur in buildings such as Nos. 73-75. This handsome neoclassical mansion was built in the 1760's by the architect Laurent Benoît Dewez, who designed several baroque abbeys during the Austrian period.

If we turn left, we gain a more positive impression further along the street. An ambitious urban renovation project financed by the AG insurance company has created the row of buildings we see at Nos. 91 to 125. These houses – some restored and others newly built – were designed by seven international architects selected by jury after an open competition. Though each building is distinct, they blend together to recreate a handsome neoclassical streetscape. Prince Charles was impressed with the project when he visited in 1992 and I imagine Dewez would also find reason to applaud this revival of his favourite style. The architects have added the occasional exotic touch such as the caryatid we glimpse through a doorway at No. 111.

Further along the street, we come upon the extraordinary Vlaamse Schouwburg, the Flemish theatre of Brussels, which occupies an overblown Flemish renaissance building laden with ironwork, gables and busts of playwrights. Yet this is no slavish imitation of old Flemish architecture. The tiered iron balconies on either side give the building an industrial look not too distant from a 19th-century factory. Nowadays the theatre struggles to find an audience for its evening performances, as most Dutch speakers now live in rural Brabant. The interior remains in perfect condition and is worth a visit if only to enjoy the unspoilt charm of the Flemish renaissance bar. The theatre occasionally puts on British and Irish plays, in an attempt to find an audience to fill its spacious auditorium without committing the heresy of staging performances in French.

A brisk walk back down Rue de Laeken brings us once again to the restaurant district around Sainte Catherine, where neon signs glow invitingly after dark. We may, however, be diverted by the music that spills out of Rue de Laeken 28. The old sign that reads 'La Tentation' survives from the time when this corner building was a garment factory. It was recently converted into a cultural centre for the Galician community in Brussels. The lofty industrial interior is now occupied by a ground-floor café and an upstairs restaurant serving specialities from northern Spain. The centre has become a popular meeting place for Spanish families, artists and music fans drawn by the folk concerts every Friday evening. Once we have found this place, we may never want to leave.

WALK 3

The Museum Quarter

THE GALERIES SAINT HUBERT TO THE MUSÉE D'ART MODERNE

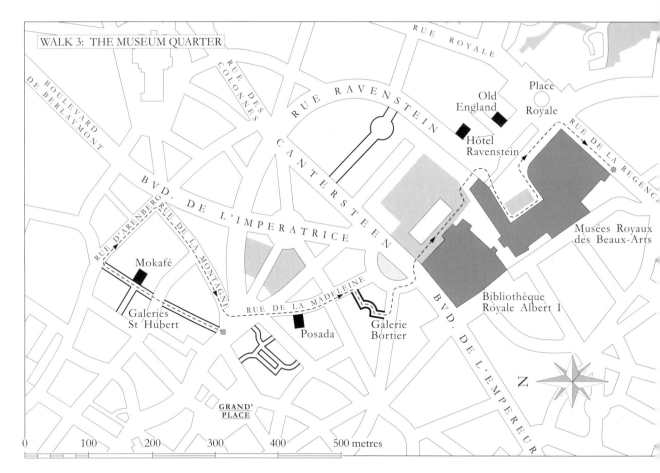

WALK 3: THE MUSEUM QUARTER

RUE ROYALE

RUE DES COLONNES

RUE RAVENSTEIN

CANTERSTEEN

Old England

Place Royale

Hôtel Ravenstein

RUE DE LA REGENCE

BOULEVARD DE BERLAYMONT

BVD. DE L'IMPERATRICE

RUE D'ARENBERG

RUE DE LA MONTAGNE

Mokafé

Musées Royaux des Beaux-Arts

Galeries St Hubert

RUE DE LA MADELEINE

Posada

Galerie Bortier

Bibliothèque Royale Albert I

BVD. DE L'EMPEREUR

N

GRAND' PLACE

0   100   200   300   400   500 metres

The Museum Quarter

THE GALERIES SAINT HUBERT TO THE MUSÉE D'ART MODERNE

This is a walk for a rainy day. It takes us into the Musée des Beaux-Arts (closed on Mondays) where we find Bruegel's *Fall of Icarus*, Bonnecroy's *View of Brussels* and the largest collection of Magrittes anywhere. We should try to be at the museum soon after it opens at ten if we are to see everything.

I. The Galeries Saint Hubert. We might familiarise ourselves with our route over coffee in Mokafé, a 1930's café with wood-panelled walls and old paintings. The café is at Galerie du Roi 9 in the Galeries Saint Hubert, a grand 19th-century arcade reached from the Rue Marché aux Herbes through a fine classical entrance inscribed *Omnibus Omnia*. This motto –

everything for everyone – came from one of the many old shops that were torn down when the arcade was built. Inspired by the novel iron-and-glass arcades of Paris, the Dutch architect Jean-Pierre Cluysenaer designed three intersecting passages named Galerie du Roi, Galerie de la Reine and Galerie des Princes. The Milanese were so impressed that they used it as a model when they built the much larger Galleria Vittorio Emanuele II twenty years later.

The arcade has hardly changed since it was opened by King Léopold I in 1847. Restored on its one hundred and fiftieth anniversary, it is elegantly decorated with expressionless female statues, marble shop fronts and oddly-shaped lamps. Just how little has changed can be seen from this 19th-century photograph, taken near the far end of the Galerie de la Reine looking back towards the Rue des Bouchers. The photographer must have stood near No. 29 to take the shot. If we were to stand on the same spot now, we would see the theatre on the right where Ali Baba was playing at the time. It is now likely to have a French farce announced on the billboard outside, though that is the only significant difference.

Many of the shops in the arcade have remained steadfastly unaltered, such as the Neuhaus shop at Galerie de la Reine 25, whose chocolates have been tempting the Belgian sweet tooth since Jean Neuhaus invented the praline here in 1857. The Ganterie Italienne at No. 3 has been there since 1890 and still politely insists on customers putting on special thin gloves before trying on any of the stock. The Librairie des Galeries at Galerie du Roi 2 stocks thick tomes on art, while the Tropismes bookshop at Galerie des Princes 11 occupies a handsome neo-renaissance interior.

The arcade became a popular meeting place for the exiled French community in Brussels during the second half of the 19th century. The gaunt Baudelaire was a regular visitor here during his stay in Brussels, pacing the arcade every day – two hundred and fifty steps in each direction – or so he claimed (I can do it in no fewer than two hundred and seventy steps, suggesting that Baudelaire either lost count or had a long stride). Another habitué was Victor Hugo, who walked through the arcade from his apartment on Grand'Place to visit Juliette Drouet, his mistress. She occupied one of the apartments above the Galerie des Princes, near Tropismes bookshop. Hugo praised Drouet as his muse, though she also served as a useful secretary when he needed a manuscript copied out. Hugo also had a weakness for the local prostitutes, as we know from his diaries where he carefully noted down the exact amount paid. He even persuaded his Dutch maid Hélène to sleep with him, savouring the fact that he made the conquest on 17 June 1861, precisely forty-six years after his favourite battle was fought. 'Hélène naked. Anniversary of Waterloo. Battle

won,' he noted drily in his diary.

It is quite possible to spend an entire rainy day in the arcades, buying a novel in Tropismes, eating lunch in the old-fashioned Taverne du Passage, and going to a film in the Arenberg cinema. The atmosphere is especially charming after dark, when the passage is lit by antique lamps and a violinist will perhaps be performing to a small audience.

We leave the gallery at the end opposite Rue Marché aux Herbes. The modern building opposite the exit was once the Vanderborght furniture shop. It was restored for Brussels 2000, the body responsible for the programme of events during Brussels' year as cultural capital of Europe, but now lies empty after plans to turn it into a centre for contemporary art were abandoned.

We now turn right up Rue d'Arenberg, crossing to the other side to admire the rugged neoclassical bank at No. 7, with its curious decoration of bees, rabbits and crabs. Begun in 1912 for the Deutschebank, it was still unfinished when war broke out, and remained so until it was completed in this heavy style in 1932. The building at No. 11 was designed by Victor Horta in 1906 for the Wolfers department store. We have to look hard to spot the Art Nouveau details such as the metal frames of the awnings and the marble cornice above the entrance. Some of the wood and glass interior has been reconstructed inside the Musée du Cinquantenaire.

Continuing up the street, we come to a plaque on No. 52 which recalls that the Dutch author Multatuli wrote his great novel *Max Havelaar* in a building that once stood near this spot. Multatuli (his real name was Eduard Douwes Dekker) had been fired from the Dutch colonial service after he protested at the corrupt administration. Desperately impoverished, he wrote the novel in 1859 in a cold attic room above a café. The novel describes the chronic corruption of Dutch colonial rule in Indonesia.

We now turn right down Rue de la Montagne, past a bookshop at No. 72 devoted to Flemish art and architecture. Baudelaire lived further along this street from 1864 to 1866, renting an ill-lit room on the second floor of the dingy Hôtel du

Grand-Miroir at No. 26. The hotel has gone, but the building on the site retains its name. Baudelaire had fled to Brussels at the age of 43 soon after publishing the scandalous *Les Fleurs du Mal*. During his stay here the poet irritated the wife of the hotelier by keeping a bat in a gilded cage and feeding it on milk and breadcrumbs. He scratched a living by giving lectures in the Maison du Roi on Grand'Place. His second lecture, on Delacroix, was attended by a contingent of English and American girls from Madame Goussaert's ladies' boarding school in Koekelberg (which, incidentally, was the school where Charlotte Brontë had rushed in 1842 after her friend Martha died there). Choosing his words with the utmost precision, Baudelaire began by thanking his audience for helping him to overcome his nerves: 'I find that the virginity of the novice speaker is no more difficult to lose than the other kind of virginity, and no more to be regretted,' he said. There was a shocked silence, then a scraping of chairs as the young girl boarders were ushered out of the hall. By the time Baudelaire delivered his third (and final)

lecture in a hall on Rue Neuve, it was to an audience of ten. 'If only you knew the stupidity of these people,' he complained to a friend.

Racked by the effects of syphilis, Baudelaire sat in his gloomy hotel room or paced the nearby Galeries Saint Hubert composing bitter books on Belgium with titles like *Grotesque Belgium* and *Poor Belgium*. The Bruxellois were scarcely human, the Antwerpers ugly as sin, and so on. Disgusted by everything he saw, Baudelaire jumped at the offer of a trip in Nadar's Montgolfière. 'To flee from this dirty people in a balloon, to land in Austria, or Turkey perhaps,' he mused. But Nadar had got his calculations wrong. The balloon turned out to be too heavy, and Baudelaire had to get out. He collapsed with a stroke in 1866 while he was visiting the Eglise Saint Loup in Namur. Brought back to Brussels by his friends Alfred Stevens and Félicien Rops, he was taken to a local hospital to recover. His mother later travelled to Brussels and escorted him back to Paris, where he died the following year. The hotel never received the 1,500 gold francs that Baudelaire owed.

We now come to a little square numbered 74 on this detail from a 17th-century map of Brussels. The map – which we will refer to on other walks – was made by Martin de Tailly in 1640. It is filled with fascinating details such as fountains, secret gardens and tiny figures in the streets. We turn left up Rue de la Madeleine (numbered 80 on the map). The lower stretch of this street has not changed too much since De Tailly drew his map. We can distinguish the houses on the right side, though the buildings on the left have been replaced by a modern hotel.

The little chapel we pass on the left of the street, the Chapelle de la Madeleine, appears on the De Tailly map next to the number 80. As we can see from the map, it was then surrounded by houses, but they were demolished during the construction in the early 20th century of the railway tunnel between the Gare du Midi and the Gare du Nord. The 15th-century chapel was rebuilt near its original site in 1957, but it was not quite the same building as before; the baroque façade of the Chapelle Sainte-Anne, which was also torn down, was added to the north side of

La Madeleine to create a curious architectural medley.

Before we climb the hill, we might browse in Book Market at No. 47, an eclectic shop that sells second-hand books in several languages (including English), battered tin cars and prints of Brussels.

Nor should we ignore Posada, a remarkable art bookshop at No. 29. Named after a Mexican artist, this creaky 18th-century building is filled with books on the most eclectic of subjects. Mr Posada (as the owner likes to call himself) receives requests from all over the world to hunt out rare books on subjects like Bruegel or Funk Art. The staff have to climb tall ladders to reach the more elusive volumes, which are shelved under the rafters, lowering the precious tomes to the ground floor in a pink wicker basket.

We can explore another arcade designed by Cluysenaer, now rather forgotten, just beyond here. Entered by a neoclassical portal at Nos. 23-25, the Galerie Bortier was built soon after the Saint Hubert arcades, but it never became quite so fashionable. Yet it is a seductive place, with its dark wood-panelled walls and cramped shops filled with novels and prints. If we glance in the window of the Vander Elst bookshop at No. 3 we can see some old photographs of the Rue de la Madeleine before it was torn down. Miraculously, the arcade has survived intact, as we discover by following the curving passage that connects with Rue Saint Jean.

We turn left at the end of the arcade to reach the broad Boulevard de l'Empereur. As we wait for the lights to change, we can look at the statue opposite of Albert I on horseback, separated from the statue of his wife Queen Elisabeth by the boulevard. The gardens behind Albert are an attempt to solve an old problem – how to link the Lower and Upper Towns. We sometimes come across postcards showing this slope in the 19th century, when it was a terraced garden with a tumbling waterfall. This picturesque creation was replaced in 1958 by these gardens designed by René Pechère in formal renaissance style. The beauty is only skin-deep: gardens and fountains are in fact planted on the concrete roof of an underground car park. The site, known as the

Mont des Arts, is occupied by the national library, several museums, a concert hall and a conference centre. The quarter has a slightly gloomy air, especially at night, but new lighting, imaginative replanting of the gardens in a semi-wild style and the creation of a public skate park have brought more people here.

Once across the road, we climb the steps on the right leading to the Bibliothèque Royale Albert Ier. This is the national library, built in a sober neoclassical style in 1954-69. The collection includes many illuminated manuscripts from the Burgundian court, some of which are occasionally displayed in the Nassau Chapel. This ornate late gothic chapel once formed part of the Nassau Palace, a splendid residence built in the late 15th century for Engelbert of Nassau, Governor of the Netherlands under Philip the Fair. It was inherited by William the Silent but confiscated after he led the revolt against Spain. If we look at the De Tailly detail overleaf, we can see the palace numbered. 58, with its long renaissance garden stretching to the south. After the ducal palace burnt down in 1731, Governor

Maria-Elisabeth moved here. A later governor of the Austrian Netherlands, Charles of Lorraine, had it rebuilt in his favourite neoclassical style, but piously spared the 15th-century chapel. Nor, miraculously, did the chapel perish in 1954, when much of Charles's palace was demolished to make way for the library. Instead, it was incorporated into the fabric of the building, making it one of the oddest architectural sights in Brussels. If we look to the left of the entrance, we can see a relief added in 1969, which shows the *Pristinus Capellae Nassauiensis Situs*.

We can go inside the library, drop off our bags and umbrellas at the *garderobe*, and visit the Nassau chapel (only open for exhibitions), then follow the signs to the Printing Museum (at level minus 1), where 19th-century iron printing presses and cases of inky typeface are displayed in the corridors. If we are here on the right day (a Monday, Wednesday or Saturday) we can look into the almost unknown Donations Cabinet, where several Belgian writer's rooms and private libraries are preserved. One room contains mementoes of the architect Henry van de Velde.

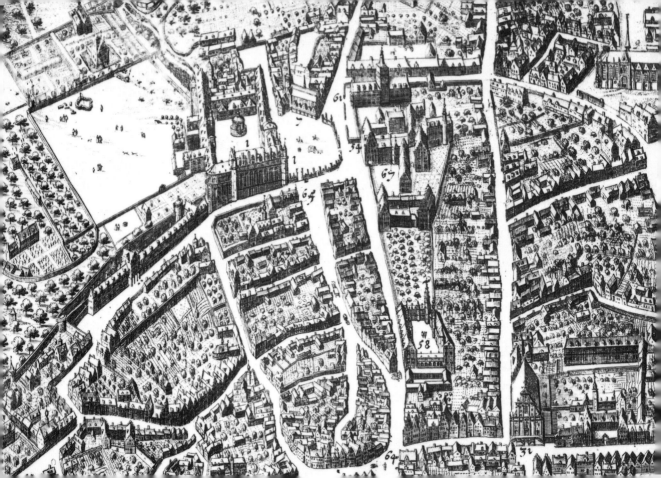

Another cluttered room is full of Michel de Ghelderode's possessions, including carnival masks, shop dummies dressed in theatrical costumes and his childhood rocking horse. Elsewhere, a window lets us see into the study where Emile Verhaeren once wrote poems and art essays at a desk strewn with notes. If we peer inside, we can two portraits by Theo van Rysselberghe on either side of the fireplace, and, almost hidden in a corner, a sketch by Ensor showing Verhaeren sharpening his pencil.

On leaving the library, we climb up to the breezy terrace situated on the flanks of Coudenberg. Looking down on the Lower Town, the eye is caught by the gilded figure of St Michael, patron saint of Brussels, on top of the town hall spire.

The street running up the hill at our back is the Rue Montagne de la Cour (Mountain of the Court Street), one of the roads Gérard de Nerval puffed up in 1840. 'Imagine in the middle of the flattest country on earth,' he wrote to a friend, 'a city consisting almost entirely of mountains: Montagne du Parc, Montagne de la Cour, Montagne des Larmes, Montagne aus Herbes Potagères; horses and dogs are exhausted after a ten-minute trot, and anyone on foot soon runs out of breath.'

Notice the mobile by Alexander Calder called *The Whirling Ear*, which slowly rotates above a circular pond. Shown at the 1958 Brussels Expo, it lay forgotten in a museum storeroom until it was installed here in the summer of 2000. Standing in front of it, we can see several interesting buildings running up the right side of the hill, three of which were designed by Paul Saintenoy. His first project was the restoration of the 15th-century Hôtel Ravenstein at No. 1. This brick gothic mansion, once owned by the Clèves-Ravenstein family, is the last surviving aristocratic residence from the Burgundian period. The building is now occupied by a restaurant and several cultural organisations.

In front of the mansion, next to an old lamppost, is the top of a flight of steps. This is all that remains of the Escalier des Juifs, one of several flights that climbed through the medieval Jewish quarter to the ducal palace. The Jews, who had

settled below the palace walls for safety, were driven out of this quarter by a pogrom in 1370. The abandoned houses were torn down and aristocratic palaces built on the site.

Now for Saintenoy's second project, the Pharmacie Anglaise at No. 68. Built in 1897, and signed, it is an intriguing revival of Flemish gothic architecture which harmonises perfectly with the Hôtel Ravenstein. The façade is crowded with gargoyles, tiled panels advertising bandages and girdles, elaborate wrought iron-work and a beautiful blue sundial that shows the hours from two to eight. In old advertisements, the Pharmacie Anglaise could boast that one of its members of staff was a 'genuine Englishman'.

After stocking up on medicines, English residents could have sipped tea in the rooftop terrace of the Old England department store, further up the hill at No. 94. Oddly enough, this spectacular Art Nouveau store was built by the same architect as the Pharmacie Anglaise and the Hôtel Ravenstein. Odder still, Old England, despite the name, was founded by a Scot – James Reid of Aberdeen. The original Brussels shop opened in 1886 and moved in 1899 to this prestigious site near the royal palace. This old photograph shows fashionable Brussels women sipping tea on the roof terrace. Perhaps they are gossiping about Léopold II's love affairs, though the husbands seem to be more taken with the view through the telescope. In 1938, Old England was ordered to paint its façade white to harmonise with the buildings on Place Royale. The business finally closed down in the 1970's, and the six-floor store remained empty for years. The ironwork has now been restored and the tiles cleaned to reveal the original thistles, crowns and shells. The Museum of Musical Instruments moved into this lovely building in 2000. This outstanding collection has about 1,500 historic musical instruments on display, a music library, concert hall, shop and restaurant. The most innovative feature is the use of infra-red headphones to allow visitors to listen to about 200 instruments and songs, including such marvellous curiosities as a Flemish hurdy-gurdy, a rasping Tibetan trumpet crafted from a human femur and a sublime song based on the medieval Cantigas de Santa Maria.

As well as these delights, the new museum allows us to visit the rooftop café and gaze down on the cathedral towers through a frail curtain of Art Nouveau ironwork. Nowhere else does Brussels seem quite so romantic.

The narrow Rue Villa Hermosa, to the left of Old England, was once famous for its taverns and night life. French exiles such as Victor Hugo and François Raspail gathered in the Café du Pot d'Or, while the British colony drank draught Bass ales at the Prince of Wales Hotel and Tavern at No. 8. This famous bar, once the haunt of Thackeray and Dickens, has been replaced by a 1949 concrete building now occupied by the Brachot Gallery.

Our aim now is to visit the Musée des Beaux-Arts, which we reach by a flight of steps near the Calder, next to a statue of Charles of Lorraine which used to stand on Place Royale. We enter a strange, empty courtyard, the Ancien Cour, part of the neoclassical palace built for Charles of Lorraine in the 1760's (his apartments are one day to be turned into a Museum of the Eighteenth Century). The most astonishing feature of the cobbled square is the subterranean courtyard of the Musée d'Art Moderne. Many hasty tourists miss this controversial feature, which is concealed behind a stone wall. Peering through the oval loopholes, we can glimpse the underground rooms of the art gallery which we are soon to visit.

The concave entrance on our right was designed in an elegant Louis XVI style. It is decorated with baroque statues including figures of War and Peace on the left balcony, Prudence and Religion, on the right balcony, and Magnanimity, with a tamed lion at her feet, in the centre of the balustrade.

A door to the right of the main entrance leads into the Chapelle Royale where Charlotte worshipped. In *The Professor*, she described the English spilling out on a Sunday afternoon: 'Gracious goodness! why don't they dress better? My eye is yet filled with visions of the high-flounced, slovenly and tumbled dresses in costly silk and satin.' Francis Coghlan's *New Guide to*

Belgium, published in 1837, said the chapel 'contains nothing remarkable,' so we can perhaps ignore it and continue up the hill, then turn right to enter the Musées des Beaux-Arts.

II. The Musée d'Art Ancien.

Alphonse Balat built the original Museum of Fine Arts in 1887-80. With its colossal Scots granite columns and oversized bronze statues, it is typical of the grand neoclassical architecture favoured by Léopold II, who wanted his capital to be as spectacular as Napoleon III's Paris. The First World War put an end to any such delusions of grandeur, and the building, like so many in Brussels, is now a burden on the state. The museum was originally free, like the great London and Berlin museums, but it has now been forced to impose an entry charge.

After buying our ticket, we enter the forum, an airy neoclassical hall filled with 19th-century sculptures. Let us sit down here and plan a visit. We are aided by four colour-coded routes that lead us into different periods. The blue route (closed 12-1) is the one that most people follow.

This leads through the 15th and 16th century rooms, where we find works by Memling, Van der Weyden and Bruegel. The brown route (closed 1-2) takes us into the 17th-century rooms we can see above us where we find Rubens and Van Dyck, along with a surprisingly good Dutch collection that seldom gets a mention. Many people end their visit here, which is a pity as the yellow route reveals some wonderful surprises of 19th century Belgian art (closed noon-1). Finally, the green route (closed 1-2) takes us to the modern collection in the circular galley we saw from the Ancien Cour. Just as we might be flagging, our spirits are lifted by the world's largest Magritte collection, six floors underground.

The collection gathered here was begun in the early 19th century as a miscellaneous assortment of rejected paintings. After conquering the Southern Netherlands in 1794, the French army plundered the chuches and abbeys, taking the best paintings back to Paris to fill the Louvre and leaving the remnants to gather dust in Brussels. A small museum was set up in the former palace of Charles of Lorraine where these unwanted works were originally hung. But the Louvre eventually became so crowded with booty that Napoleon decided to create fifteen provincial museums throughout the Empire to take the overflow. Fifty paintings were returned to Brussels and many other works were repatriated after the Emperor's final defeat.

The museum we are about to explore was opened in 1880 as part of the celebrations to mark fifty years of independence. The modern art museum was added in 1984 by digging out the cobbled courtyard of the old palace of Charles of Lorraine. We will visit this later, but in the interests of chronology we ought to begin by following the blue signs up the main staircase, pausing to admire Gabriel Grupello's *Fountain with Two Sea Gods*, carved in 1675 for the Fishmongers' Guild House. An angry Neptune is sitting in the basin glaring at a sea horse which once spurted jets of water, while a demure Juno is holding her nipple to direct a trickle of water into the basin where the wine bottles were cooled.

After passing two views of Antwerp hung on the stairs, we turn right into the medieval rooms.

A dented old panel showing *Scenes from the Life of the Virgin* in Room 10 has survived from about 1400. Or almost. Someone has hacked off a panel on the right side, removing one of the five scenes. So we are left only with the meeting of Joachim and Anne outside the Golden Gate in Jerusalem, the Nativity of the Virgin, the Coronation of the Virgin, and the Presentation in the Temple. Notice the details: a tiled floor in the first scene; a patterned bed cover and sunlight glinting on an ornate glass vase in the next scene. The elegant gothic vaulting has been lovingly painted to provide a frame for each scene. The more we look, the more we see that reminds us of later Flemish and Dutch paintings. The organ behind the central column is like the one in the Van Eyck brothers' Ghent Altarpiece. The pewter jug could be the Master of Flémalle. We are seeing here the hesitant beginnings of a tradition that links Van Eyck, Van der Weyden and the 17th-century Dutch artists.

We find this style taken further in the Master of Flémalle's *Annunciation* in Room 11 (reproduced opposite). Set in a typical Flemish interior,

this painting shows the angel Gabriel appearing to the Virgin Mary as she is reading a book. Yet the artist is as much concerned with the background minutiae such as wooden shutters, a tiled hallway and a vase of lilies on the table. The shadowy light falling on the plaster walls could almost be Vermeer. This panel was the model for a well-known later altarpiece, the *Mérode Annunciation*, now hanging in the Cloisters in New York. We know almost nothing about the Master of Flémalle who produced these paintings, except that he has been wrongly named. He was identified as such by a 19th-century critic who claimed that three of his paintings once hung in the Abbey of Flémalle. It took a sharp 20th-century mind to establish that there never had been any abbey at Flémalle. So who was this extraordinary painter? Some critics identify him with Robert Campin, an artist who worked in Tournai from about 1410 to 1440, though the official records that survive are too vague to provide us with a definite answer.

Van der Weyden probably studied under the mysterious Robert Campin; he certainly seems to have married Campin's niece. Yet Van der Weyden's style represents a new direction. The *Portrait of the Grand Bâtard de Bourgogne* (opposite) ignores background details altogether, concentrating entirely on the face of Anthony, the illegitimate son of Philip the Good. His eyes, full lips and high cheekbones make this portrait exceptionally striking, almost like a fashion shot in a 1950's Vogue. Van der Weyden spent most of his life in Brussels, painting portraits of the Burgundian nobles who lived in the gothic palaces built, but no longer standing, near here. He presumably earned a good living, for he lived near his clients in the steep Rue Montagne de la Cour, rather than among the craftsmen in the Lower Town. One of the few works left in Brussels is the *Portrait of Laurent Froimont* we see in this room, which originally formed part of a diptych. The other panel, featuring the Madonna, now hangs in the museum in Caen. The double portrait was originally hinged, so that it could be shut and taken on journeys. If we look around the back, we can see a grisaille

picture of the martyrdom of Saint Lawrence –
Laurent's patron saint – which he could contemplate when the diptych was closed. Froimont's
coat-of-arms was also painted on the back until
a zealous French revolutionary scratched off
this aristocratic symbol.

Van der Weyden's indifference to things is
seen again in his *Pietà*. He cuts out most of the
cross, reduces the number of people to four and
includes a solitary skull to symbolise death. His
interest is entirely focused on the faces of the
mourners and the precise line of the muscles on
the dead Christ's arms. We need only walk into
the next room and look at the Petrus Christus
Pietà to see the more orthodox Flemish style.
Though the cross is also omitted in the Christus
painting, we can see the holes in Christ's hands
where the nails went through, and the various
carpenter's tools used to pull the nails out. The
women in Christus may cry, but there is no feeling there. Return to the Van der Weyden, and we
see the deepest grief imaginable.

A side room (No. 13) has been specially built
to display Dieric Bouts' two large paintings

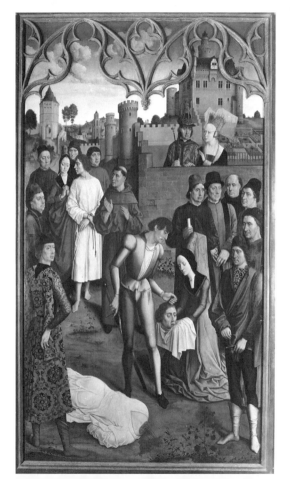

showing *The Judgement of the Emperor Otto*. This remarkable double work hangs on a stone wall intended to evoke the original location in Leuven's gothic town hall. Bouts was commissioned late in his career to paint four large works to hang in the court of law. He died in 1475 having only completed the third panel – the one on the right – and part of the second. The latter, entitled *The Execution of the Innocent Count*, was completed by one of Bouts' pupils. It shows the Emperor Otto III and his beautiful wife looking out from the walls of a gothic castle as the empress maliciously accuses a count of having tried to seduce her. The innocent man, dressed in white, is led to his execution, accompanied by his wife in a red dress. Turning to the right panel, which Bouts completed himself, we see *The Ordeal by Fire* in which the wronged wife, still holding her husband's head, submits to an ordeal by red-hot iron to prove his innocence. Satisfied by the evidence, Otto orders his wife to be burned at the stake. Not one for blood and gore, Bouts places this scene discreetly in the distance.

But what did the other two panels show? We will probably never know. It seems as if Bouts has said everything in two panels we see here, which form one of the great masterpieces of Flemish art, combining closely observed detail with a strong sense of character. It is worth getting up close to observe the floor tiles, folds of cloth and miniature trees growing in the medieval garden. Notice that Bouts matches the gothic arches of the wooden frame with the architecture in the painting to increase the illusion of depth.

We find several works by Hans Memling of Bruges in Room 14, including the *Portrait of William Moreel and his wife Barbara van Vlaenderbergh*, two wings of a triptych which has lost its central panel. Moreel was a wealthy spice merchant and banker who may have taken the small folding work on his travels. The couple sat again for Memling six years later for another triptych which now hangs in the Groeningemuseum in Bruges.

Nothing is known of the Master of 1473, apart from the date that gives him his name, inscribed

on the bottom of a curious triptych. The full date, in gothic letters, is July 27, 1473. Perhaps Jan de Witte, the man in the painting, married Maria Hoose on that summer day more than five centuries ago. He was thirty at the time, while she was just thirteen, according to the gothic inscriptions under their portraits. De Witte, who was marrying here for the second time, became burgomaster of Bruges in 1482.

A painting by the Master of the View of Saint Gudule may catch our eye in room 15. This anonymous Brussels artist often included views of Saint Gudule – the cathedral of Brussels – in his paintings, though the *Marriage of the Virgin* we see here in fact shows the south transept of the Eglise Notre-Dame du Sablon. We will pass this church on our next walk, though the portal is now so black with grime that it is scarcely recognisable.

It can be instructive to compare the fashions we see in the paintings from Bruges and Brussels hung in this room. The Master of the Legend of Saint Ursula and the Master of the Legend of Saint Lucy probably came from Bruges, where the women dressed in rich brocades and sumptuous green velvet. The Master of the View of Saint Gudule and the Master of the Life of Saint Barbara worked in Brussels, where the clothes seem plainer, not quite the height of fashion. Yet one man in the foreground of the Master of Sainte Gudule's painting is wearing an astronishing pair of long pointed shoes.

A darker mood engulfs Flemish art as we move into Room 17, where renaissance themes begin to seep into the Flemish gothic mind. The Temptation of Saint Anthony was a favourite subject, inspiring one anonymous artist to paint a tiny panel showing the tormented saint in the midst of a dark forest. Hieronymous Bosch produced a large triptych on the same theme, a 16th-century copy of which hangs on the opposite wall. Bosch's apocalyptic mind created a haunting image of burning cities and perverse sexuality that appealed particularly to Philip II of Spain. Most of his paintings consequently now hang in Spain (though the original of this one is in Lisbon). One Bosch that escaped Philip's clutches, the *Calvary with Donor* in this room, is a curiously tranquil painting of the Crucifixion in which the donor is dressed in fashionable Burgundian clothes. Some critics have identified the city in the background as Bosch's home town of 's Hertogenbosch, though the architecture seems too fantastic to be real.

The next rooms (18-20) contain paintings by German renaissance artists, including several works by the strange Lucas Cranach. He painted numerous portraits of prominent figures in 16th-century Saxony, including the bearded, cruel-looking man we see in the work known as the *Portrait of Dr Johann Scheyring*. Cranach painted this in 1529, as we can tell from the tiny inscription to the left of the man's shoulder, which incorporates Cranach's artist's mark of a dragon with raised wings. We know nothing about the identity of the sitter, but he was certainly not Dr Johann Scheyring. There is another portrait by Cranach of Dr Scheyring and it shows an entirely different person. Max Friedländer argues that the man we see here may have been Dr Johann Schöner, a mathematician and astronomer. The false name was probably added at the top of the painting by a later artist.

We can spot Cranach's dragon with raised wings concealed on the tree trunk in his 1531 *Venus and Cupid*. He painted this work for the Elector of Saxony to hang in one of his castles. The Latin inscription at the top tells the fable of Cupid, who was stung by bees after stealing some honey. Cupid ran to his mother, who told him that the wounds he inflicted on lovers were far more painful. The woman posing as Venus, wearing nothing but a necklace and a wide hat, was Cranach's model in several other paintings such as the *Lucretia* in Berlin. Cranach seems to have based the face on Princess Sibylla of Saxony, whose portrait he painted in 1528. The large double portrait of *Adam and Eve* we see in the same room is one of several works he did on this theme in the 1570's, this version providing us with a glimpse of Cranach's studio reflected in the stag's eye.

Leaving these rooms of German art, we come to the more innocent Flemish art of Gerard David in Room 21. His *Virgin and Child*, otherwise known as *The Madonna with the Porridge Spoon*, shows the Virgin feeding porridge to the infant Jesus with a wooden spoon. Painted in 15th-century Bruges, after the great port had declined into a quiet backwater, this work reveals a typical Flemish realism. Its mood of quiet domestic contentment anticipates the 17th-century Dutch interiors of Vermeer and De Hoogh.

The large *Altarpiece of the Brotherhood of Saint Anne* in Room 22 was painted by Quentin Metsys in 1509 to hang in a chapel of the Sint Pieterskerk in Leuven. Metsys illustrates the life of Joachim and Anne – the left panel shows Joachim being told by an angel that Anne is to bear a child, the future mother of Christ, while the middle panel illustrates Anne holding the Virgin Mary. Metsys had seen drawings by Leonardo da Vinci, which probably influenced the rocky outcrop in the middle panel, though the human details in the painting are typically Flemish in spirit – the little girl in the foreground is reading a book upside down and, almost unnoticed, a shepherd is watching his flock in the left panel.

The *Portrait of a Man* by Jan Mostaert in Room 24 tempts us into speculation. Who was this bony-faced and anxious man and what on earth is happening in the background? A careful study of the painting recently revealed the initials A. C. on the cushion in the foreground and again (though this is difficult to see) on the coat of arms held aloft by cherubs. This has enabled scholars to identify the sitter as Abel van de Coulster, a Councillor to the Court of the Netherlands in Brussels. But what is the meaning of the chained ape in the background or the walnut shell on the ground?

Jan Gossart painted the *Venus and Cupid* in Room 25 in 1521, ten years before Cranach tackled the same subject. Gossart makes no reference to the legend of the bees, but concentrates instead on the fleshy figure of Venus. Gossart had travelled to Italy in 1508, returning to Antwerp with a new idea of rotund female beauty quite different from Cranach's slender gothic waifs. Gossart also painted the remarkable *Portrait of a Donor and his Wife* in which the man is fiddling with his coat in a way that suggests he has committed a secret crime. Trompe-l'œil labels (which we cannot see as they are on the back of each panel) beg for divine forgiveness, but for what offence?

Room 25 contains the wonderful *Girl with a Dead Bird*, painted by an unknown 16th-century Flemish artist. Art historians have tried, but so far failed, to identify this troubled blue-eyed girl in a bonnet, holding a dead fledgling in her hands.

Bernard van Orley lived in Brussels near the Place Saint Géry in the days when the square looked as it does on page 102. A young doctor called Georges Zelle who lived in the same square commissioned him in 1519 to paint the portrait we see in Room 26. The pattern of crossed hands on the hanging behind the doctor seems to suggest that the artist and the doctor were close friends, though the meaning of the interlocked letters remains a mystery. Van Orley also painted a melancholy portrait of Margaret of Austria, which pleased her so much that she had seven copies made (including the one we see here). Her mother had died after falling from her

horse when Margaret was just two. One year later, her father, Maximilian of Austria, married her to the future Charles VIII of France, but the marriage was dissolved nine years later to allow Charles to be paired off with the more useful Anne of Brittany. Maximilian then selected Don Juan of Castile as a suitable husband, hoping to link the Austrian and Spanish Hapsburg territories. Margaret, by then seventeen, was sent off to the Spanish court, but her new husband died nine months later, allegedly as a result of excessive lovemaking. At the age of twenty-four, Margaret married Philibert the Handsome, Duke of Savoy, but he died of pneumonia three years later after falling into an icy pond. It is hardly surprising that in 1521, when Margaret commissioned Van Orley to paint the large altarpiece in this room, she would choose the trials of Job as a subject. Bearing the title *The Virtue of Patience*, it shows a hurricane destroying the house where Job's children are feasting. It is often arguable whether a painting was executed by Van Orley or his workshop, but here there seems to be little doubt, as the artist has signed his name twice –

once on the edge of the step at the bottom of the painting, and again in a tiny inscription on the pillar to the left. If we peer closely, as we are so often required to do by Flemish artists, we can also see on the pillar the date 1521 and the motto '*Elx syne tyt*' (a time for everything) above the artist's signature.

We might pause in Room 28 to look at Jan van Coninxloo's *Saint Benedict's Altarpiece* of 1552. The scenes from the life of Saint Benedict include the miracle of the broken cup, in which an attempt to murder the saint is thwarted after he blesses the poisoned cup and it shatters. Van Coninxloo has set this scene in a 16th-century Flemish kitchen containing gleaming brass pots and a caged bird.

The museum is particularly proud of its collection of paintings by Pieter Bruegel the Elder, which are hung on rich burgundy walls in Room 31. The most famous of these is *The Fall of Icarus*, opposite, painted in the 1550's. Or so it was thought. The museum is now reluctantly admitting that this painting could not have been done by Bruegel, as it is painted on canvas which

dates from about 1600 and Bruegel died in 1569. Perhaps it was by his son, who copied all his father's works, but if so then what happened to the original? There is another version of the painting in the Van Buuren Museum (see page 341), but this, too, is apparently a copy. In the beautiful poem *Musée des Beaux-Arts* ('How right they were, the old masters'), W. H. Auden dwells on Brugel's Icarus as an illustration of the way that suffering 'takes place/While someone else is eating or opening a window or just walking dully along'. At first, we do not see Icarus at all; we see a ploughman, a daydreaming shepherd and a sailing ship. We have to look closely to see a tiny splash in the water and a leg about to disappear below the waves. Auden suggests that Icarus is ignored because 'the expensive delicate ship that must have seen/Something amazing, a boy falling out of the sky,/Had somewhere to get to and sailed calmly on'. Perhaps Auden saw the painting as a metaphor of the times. He wrote the poem during a stay in Brussels in the winter of 1938, when Jews were being persecuted in Germany as the world calmly looked on.

We have to search even more diligently to find the census-taker in Bruegel's *Census at Bethlehem*. This is definitely a Bruegel, painted in 1566 a few year after he had moved to Brussels. It is set in a snow-bound Flemish village of the Pajottenland, west of Brussels, on a crisp winter's day. At first, we are seduced by the charming scenes of children playing on the ice, the dilapidated village, and the fiery sphere of the setting sun. Only later do we discover the seated man in the fur coat noting down children's names, and the figure of Mary seated on a mule in the foreground. Bruegel has signed and dated the work in the bottom right-hand corner.

The other important work here by Bruegel, *The Fall of the Rebel Angels*, was painted in Antwerp in 1562. Like a scene from a horror film, it is crowded with bloated fish and winged monsters.

Is the name spelt Bruegel or Brueghel (or even Breughel)? It depends on the artist we are talking about. Pieter the Elder was born *Brueghel* but he later dropped the *h*. His sons Pieter the Younger and Jan restored the original family

name, which is sometimes confusingly spelt Breughel. In an attempt to clear up the confusion, art critics have given nicknames to the different family members. Thus, Pieter the Elder is known as 'Peasant Bruegel', his son Pieter the Younger is 'Hell Brueghel' and his other son Jan, who painted flowers, is 'Velvet Brueghel'.

Bruegel's painting of *The Massacre of the Innocents* is in Vienna, like many of his best works, but the Musée d'Art Ancien has a copy made by his son, Pieter Brueghel the Younger, who painted faithful copies of many of his father's works as well as landscapes on his own account. He has signed this canvas in the same place as his father, but reverted to the old-fashioned spelling of Brueghel. We also find Pieter the Younger's copy of his father's *Wedding Dance*, which hangs in Vienna. Despite his nickname of Hell Brueghel, however, there are no known paintings by him in which Hell appears. Perhaps 'Fake Brueghel' would be a better moniker.

Room 32 contains a painting by Denijs van Alsloot showing *The Festival at the Vivier d'Oye* which may have belonged to the same series as the Ommegang paintings on pages 12-13. As usual, Van Alsloot gives us a crowded scene filled with fascinating details such as the man wielding a sword in the middle of the lake and the spectators (Albert and Isabella among them) watching the festivities from a curious covered grandstand created from clipped hedges.

We come across another painting by Van Alsloot in Room 34. His *Winter Landscape with the Castle of Tervuren* was painted in 1614 looking across the frozen lake to the old ducal castle rebuilt by Albrecht and Isabella. But the strangest paintings in this room are two 16th-century *Anthropomorphic Landscapes*. We know nothing about the artist, or indeed these two paintings, apart from the fact that they conceal the faces of a man and woman. A green hill in one painting turns out to be a woman's head ingeniously formed out of strategically positioned rocks and shrubs. A line of sheep forms a fairly convincing pearl necklace and a little red chapel turns out to be her lips. The man's head is also formed from a hill, with a craggy rock as his chin and a clump of bushes as a beard. His ear, looked at closely, is a hollow rock, and his nose is formed by a house.

The next rooms (Nos. 37 to 45) contain the Delporte-Livrauw Bequest. Almost a museum in its own right, this collection of Flemish art was given by Franz Delporte and his wife Marguerite Livrauw. It is arranged chronologically, like the main collection, so we find ourselves going back to the early middle ages. In Room 44 we come upon a painting by Pieter Bruegel the Elder that many visitors fail to find. Bruegel painted *Winter Landscape with Skaters and a Bird-Trap* in the winter of 1565. It shows a typical Brabant village in the rolling Pajottenland. It might be the church of Pede-Sint-Anne which we see on the edge of the lake, with the spires of Brussels visible in the distance. The scene looks innocent enough, with villagers skating on the ice and children immersed in games. Yet there is a hint of menace concealed in the scene, for some birds in the bottom right-hand corner are pecking at crumbs beside a crude wooden bird trap.

Pieter Bruegel the Younger painted *The Village Wedding* we see in this room in 1607. He based it on one of his father's paintings which no longer exists, and signed it BRUEGHEL 1607 to avoid it being confused with the original work. The scene is again set in one of the villages to the west of Brussels where Bruegel the Elder painted many of his most famous works. It shows a plump bride sitting down at a table to receive various gifts, while guests dance to bagpipe music and three men relieve themselves against a cottage wall.

We now follow the brown route, which leads us up the stairs past a fascinating painting by Antoon Sallaert, *The Infanta Isabella shoots down a wooden bird during an archery contest on the Sablon*, reproduced opposite. Isabella is said to have brought down a wooden parrot from the spire of the Sablon church with her first arrow. We can see her standing in front of the tent on the left, wearing a stiff lace collar that must have made it difficult to aim a heavy crossbow. Looking more closely at the painting, we can see that the sky is full of arrows, which must have made it virtually impossible to judge who fired the winning shot.

Hanging at the top of the stairs, we find Jan Baptist Bonnecroy's luminous *View of Brussels*, reproduced on page 4-5. Bonnecroy stood on a hill to the north of Brussels on a breezy spring day with dappled sunlight falling on the red pantiled roofs. The exact date of the painting is uncertain, but it was probably in 1664 or 1665, judging from the buildings visible. We can see the cathedral with its twin towers on the hill opposite, and the tall spire of the town hall near the centre of the city.

Pieter Bruegel the Elder, whose *Census at Bethlehem* we have just seen, was buried in the large gothic church to the right of the town hall, which we can visit on Walk 5. Bruegel often left the city by the Porte de Hal, on the far right, to paint scenes such as *The Bird Trap*. The road below Bonnecroy's vantage point is the Chaussée de Gand, along which Charlotte Brontë's carriage bumped when she entered Brussels in 1842.

We know almost nothing about the life of Jan Baptist Bonnecroy. He was born in Antwerp in 1618, studied landscape painting under Lucas

van Uden and joined the Brussels painters' guild in 1665. His only son died at the age of twenty-two, leaving his eldest daughter Anna Maria to inherit his unsold paintings. When she died in 1761, her estate included a large painting of Brussels and a view of Antwerp. These two works were bought by the Duke of Arenberg, whose descendents sold them in 1960 to a New York book dealer who hung them in the family mansion in Ridgefield. When they came on the market in 1990, the King Baudouin Foundation snapped up the Brussels view, and Antwerp city bought the view of Antwerp, which now hangs in the Maritime Museum. Amsterdammers failed to pick up a third Bonnecroy panorama, showing their city from the north, which now hangs in the Musée d'Ixelles (described on page 339).

If we now go through the door to the right, we can follow the sign pointing to the Rubens collection in Rooms 52 and 62. If we are bracing ourselves for Rubens' fleshy nudes, we are in for a pleasant surprise, for the works in Room 52 are small and intimate. We find a charming *Portrait of Helena Fourment*, Rubens' vivacious second wife, with her rippling blonde hair and neat black hat. The *Portrait of Paracelsus* next to her is a copy of a lost work by Quentin Metsys.

We find a curious portrait of *Four Negro Heads* which shows the face of an African man in four different moods. We know nothing about the identity of the sitter, apart from the fact that he posed again in Rubens' *Adoration of the Magi*, which hangs in the next room, and again in Jacob Jordaens' painting of *St Martin* in Room 57. The set of twelve chalk drawings in the middle of Room 52 may surprise us with their delicacy. Rubens drew in 1636 these studies for a series of paintings to decorate the Torre de la Parada, a royal hunting lodge outside Madrid. They include a *Fall of Icarus* in which Rubens, unlike Bruegel, picks on the dramatic moment when the boy begins to plunge to earth.

The dark *Landscape with the Hunt of Atalanta* is a romantic country scene painted by Rubens near his country retreat of Het Steen, north of Brussels. Paintings such as this were popular with British collectors and influenced 18th-century English landscape artists such as

Gainsborough and Constable. Rubens' religious works had more impact on French 18th-century artists such as Delacroix. The debt is clearly shown by Delacroix's copy and Rubens' original version of *The Miracles of Saint Benedict* which hang near each other in this room. We have already met this theme in Room 28, though Rubens had no time for the episode with the broken cup we saw earlier.

Rubens painted a double portrait of *Archdukes Albrecht and Isabella* some years after Isabella's triumph with the crossbow. It seems odd that they have been hung at opposite ends of the room. If they were together, we could see more easily that the two paintings are linked by a common wall at the bottom and a dark red cloth draped in the background. Another couple – Jean-Charles de Cordes and Jacqueline van Caestre – are also hung in opposite corners, though this dour pair look as if they might well have chosen not to be together for long periods.

The next room (No. 62) contains several large altarpieces painted for churches in Ghent and Tournai. Plundered by the French and taken off to Paris, these were later returned to Brussels, where they now hang without frames, looking rather out of place. We have to imagine them suspended above an altar with candles flickering and a whiff of incense in the air. We might notice the familiar face of Helena Fourment wiping Christ's brow in *The Bearing of the Cross* and the African we saw earlier wearing a turban in the *Adoration of the Magi*.

The next room (No. 54) contains several works by Frans Snijders, including *The Larder* which is reproduced on page 387. Snijders spent his youth in an Antwerp tavern famed for its good food. This had a profound influence on his paintings, which lovingly depict plates of oysters and overflowing baskets of fruit.

On leaving this room, we reach the open gallery overlooking the main hall (No. 53). Several Flemish paintings hung here show the interiors of 17th-century private picture galleries. This genre flourished Antwerp and Brussels, permitting collectors to show off all their art treasures in a single canvas. One such painting by Hieronymus Francken the Younger shows

The Cabinet of Jan Sellinck in Antwerp. Another painting of this type, opposite, hangs on the other side of the hall (Room 60). Painted by David Teniers, *Archduke Léopold-William in his Gallery* gives us an intriguing glimpse inside the picture gallery of the ducal palace at Brussels in 1651. Teniers has usefully painted the artists' names on the frames so that we know that the painting protected by a green curtain is a Raphael (it shows Saint Margaret) and that most of the other works admired by the Archduke are by Italian artists.

Before we look at the Teniers, we should look for Anthony van Dyck's *Genoese Lady with her Daughter* in Room 53, painted during a six-year stay in Genoa. Van Dyck travelled to Rome to paint the portrait we see of Frans Duquesnoy, a Flemish sculptor resident there. We now come upon an unexpected collection of 17th-century Dutch paintings in Room 60, including a luminous *Market Square at Haarlem* by Gerrit Berckheyde and Rembrandt's *Portrait of Nicolaes van Bambeeck*, which once hung alongside the portrait of his wife Agatha Bas (she is now in Buckingham Palace).

After we have looked at Van Bambeeck, we can leave this floor and return to the main hall. Several large paintings hang here, including Jacques-Louis David's *Mars Disarmed by Venus*. This almost painfully bright picture was painted while David was living in exile in Brussels at Rue Léopold 5. He apparently used actresses from the Monnaie theatre, opposite his house, as models. The work dates from the year before he died, as we know from the inscription partly hidden by a dark cloud.

We are now ready for the yellow route, which we reach through a room containing five paintings of 17th-century battles by Pieter Snayers, including a remarkable view of the *Siege of Kortrijk*. Snayers was a highly skilled war artist who painted dozens of works showing troop formations and siege techniques in astonishing detail. He supplied twenty-one of these battlefield paintings to the Duke of Amalfi, who led the imperial army in the Netherlands, and a set of twelve to Archduke Léopold-William (including the five here). Perhaps these were the

paintings that Evelyn saw when he visited the ducal palace, which he described in his diary as 'stories of most of the late actions in the Netherlands'.

III. The Musée d'Art Moderne. We now take an escalator down to the Musée d'Art Moderne, passing Arman's *Hommage to Jackson Pollock*, which the artist created by squeezing paint tubes onto a canvas. Turning right at the bottom, we enter the 19th-century department which occupies the basement and three floors of a neoclassical town house at Place Royale 1. Originally built in 1779 to house the administration of the imperial lottery, this building became the Hôtel Britannique in the early 19th century, later changing its name to the Hôtel de l'Europe. We begin in the basement (level minus 2) where Jacques-Louis David's *Marat dead in his bath* shows the murder of the revolutionary Jacobin doctor Jean-Paul Marat. Afflicted by a debilitating skin disease that could only be alleviated by immersion in water, Marat spent long hours in the bath writing political tracts. He

was in this vulnerable position when Charlotte Corday, a Normandy woman who supported the more moderate Girondist cause, burst in and stabbed him to death. Marat is shown holding the bloodstained begging letter dated 13 July 1793 that Corday wrote as a ploy to gain access to the bathroom. David painted the dead body at the scene of the crime, adding the date 1793 at the bottom of the wooden crate which Marat had been using as a writing table. (Scrubbed out but still visible is the original date - *l'An II* - in France's short-lived Revolutionary calendar.)

Also in this room is a preliminary study by Antoine Wiertz of *The Apotheosis of Queen Marie-Louise*. This enormous painting was commissioned to celebrate the Belgian Silver Jubilee in 1856. Had it been executed, the work would have been considerably taller than the Colonne de Congrès, but the project was abandoned. The more macabre side of Wiertz is seen in *La Belle Rosine* in which a voluptuous Rubensian woman confronts her own skeleton.

One floor up (level minus 1), we find several paintings by Alfred Stevens, a Belgian artist who enjoyed considerable success in Paris. His *Autumn Flowers*, painted in 1867, illustrates a style that appealed to the well-off Parisian women of the Second Empire. We also find several sombre Flemish interiors by Henri de Braekeleer, who specialised in nostalgic scenes such as *The Card Game* in which two children are playing cards in a sunlit neo-renaissance interior.

Climbing to the next floor (level 1), we find paintings by Henri Evenepoel, a Belgian artist who, like Stevens, spent most of his life in Paris, painting portraits such as *The Man in Red* of 1894, which shows the artist Paul Baignières posing with his easel and paint brushes in front of a bucolic fresco. He appears to be painting, though it seems unlikely that he would go to work wearing such a neat red suit and pink shirt. Evenepoel died in 1899 at the age of twenty-seven, soon after painting the sullen girl we see in *Henrietta wearing a Large Hat*.

We should find Anna Boch looking dark and mysterious in an 1884 portrait by Isidore Verheyden in this room. Boch was a talented artist, as we see in her 1901 painting of *The Shores of Brit-tany*. She joined Les Vingt and became friends with several Belgian artists, helping them find work designing tiles for her father's ceramic factory. Boch built up a large collection of modern paintings including Van Gogh's *Red Vineyard* of 1888, which she bought for four hundred francs at an exhibition of Les Vingt in the winter of 1890. This turned out to be the only painting Van Gogh sold in his lifetime.

The next floor (level 2) contains a small bronze version of Jef Lambeau's *Human Passions*, dating from 1889. The full-size version was installed in a pavilion built by Victor Horta in the Parc du Cinquantenaire, but it caused such moral outrage that it was quickly closed to the public, and has remained so ever since. It seems odd, therefore, to be allowed to look at the miniature.

The next room has walls painted a rich blue tone that echoes the blue in Edward Coley Burne-Jones' *Psyche's Wedding*. This alluring room contains symbolist works by Fernand Khnopff, who spent the first six years of his life in Bruges, where his father was a local magistrate. The family moved to Brussels in 1864, settling in a large town house at Rue Saint Bernard 1, which later suffered the indignity of having its ground floor converted into a petrol station, but has now been restored to its original state. Khnopff remained haunted by the misty atmosphere of Bruges, though he rarely returned to the city, preferring to use tourist postcards for inspiration. A photograph of the Memlingplaats reproduced in the novel *Bruges-la-Morte* inspired *An Abandoned City*, painted in 1904. Khnopff meticulously copied the building with the double step gable from the photograph, but omitted the figure of Memling from the stone plinth and added a mythical sea lapping the brick walls. The melancholy mood of Bruges was not Khnopff's only obsession. He made endless portraits of his younger sister Marguerite, such as the one hanging here, painted in 1887 in cool tones of grey and white. The strange *Memories of Lawn Tennis* of 1889 shows seven women – all modelled on Marguerite – playing tennis. Opposite is his equally unsettled picture, *Listening to Schumann*.

By the time we reach level 3, Belgian art is beginning to shake free of French influences. A room on this floor contains paintings by James Ensor, who was in the same class as Khnopff at the Brussels Academy of Fine Arts. While Khnopff moved in with his parents in Brussels, Ensor returned to Ostend to work in a studio above his mother's souvenir shop. His early works were melancholy portraits set in bourgeois interiors, such as the 1881 portrait of his English father, the portrait of his Flemish mother from one year later, and *The Russian Music*, painted in 1881 for Anna Boch, and apparently showing Boch sitting at the piano with her back to us, while the painter Alfred William Finch listens to her playing Russian music. By 1883, Ensor's style had changed dramatically, as we see in *Scandalised Masks*, in which two locals are wearing Carnival masks in a bare interior.

Ensor's art became increasingly eccentric over the next twenty years, leading to the vibrant colours of *Odd Masks* in 1892 and the bizarre vision of *Skeletons quarrelling over a Kipper* of 1891, which makes more sense when we discover that the French word for a kipper (*hareng saur*) sounds vaguely like Ensor. By the 1920's Ensor was

considered the grand old man of Belgian art. He was visited in Ostend by Einstein, and made a Baron by King Albert in 1929. Yet this did not prevent his greatest painting from being sold to the J. Paul Getty Museum in 1983. Painted in 1888, Ensor's *Entry of Christ into Brussels* used to hang in Antwerp's Museum of Fine Arts, but the Belgian government was unable to match the Getty offer when it came on the market and the painting now hangs prominently in the new Getty Museum in Los Angeles. All that remains in Belgium is a small detail we see in this room showing *Figures in front of the Poster for 'La Gamme d'Amour'*. If we look closely at the poster we can read that it is advertising a ballet with music by Ensor staged in 1914.

The next room contains a small collection of French Impressionism, including Bonnard's *Nude against the light* of 1907 and Gauguin's *Portrait of Suzanne Bambridge*, painted in 1891 in Tahiti, and showing an eccentric English expatriate who married a Maori chief on the island. Three of the paintings in this room once hung in Anna Boch's house alongside the Khnopff we saw two floors down and the Van Gogh she bought in 1890 – Seurat's *The Seine at La Grande-Jatte*, painted on the same island as the famous *Sunday at the Island of La Grande-Jatte* in the London National Gallery, Gauguin's *Conversation in the Fields* and Signac's *The Creek*.

We return to Belgian art in a room containing part of the Rik Wouters collection (the rest is in the modern department). Born in Mechelen, Wouters studied sculpture at the Brussels Academy. It was here that he met Hélène Duerinckx, or Nel as she was known, a young woman who posed for art classes. They married and lived together in the Brussels suburb of Watermael-Boitsfort. Wouters later took up painting and used Nel as a model in many of his works, such as the wistful *Woman with a Yellow Necklace* of 1912.

Before we leave this room, we should note the strange Impressionist *View of London* painted by Emile Claus on a day of watery sunshine in 1917. Claus fled to London during the First World War, where he painted several views of the Thames in a style that was by then rather old-fashioned. Other works in this room, such as

Albert Servaes' *Lamentation*, illustrate the religious leanings of the First Latem School. This colony of artists – which included Gustave van de Woestijne and Valerius de Saedeleer – settled in the village of Sint-Martens-Latem to the west of Ghent in the early 20th century.

We now return to level minus 2, and follow the signs to the green route. After a long and heated debate, it was decided to house the modern art collection in a modern building sunk eight floors below the cobbled courtyard of Charles of Lorraine's palace. We begin our tour at level minus 2, then descend by a circular route to the lowest floor at level minus 8. On the way, we will discover Léon Spilliaert, Paul Delvaux and René Magritte. Some of the sections are devoted to particular movements, but by the time we reach level minus 8 the museum curators have the honesty to admit that they are at a loss to label the diverse works. We can perhaps see why, as our attention wanders from wooden posts leaning against a wall to the two smashed violins glued onto a canvas in Arman's *Angry Violins*. Even the names of several artists are a source of confusion: Panamarenko takes his name from the Pan Am airline, and another sculptor for some reason signs himself Denmark.

We begin by descending to level minus 3, where Dennis Oppenheim's *Attempt to Raise Hell* features a brass bell suspended above a puppet lit by an eerie blue spotlight. The bell is struck at random intervals, echoing through the museum. Oppenheim was notorious in the 1970's for performances that involved props such as a live tarantula, and a dead dog laid out on an organ keyboard to produce a sound that changed subtly as rigor mortis set in. Further down the corridor, we come upon Vic Gentils' *Rua de Amor*, a strange wooden sculpture made from bits of old piano and representing two prostitutes and a client in a Brazilian brothel.

Down one level (minus 4), we discover the rest of the Rik Wouters collection, including a sullen Nel posing for the statue *Household Cares* of 1913-14 and Nel again studying her reflection in a mirror in *Woman in Blue*. In *The Flute Player* of 1914, Wouters has clearly fallen under the spell of Cézanne. One of his last works, this was painted in his house in Watermael-Boitsfort looking out onto suburban roofs and the distant Forêt de Soignes. Wouters was imprisoned in the Netherlands after the outbreak of war, and died of eye cancer in an Amsterdam military hospital in the summer of 1916, aged only 34.

The appealing school of Brabant Fauvism is represented by Ferdinand Schirren's *Woman at the Piano*, a strangely tranquil work painted during the First World War. A portrait by Willem Paerels shows the Brussels gallery dealer Georges Giroux, who organised a Wouters exhibition in 1912 and a Schirren show in 1917.

The edgy Symbolist paintings of Léon Spilliaert, whose father ran a perfume shop in Ostend, occupy a separate room. Here we find a 1908 view of the Royal Arcades in Ostend, *The Bather* of 1910 and an ominous painting from the same year of a vast airship. Unable to sleep at night, Spilliaert wandered the lonely streets of Ostend, painting dark restaurants and the deserted promenade. This haunted *Self-Portrait* of 1904 was done on one such sleepless night when he sat in his living room looking at his reflection in a

mirror lit by moonlight.

Now for the Latem School or, rather, the *Second Latem School*, for we have already met artists such as Gustave van de Woestijne and Albert Servaes from the first school. Looking for an escape from the industrial Belgian cities, the artists of the Second Latem School were drawn to the simple peasant life of East Flanders. Some arrived in the 1910's, while others, often shell-shocked from the trenches, came to Latem in the 1920's to paint some of the works we find here. They tended to produce melancholy works in muddy tones of brown and grey, as we can see in Constant Permeke's 1916 painting of *The Stranger*. Considered the first work of Flemish Expressionism, it was in fact painted in Britain, where Permeke had been sent to recuperate after being wounded in 1914 during the siege of Antwerp. Another gloomy painting by Permeke titled *The Potato Eater*, 1935, hardly makes peasant life seem attractive. Frits van den Berghe's *Sunday* of 1924 gives a more cheerful vision of rural life on the banks of the River Leie. But perhaps the most appealing artist of the group is Gustave de Smet who painted *The Dressing Room* in 1928, showing a circus artiste with rouged cheeks being visited by a mysterious stranger.

The next level down (minus 5) is devoted to the eerie Surrealism of Paul Delvaux. Most of the paintings here date from his melancholy middle years in Brussels, when he became increasingly obsessed by skeletons, night trains, empty trams and nude women. He was still living with his parents in the Rue d'Ecosse in 1928 when he met Anne-Marie de Martelaere, known for some reason as Tam. Delvaux ended the relationship after his overbearing mother made him promise never to marry her. One year later, his fear of women was intensified by a visit to the Spitzner Museum, a travelling exhibition at the Midi Fair organised by a Doctor Spitzner and featuring ghastly wax figures of naked women showing the effects of venereal disease. Already warned off women by his mother, Delvaux found himself staring at a nude waxwork with a hidden machine that moved her chest to create the impression of breathing. It was an image that

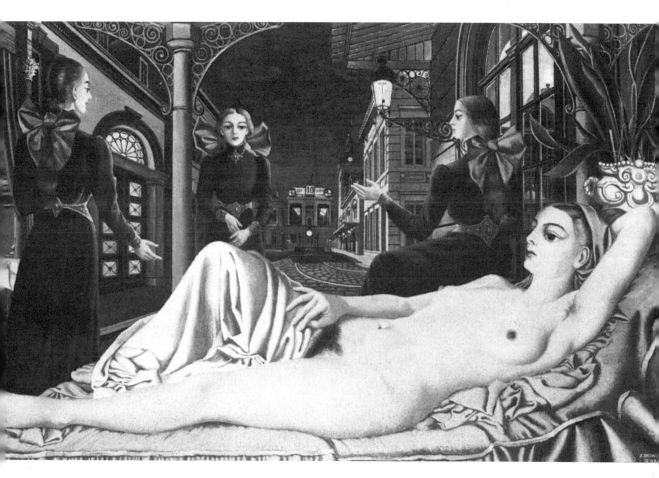

was to haunt him for the rest of his life. 'All the sleeping Venuses I have painted originated there,' he once confessed. Delvaux's 1943 painting *Musée Spitzner*, which dates from the German Occupation, shows the lingering memory of the fairground attraction he had visited eleven years earlier. A naked boy stares at a voluptuous woman while a group of academics stand in an empty street outside the old Gare du Midi.

Delvaux, seen here in later life, discovered Surrealism in 1934 at the Minotaur exhibition in the Palais des Beaux-Arts, which included paintings by Dalí, Magritte and De Chirico. His *Pygmalion* of 1939 is set in a barren Mediterranean landscape similar to De Chirico's scenes. Many of Delvaux's works echo classical works, such as *La Voix Publique* of 1948, on the previous page, in which a naked female reclines in the style of a Titian nude. The setting, though, is a 19th-century Brussels street near a station, and the woman resembles one of the wax models in the Musée Spitzner.

The world's largest collection of Magritte is hung in a series of small rooms at level minus 6.

This collection was recently boosted by paintings left to the museum by Magritte's wife Georgette, who died in 1987. Many of the works once decorated the Magritte's suburban home in the Rue des Mimosas. The nude portraits of Georgette in *La Magie Noire* and *Le Galet* were hung in a corner of Magritte's studio above an ugly green sofa. We may wonder if the enigmatic titles provide a clue to Magritte's art, but this is probably a blind alley. Many of the names were playfully coined by friends who met regularly at the Magritte's house. Perhaps it is more fruitful to look for clues in Magritte's strange childhood in southern Belgium. He was once sitting in his pram when a balloon crashed on the roof of the family home in Lessines. A more horrific experience occurred in 1912, at the age of 14, when he found his mother's naked body floating in a river. Stricken by the suicide, the family moved to Charleroi the following year. Magritte met Georgette at the local school and married her nine years later in Brussels. He studied art at the Brussels Academy during the First World War and left in 1922 to work briefly in a wall-paper factory. Two years later, he was converted to Surrealism after seeing Giorgio de Chirico's *Le Chant d'Amour*.

One of the most famous paintings in the collection is the *Empire de la Lumière* (Empire – or Power – of Light) in which we see a house at night lit by a solitary street lamp. It seems a perfectly normal suburban scene until we notice that there is daylight above the trees. The title was invented by Paul Nougé, a Surrealist writer who appears in a strange double portrait painted by Magritte in 1927. Georgette can be seen in a portrait of 1935 surrounded by a bird, a key and a scrap of paper with the word 'vague'. It is perhaps futile to search for any meaning in this painting. 'The objects are not symbols, nor is her face,' Magritte once declared.

There are paintings by other Surrealists in the next room, including Giorgio de Chirico's *Melancholy of a Beautiful Day*, painted in 1913 and showing an empty Italian square lit by a harsh afternoon sun. Salvador Dalí's *Temptation of Saint Anthony* tackles a theme we have already met in Room 17. Dalí shows the naked saint on a

Catalan beach as a procession of three elephants with spindly legs approach him laden with symbols of temptation. This work was painted for a competition organised in 1946 by the American film producer Albert Lewin, who was looking for a painting of the Temptation of Saint Anthony to use in a screen adaptation of a Maupassant novel. Dalí, who had already designed sets for Hitchcock's *Spellbound*, was one of twelve artists who submitted entries. Neither he nor Delvaux, another entrant, won. Lewin finally chose a work by Max Ernst (now in a museum in Duisburg). It appears briefly in Lewin's now forgotten film *The Private Affairs of Bel Ami*.

We find gloomy works by the Jeune Peinture Belge movement on the next level down (minus 7). The pessimism immediately vanishes when we come to the COBRA group, who coined their name in a Paris brasserie in 1948 by taking the initial letters of their home towns Copenhagen, Brussels and Amsterdam. The Belgian artist Corneille's *A New Dawn Full of Birds* reflects COBRA's post-war optimism in its very title.

Another Belgian, Pierre Alechinsky, teases us with a whimsical painting titled *Sometimes it's the Opposite*. Sadly, this exuberant group wound up its affairs in 1951, though many of its members are still active.

The deepest level, eight floors below ground level, is occupied by an enjoyably irreverent collection of recent art. The Belgian Surrealist Marcel Broodthaers entertains us with his solemn attempts to create a Museum of Modern Art containing a Department of Eagles. His mock museum cabinets contain exhibits such as a blank canvas and a lump of coal wrapped like a precious jewel. Much of Broodthaers' energy went into mocking his fellow Belgians, as in his red cooking pot overflowing with mussels, and the bone he has painted with the colours of the Belgian flag. A useful compendium of his motifs can be seen on his gravestone, reproduced on pages 369 and 370.

The most recent works in this museum reflect some oddly obsessive artists, such as the German Bernd Lohaus, who now lives in Antwerp and spends much of his time gathering driftwood from the Scheldt to create works such as the row of sixteen planks leaning against a wall to form *Wandskulpturen*. Christian Boltanski, a French-Polish artist who survived the war hidden under floorboards, clipped photographs of murder victims from a sensational Spanish magazine to create the morbid *Shrine: Murders* and Wim Delvoye has produced a cabinet of mock Dutch Delftware using gas cannisters and saws in his *Installation with Two Gas Cylinders and 29 Saws*. But the most obsessive is the French painter Roman Opalka, who produces works such as the one here titled *Detail n°s 1556343-1574101*, which he creates by adding successive numbers to a canvas and photographing the result at the end of each day.

All that remains is to make our way to the Sculpture Gallery in the basement, where we find two robust figures that may have been carved by Rodin for a house near the Bourse. We can also admire Guillaume Geefs's romantic statue of the dying Count Frédéric de Mérode, wounded during the 1830 revolution near Antwerp. 'At about 4 o'clock in the afternoon,

a bullet went straight through his right thigh,' an eyewitness wrote. And there's the bullet hole clearly visible in Mérode's thigh, as clear as the gash in Marat's chest. The vaulted brick cellar beyond is lined with 19th-century busts lit skilfully to allow us to appreciate the folds of cloth in Charles Geerts's *Deipara Virgo* and the sensual profile of Charles-Auguste Fraikin's bust of Justa de Potter. We also find a bronze bust by Ollivier de Marseille of Charles of Lorraine, looking wilder than he appears in the statue we passed earlier.

As we pass through the cloakroom on our way out, we should pause a moment in front of Gustave Wapper's *Day in September 1830*, which shows rebels hoisting the Belgian flag on Grand'-Place on 20 September. Wappers may have been inspired by Delacroix's famous painting in the Louvre of *Liberty leading the People*, which also has a date in its title (28 July 1830). The main difference is that Delacroix painted his work soon after the event, whereas Wappers waited until five years had elapsed. In *Villette*, Charlotte Brontë dismissed the Belgian revolution curtly as:

163

'a kind of struggling in the street – a bustle – a running to and fro, some rearing of barricades, some burgher-rioting, some calling out of troops, much interchange of brick-bats, and even a little of shot.' The Belgians see it differently.

WALK 4

The Sablon

PLACE LOUISE TO NOTRE-DAME DU SABLON

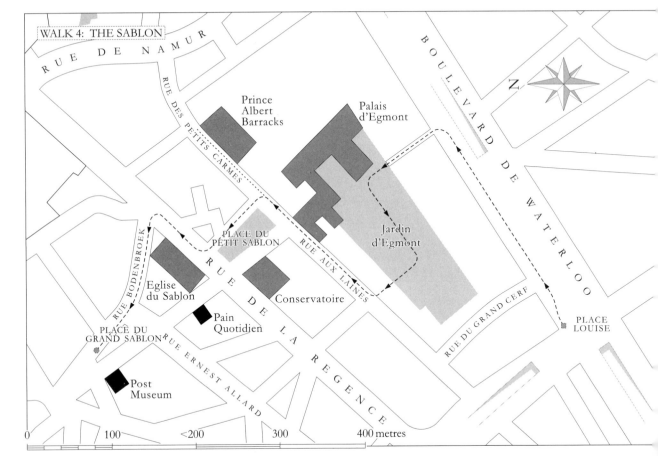

WALK 4: THE SABLON

RUE DE NAMUR

RUE DES PETITS CARMES

Prince
Albert
Barracks

Palais
d'Egmont

BOULEVARD DE WATERLOO

N

RUE BODENBROEK

PLACE DU
PETIT SABLON

RUE AUX LAINES

Jardin
d'Egmont

RUE DE LA REGENCE

Eglise
du Sablon

Conservatoire

Pain
Quotidien

PLACE DU
GRAND SABLON

RUE ERNEST ALLARD

RUE DU GRAND CERF

PLACE
LOUISE

Post
Museum

0   100   <200   300   400 metres

WALK 4

The Sablon

FROM PLACE LOUISE TO NOTRE-DAME DU SABLON

This short walk, which lasts about two hours, takes us through one of the most attractive quarters of Brussels, where we still find the occasional aristocratic mansion to admire. The walk is best done on a Saturday or Sunday, when an antique market occupies the square where we end our walk. We start by taking the metro or tram to Place Louise, or by catching bus 34 from the Bourse. A pause for coffee can be made at La Crèmerie de la Vache, off Avenue Louise at Rue Jean Stas 6 (closed Sundays). The interior is like an old-fashioned French cheese shop, with white tiled walls, bare wooden floors and blue-and-white checked tablecloths. The coffee comes on a silver tray with a little bottle of milk and a chocolate. On leaving we retrace our steps to Place Louise and cross to Boulevard de Waterloo, then turn right past the Versace shop.

I. The Parc d'Egmont. We continue along the Boulevard de Waterloo, past the Hilton doorman, then turn left down a cobbled lane that leads to the Egmont Park, a forgotten patch of greenery where elderly ladies walk their dogs in the afternoon. When Coghlan wrote his 1837 guide this was a 'spacious and magnificent garden, where the richest and rarest flowers are cultivated, especially the *camellia* species.' The camellias have gone, but the park is still dotted with the odd interesting feature, such as the recently restored Orangerie, the bronze replica of the Peter Pan statue in London's Kensington

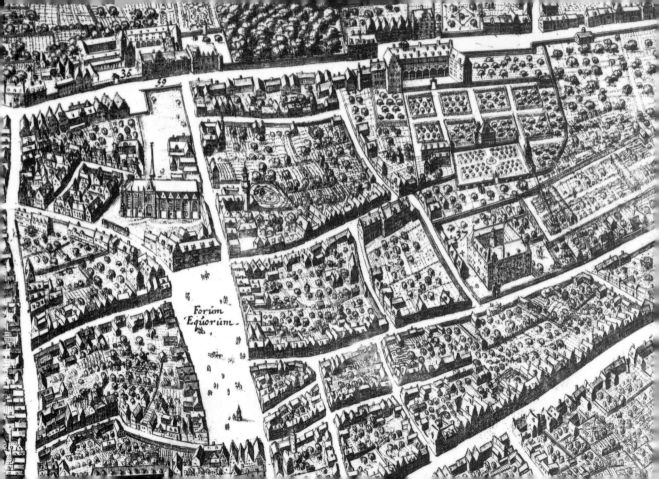

Forúm
Equorum

Gardens, and six mysterious Doric columns. Perhaps the strangest relic is an ancient well known as the Groote Pollepel (the great wooden spoon) which still provided water for the Isabelle Quarter in Charlotte Brontë's day. The well used to stand to the north of the Pensionnat Heger, but was moved to a corner of the park in the 1950's when the Galerie Ravenstein was constructed. The neoclassical building overlooking the park stands on the site of the 16th-century palace of Count Egmont. It was here that the British and Irish prime ministers signed the Treaty of Rome in 1973, an occasion for which Heath was decorated, with eggs thrown at him by a protestor.

We leave the park by a new entrance opposite the Hilton Hotel, where lines from a poem by Marguerite Yourcenar are reproduced on the paving stones. Yourcenar was born in a house on Avenue Louise in 1903. She made her name with the publication of *Memoirs of Hadrian*, a novel in the form of a long letter written by Emperor Hadrian to Marcus Aurelius as he becomes aware of death approaching.

We now go right along the Rue aux Laines, where the Duke of Arenberg commissioned the architect Löw to build a row of twenty-one neoclassical mansions along our side of the street; each one is signed 'Guillaume Löw 1903'. On the opposite side, Benjamin de Lestré added his distinctive signature on the corner of the elaborate neo-baroque building at No. 15.

The gates of the Palais d'Egmont are a little further on the right. An older palace than the one we see now was built here in the 16th century by the Princess of Gavre, widow of Count Jean d'Egmont. This palace – numbered 39 on the De Tailly map opposite – passed to her son, the unfortunate Lamoral d'Egmont who was beheaded in 1568. The building was confiscated by the King of Spain, but returned to the family in 1576. It eventually passed to the Duke of Arenberg, who in 1753 employed the architect Jean-Nicolas Servandoni to build the neoclassical main wing we see in front of us.

Coghlan wrote enthusiastically about the Arenberg Palace, as it was then called, in his 1837 guidebook. It had a splendid picture-gallery and a valuable collection of Etruscan vases. But one feature particularly impressed Coghlan. 'The family of Arenberg are said to be in possession of the real head of the Laocoon.' One of the major archaeological discoveries of renaissance Italy, the sculpture is now kept in the Vatican.

The Palais d'Egmont looks like a perfectly symmetrical neoclassical building, yet the three wings in fact date from three different centuries. The building straight ahead of us was built in 1753 by Servandoni, while the left wing was added on the site of an old church in 1832-7, and the right wing tacked on in 1905 after the gothic Egmont palace seen in De Tailly's map burned down. The three architects have succeeded in creating total harmony, which is something of a miracle in Brussels.

We are about to enter the park opposite, but there are two more buildings to look at first. If we continue along Rue des Petits Carmes, we pass the massive Prince Albert Barracks on the right. This stands on the site of the prison where Verlaine was taken after he had shot Rimbaud. Further along the street, we can see a plaque high on the wall next to the gate at No. 20. It is virtually impossible to read the inscription, but if we could we would discover that this is the site of Culembourg Palace, scene of the banquet that sparked off the Revolt against Spain. We now go back into the park where, if the weather is fine, we can sit on one of the benches facing the fountain to read the history of this neighbourhood.

II. The Place du Petit Sablon. We are now in the heart of the quarter where the Revolt of the Netherlands began in 1566. A group of nobles, about three hundred in all, gathered in the Culembourg Palace in Rue des Petits Carmes. Led by Count Brederode, they set off for the ducal palace, marching along the street behind us where the trams now run. After passing through the great hall, the foundations of which are preserved in a museum below Place Royale, they entered the council room where Margaret of Parma was sitting. Brederode presented their petition, in which the nobles called on Margaret to end the inquisiton and respect freedom of religion. After it was over and the nobles had left, Count Berlaymont uttered his famous quip, 'Is it possible that your Highness can be afraid of these beggars?' Two days later, Brederode organised a banquet in the Culembourg Palace, at which he produced a beggar's bowl and purse, and uttered the cry, 'Long live the beggars!' The nickname stuck, and for the next eighty years, the Spanish found themselves hounded on land and sea by beggars.

We won't find any trace of the Culembourg Palace, which was demolished by the Duke of Alva in an outburst of rage that also led to a spate of executions. Nor have any of the other palaces survived, but we can admire the statues of some of the leading figures of the Revolt, at least as 19th-century sculptors imagined them, among the ten figures gathered in a semicircle around the fountain in front of us. The two figures on the plinth are Egmont and Hoorn, who remained forgotten until the 19th century, when the young Belgian state, searching around for national heroes, pounced on the counts beheaded by the Duke of Alva. Charles-Auguste

Fraikin designed this romantic statue of the pair to stand on Grand'Place, but it was considered too large for the square, and was moved to this site, in front of the Egmont Palace, in 1879.

On the far right of the semicircle, sword in hand, is William the Silent, who fled from Brussels just in time to escape the fate of Egmont and Hoorn, though a Spanish assassin finally caught up with him in Delft. Third from the right is Count Brederode, identified by a begging bowl hidden in the folds of his cloak, while on the far left, posed in front of a pile of books, is Philip of Marnix, the leading thinker of the Dutch Revolt who wrote an influential book on teaching languages to children. Some of the other statues may be familiar to us, such as Lodewijk van Bodeghem (on the right between William of Orange and Count Brederode) who worked with Hendrik van Pede on the Maison du Roi, though he is here commemorated for the church he designed for Margaret of Austria in Brou, southern France. He is holding a plan of the church, which was built in memory of Margaret's third husband (the one who died of pneumonia after

falling in a lake). Bernard van Orley, whose portrait of Margaret of Austria hangs in the Musée des Beaux-Arts, is third from the left. Fifth from the right, Cornelis de Vriendt, the architect of Antwerp's town hall, stands in front of a renaissance satyr. Next to him, the botanist Rombaud Dodonée is holding a flower in his hand. On the other side of Egmont and Hoorn, at the top of the path, is the Flemish geographer Mercator, though his enormous feet are perhaps not visible from where we are sitting. He is followed by Jean de Locquenghien, the Brussels burgomaster who built the Willebroek Canal and, finally, next to Marnix, Abraham Ortelius who is identified by an atlas.

The one figure oddly missing from this roll call of Flemish heroes is Pieter Bruegel. He was living in Brussels in 1566 when the nobles gathered in the Culembourg Palace, and was working on the *Parable of the Blind* at the time of Egmont and Hoorn's captivity. Bruegel is far more famous than any of the ten people we see here, but for some reason he has been omitted from this garden of fame. Indeed, there is no statue of Bruegel anywhere in the country. He has simply vanished, like poor Icarus disappearing beneath the waves.

This little park is one of the most romantic spots in Brussels, with the hedge clipped to create niches for the statues and a fountain spilling over a large basin. At night, when the figures are floodlit, it looks almost like a stage set, with Egmont and Hoorn helping each other to the scaffold, while the ten statues emerge from the shadows like a chorus. And there is more to see than that, for the park is enclosed by an elaborate fence decorated with the most fanciful wrought iron motifs in the city. Looking closely, we can see tiny animal heads and curious medieval faces peering out of the ironwork.

The stone pillars around the park are copied from the fence that once surrounded the courtyard of the ducal palace, seen in the view on page 195, next to the church labelled G, but the forty-eight bronze figures representing the Brussels guilds are a purely 19th-century touch. If we are so inclined, we can wander around the perimeter, noting the tallow merchant holding a

dead goose, the slater carrying a ladder and the painter holding a palette.

We leave the park at the bottom end and turn left. Two plaques (in French and Dutch) are attached to the corner building at Rue de la Régence 17. These mark the site of the Tour et Tassis Palace, visible on the map on page 168, but torn down when the broad Rue de la Régence was created in 1872. Europe's first postal service was run from this building in the 15th century by François de la Tour et Tassis. We can see a portrait of Charles V with his jutting jaw on the French plaque, and a rather chubby François de la Tour et Tassis on the Dutch version. The old Tour et Tassis palace was later occupied by the conservatory of music. When it was demolished to widen the road, the conservatory we see now was built by Jean Pierre Cluysenaar. Looking inside the main courtyard, further up the street, it is hard to believe that this fussy neoclassical building was designed by the same architect as the elegant Galeries Saint Hubert, and harder still to accept that Auguste Rodin was involved in the project. Several

Brussels sculptors were employed to carve cary-atids, busts, garlands and musical instruments, including Antoine-Joseph van Rasbourgh, who shared a studio with Rodin at Rue Sans-Souci 111; and it was there that Rodin produced the bust of Beethoven and the two caryatids on the wing to the left of the courtyard. The pediment was carved by Charles van der Stappen, who bodied forth the subject of *Orchestration* with a female muse of music directing a choir of children.

III. The Eglise du Sablon. We now cross the road and turn right. We are about to visit the Eglise du Sablon, but before we go inside we should continue beyond the church to stand on the spot where the photograph opposite was taken in the early 20th century. The view along the Rue de la Régence towards the looming Palais de Justice has hardly changed since then; the trams are still running and even the lamp-posts look the same. A curious late gothic sacristy was added on the south side of the nave in 1549. It was restored by Maurice van Ysendyck in

1905 so that it looked like new when the photo-graph was taken.

The church we are looking at now is far more ornate than the original gothic building. The 19th-century restoration transformed its appear-ance drastically, by tearing down the old houses built around the church and adding countless fanciful neo-gothic details, such as the florid octagonal tower attached to the sacristy and the elaborate west portal which is nowhere to be seen in older views of the church. Some critics say the restorers went too far, and turned a simple late gothic church into a fussy shrine, but the department of monuments thinks other-wise, and recently embarked on a costly restoration of the delicate white stonework.

We enter the church by the south transept, which appears in a painting by the Master of the View of Sainte-Gudule in the Musée d'Art Ancien. Let us sit down to read about the build-ing on one of the chairs near the pulpit.

The church dates back to 1304 when the guild of crossbowmen founded a chapel on this summit. In 1348, Béatrice Soetkens, a draper's

daughter, heard a voice telling her to go to Antwerp and bring an abandoned statue of the Virgin to the crossbowmen's chapel. Pilgrims started to flock to the chapel to venerate the statue, and it was paraded through the streets during the Ommegang procession. This pageant became particularly flamboyant during the 16th and 17th centuries, as we have already seen.

To cope with the flood of pilgrims, the church was rebuilt in the 15th and 16th centuries in Brabant late gothic style. It was further embellished by Burgundian nobles who built their palaces nearby in the Sablon quarter. We will find various aristocratic relics dotted around, including two magnificent baroque chapels at the east end, one on either side of the choir. The chapel on the right contains a bookshop, but it is the other one that is particularly interesting. This was designed in 1651 by Lucas Faydherbe for the Tour et Tassis family. The bust of Saint Ursula above the entrance was carved by Gabriel Grupello, whose fishmongers' fountain we saw in the Musées des Beaux-Arts. We have to hope that the chapel is open; otherwise peer through

the bars to glimpse Count Lamoral d'Egmont's mausoleum, with the figure of Fame blowing a trumpet and angels fluttering in the background.

The elaborate 17th-century pulpit was carved by a Brussels sculptor for an Augustinian church. It is supported by symbolic creatures representing the Four Evangelists – a man for Matthew, a lion for Mark, an ox for Luke and an eagle for John. A marble plaque on a column near the altar marks the spot where the poet Paul Claudel sat every day. Claudel served as the French ambassador in Brussels from 1933 to 1935.

If we now walk down the north aisle, we come to a chapel containing an alabaster monument commemorating Count Flaminius Garnier, secretary to Charles V and the very Catholic Duke of Parma. Carved in 1553, it is decorated with six panels showing *Scenes from the Life of the Virgin*. Notice the kneeling figures at the top of Garnier and his wife, Barbe de Reversé. The stained glass Mexico Window above the altar was installed much later, in 1867, in memory of Maximilian of Austria, who married Léopold II's sister Charlotte. Maximilian was briefly Emperor of Mexico until rebels captured and executed him in 1867 (Manet's engraving of the execution is on page 234). The five saints in the window include the obscure Saint Maximilian and, for want of anyone better, Charles Borromeus as patron saint for poor widowed Charlotte.

There is some fun to be had hunting in the church for representations of the legend of Béatrice Soetkens, such as the renaissance stucco detail below the organ loft at the west end, which shows the boat sailing from Antwerp with the statue on board. We also see various crossbows which symbolise the church's founders. One thing we won't find, though, is the miraculous statue, which was destroyed by Calvinists.

It is now time to stroll down the hill to the Place du Grand Sablon. As its name suggests, this square was once a sandy slope on the escarpment above the old town. Several inns were established here in the middle ages to accommodate the growing number of pilgrims who came to venerate the famous statue.

The Minerva Fountain in the middle of the square barely produces a trickle these days, though it once supplied water for the entire quarter. The figure of Minerva, minus her nose, is pointing to a shield with two busts, both rather weathered but still showing the vague profiles of Empress Maria Theresa and Francis of Lorraine. Signed on the base *J. Bergé Bruxell 1751*, the fountain was paid for by Thomas Bruce, 3rd Earl of Elgin, who fled Scotland in 1696 and lived in a mansion on the Sablon until his death in 1741. He bequeathed this fountain as a token of gratitude to the Brussels people.

Alas, the charming and creaky Musée de la Poste at Place du Grand Sablon 40 (with its interesting collection of photographs of old Belgian post offices, a post office door from Herenthals with a separate window for the local gentry, and a sturdy pair of fur-lined postman's boots), has recently closed, so we are now obliged to break off for some refreshment. The Sablon is one of the city's favourite spots for a cup of coffee, and the square is now surrounded by cafés, antique shops and chocolate shops such as Wittamer's at No. 12 and Marcolini at No. 39. We might end with coffee and cake in Les Salons de Wittamer, or head up the hill to the Pain Quotidien bakery at No. 11, which has a spacious café and a seductive walled garden. This building stands on the site of a splendid renaissance palace (numbered 66 on the De Tailly detail on page 168). Known as the Hôtel de Wemmel, it was built in the 16th century for Maximilien Transsylvanus, another of Charles V's secretaries. We can see that it had a lofty tower and a curious circular garden, but all that vanished when the building was demolished in 1828 and replaced by Nos. 9 and 11.

WALK 5

The Marolles

<pre>PLACE DU GRAND SABLON TO THE PALAIS DE JUSTICE</pre>

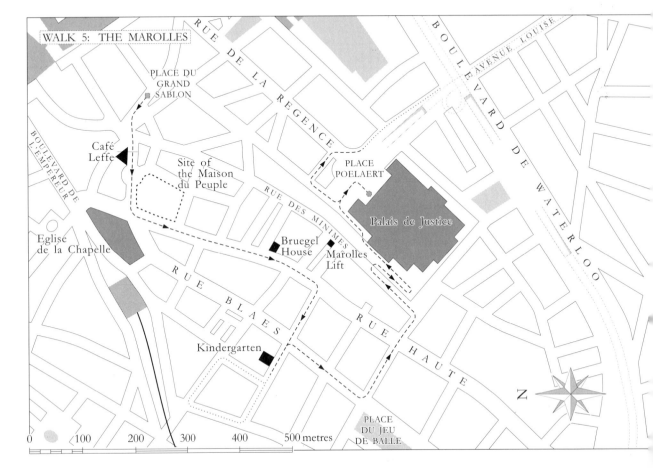

WALK 5: THE MAROLLES

PLACE DU GRAND SABLON

RUE DE LA REGENCE

BOULEVARD DE WATERLOO

AVENUE LOUISE

Café Leffe

BOULEVARD DE L'EMPEREUR

Site of the Maison du Peuple

PLACE POELAERT

RUE DES MINIMES

Palais de Justice

Eglise de la Chapelle

Bruegel House

Marolles Lift

RUE BLAES

RUE HAUTE

Kindergarten

PLACE DU JEU DE BALLE

N

0   100   200   300   400   500 metres

WALK 5

The Marolles

FROM THE PLACE DU GRAND SABLON TO THE PALAIS DE JUSTICE

This walk takes us into the heart of the Marolles, a quarter settled by cloth weavers in the Middle Ages. The weavers of Brussels, like those in Ghent, were a notoriously unruly crowd, giving the Marolles a reputation for lawlessness; even Baedeker felt it necessary to warn his fin-de-siècle readers that the streets of the Marolles 'exhibit many drastic scenes of popular life'. Nowadays we relish that kind of thing; the Marolles as a result has experienced a certain revival. This quarter still has some extraordinary shops where you can buy tripe, horse meat, doorhandles, pith helmets or church pews. It is now one of the last quarters in Brussels where we might, on a rare moment, come upon a scene evoking a Bruegel painting.

Our walk once again begins on the Place du Grand Sablon. We should try to set off early in the morning to catch the flea market on Place du Jeu de Balle before it shuts up at about midday. Before we start, though, there is perhaps time for a coffee in Pain Quotidien at No. 11 or, for a change, Café Leffe at No. 46.

We now descend to the bottom of the square, and continue down Rue Joseph-Stevens. If we keep to the right-hand side of the street, we come to a chemist shop on the corner of Place Emile Vandervelde with an elegant wrought-iron sign. The Maison du Peuple, designed by Victor Horta in 1896-9, once stood opposite. The photograph reproduced overleaf shows the spectacular curved glass-and-iron façade which

was decorated with flamboyant iron pinacles and the names (if we could read them) of great socialists such as Marx and Proud'hon. This people's palace sold books and magazines, as well as delivering groceries by horse-drawn carriage. It had a meeting hall seating fifteen hundred people and a large café.

The building was demolished in 1965 and the site is now occupied by the bleakest of office blocks, where the Belgian Ministry of the Middle Classes adds insult to injury by echoing the curve of the Horta façade. Yet all was not lost. The blocks of carved stone and iron railings were rescued and kept in a Brussels cemetery for decades as various reconstruction plans were debated. The surviving fragments have been reassembled, though not to everyone's satisfaction, in the Horta brasserie in Antwerp.

If we look at the photograph here, we can see the vague outline of the buildings opposite reflected in Horta's large glass windows. One of these is an Art Nouveau house, still standing next to the Pharmacie du Sablon. Not as bold as a Horta building, it still reveals some daring

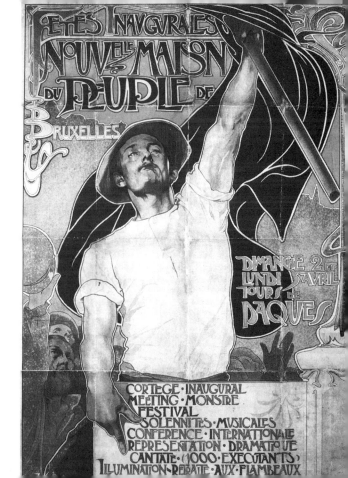

architectural features, such as its iron frame and sgraffito tiles.

I. The Eglise de la Chapelle. We are now heading for the church at the bottom of the hill (in the middle of the De Tailly detail opposite). The white stonework of the Eglise de la Chapelle was recently cleaned, and so, for a few years at least, we will be able to admire the church in pristine condition. If we stand on the corner at the foot of the hill, we can begin to understand the different stages of construction. The low choir and transepts date from the 13th century, the higher nave was built in the 15th century, and the curious belfry was added in 1699, replacing an old spire brought down four years earlier by the French bombardment. The belfry was designed by Antoon Pastorana, who also built the guild house of the boatmen we saw at Grand'-Place 6.

Entering the church by the door below the tower, we can try to picture the scene in the spring of 1563 when Pieter Bruegel married Mayken Coecke, the daughter of his fellow painter Pieter Coecke van Aelst, under the watchful eye of Mayken's mother. According to an old legend, Bruegel was forced to move to Brussels by his future mother-in-law, who wanted him safely out of the clutches of his former mistress in Antwerp. Bruegel died in his early forties, only six years after he married Mayken. He was probably buried in this church, though no gravestone survives. The only evidence we have is a memorial plaque in the third chapel on the right, erected by Jan (Velvet) Brueghel in 1625 in memory of his father. It once incorporated a Rubens painting of *Christ Handing the Keys of Heaven to Saint Peter*, presented by Rubens as a token of his admiration for Pieter Bruegel. The church authorities sold the original to a private collector in the 18th century, replacing it with the copy we see here.

The church is intriguing to explore, with its faded murals, gloomy paintings and ancient memorials. A curious fragment of the original Romanesque building has been preserved to the right of the choir. The pulpit is an extravagant baroque work carved in 1721 and showing the prophet Elijah clutching a rock to escape the wrath of Jezebel. The church's caretaker sits in a glass cabin, keeping a watchful eye on the few visitors who find their way here and ringing a loud bell at two minutes to four to chase out the last stragglers. I somehow think Bruegel would have enjoyed the scene.

On leaving the church, we go straight ahead down Rue Haute, past a narrow alley next to No. 116 named Impasse des Chansons. Bruegel and Mayken are said to have owned the brick house further along the street at No. 132. The step-gabled house, which has been carefully restored, was certainly owned by the artist's grand-daughter, Anne Brueghel, who bequeathed it to her son, David Teniers III. Local historians think that Anne probably inherited it from her father Jan (who paid for the memorial we saw in the church), and he in turn was given the house by his father. If so, this is the house where Bruegel painted most of his famous works, such as the *Census at Bethlehem* we saw earlier.

Continuing down Rue Haute, we come to a shop with an attractive old interior with mirrors

at No. 158. The neoclassical building opposite was built by the Jacqmotte coffee company, founded in 1828, and recently converted into stylish lofts and offices. One of the city's Bruegel fountains stands on the square on the left, this one modelled on Bruegel's painting of a chained monkey. The Maison Espagnole at No. 164 is an attractive brick house with a step gable, restored in 1972. If we look closely, we can see two old stones incorporated into the door frame. One is inscribed *ANN* and the other looks as if it is the number *641* laid upside down. One theory is that these are fragments of a keystone dated *ANNO 1641*, but if that is the explanation then it must have come from a different buildings as the Spanish House dates from 1607.

After pondering this puzzle, we turn off to the right down Rue Gisleins and cross Rue Blaes to look at the kindergarten at No. 40. This was built by Victor Horta at the same time as he was working on the lamented Maison du Peuple. Notice the tiny leaf-like decoration at the tops of the windows and the eccentric little turret. There was once a plan to turn this building into a museum of education, but this appealing notion seems to have been abandoned.

Our walk continues along Rue Blaes, but we can, if we are keen on Art Nouveau, and not put off by dingy surroundings, make a short detour in search of two other buildings. Turning right just beyond the school along Rue de Nancy we can find out what, if anything, has been done to save the remarkable Art Nouveau building at No. 6-8, built and signed by Léon Sneyers in 1900. Originally owned by the painter Jan Cortvriendt, the house is reminiscent of Hankar's geometrical style, with its projecting roof, abstract wrought iron balconies and sgraffito panels designed by Adolphe Crespin. We now continue to the end of the street and turn left, then left again along Rue des Tanneurs, where we find a former wine warehouse known grandly as the Palais du Vin at Nos. 58-62. We can see a relief with grapes at the top of the arch, wrought-iron vines trailing across the door and bunches of grapes hanging from carved swags on the front. The warehouse was built in 1909 by Fernand Symons in a vaguely Art

Nouveau style. The fifteen sgraffito panels designed by Géo Ponchon are now crying out for attention.

II. Place du Jeu de Balle. Our detour ends here. We continue along Rue Blaes to Place du Jeu de Balle, with luck in time to catch the flea market held here every day. Each morning at first light, dealers drive battered vans down to this square, and spread threadbare carpets over the cobblestones to display their spoils. You can find just about anything here: a stuffed bird, a copy of *War and Peace* minus the last ten pages, perhaps even a box of used toothbrushes.

As the day wears on, objects get trampled on, soaked by rain, lodged between the cobblestones, until eventually the square looks like one vast rubbish dump. Yet locals keep sifting through the debris in search of hidden treasures. Will anyone ever buy that tarnished fork with one prong? you ask yourself. The answer is probably yes. I have even seen one enterprising trader selling old copies of one of the city's free newspapers.

Once we have had our fill of gilded ballroom chairs and broken telephones, we might glance inside the café at No. 50 called De Skieven Architek, which is decorated with a large mural of the Marolles and some old family photographs. The local market traders come here at dawn for coffee and rolls, or they drop in at lunchtime for *stoemp* or *waterzooi*. The name *Skieven Architek* (dirty architect) refers to Joseph Poelaert, thanks to whom the word 'architect' is about the worst insult you can hurl at anyone in the Marolles. The building which earned Poelaert his villainous reputation is our next destination.

III. The Palais du Justice. We head up the steep, cobbled Rue des Renards, cross Rue Haute and continue up Rue du Faucon, past a passage with a trompe l'œil mural at No. 17. We now turn left to approach the Palais de Justice by a dramatic flight of stone steps. Or we can take the modern lift which opened in 2002 to link the Marolles with the Upper Town. Operated by the public transport authority, the automated lift is free. Looming above our heads is the

monstrous palace, which consumed the energies of the architect Joseph Poelaert from 1866 until his death, from utter exhaustion, in 1879. We can appreciate its impressive bulk from this photograph taken from the spire of the town hall, but even more so once we are inside (open Monday to Friday, 9 am to 12.30 and 15.30 to 16.00 pm). Once through the doors, we find ourselves in the vast *Salle des Pas Perdus* where lawyers discuss cases with their clients at heavy wooden desks. Exhausted by the Piranesian grandeur of our surroudings, we can sink onto a bench to read about the building.

The palace of justice was deliberately sited on the Galgenberg, the gallows hill, to strike terror into the lawless folk of the Marolles. It is the most potent symbol of Léopold II, who once declared his ambition to be 'to make Belgium greater, stronger and more beautiful.' Poelaert helped Léopold achieve the first two of these aims, though perhaps not the third, by modelling the court of justice on the monumental temples of ancient Babylon. The building called for 389,000 cubic metres of brick and stone,

8,735 tons of iron, 9,250 square metres of glass and mirror, 1,530 doors and 1,513 windows. It contains 34 courtrooms, 245 offices, 8 libraries, 80 archive rooms and, if local gossip is to be believed, a forgotten room that was once secretly used by a Brussels barber. It was, allegedly, Hitler's favourite building.

On leaving the Palais de Justice, we turn left to reach a terrace overlooking the Lower Town. We can identify the Midi tower on the far left near the Gare du Midi, the church on Place du Jeu de Balle, the Eglise de la Chapelle where Bruegel is buried, the spire of the town hall, the Ministry of the Middle Classes office block, and the curious 17th-century clock tower of the Eglise des Minimes. If it is a clear day, we should be able to see the Basilique de Koekelberg on a distant summit, begun by Léopold II in 1905 in imitation of the Sacré-Coeur in Paris but halted by the outbreak of war and not completed until 1969. By that date, Léopold's vision of a neo-gothic church had been supplanted by a later Art Deco design. To the right of the basilica, we might just glimpse the steel spheres of the Atomium.

189

In recent years the skyline of Brussels has changed dramatically, thanks to a new policy of reducing the height of skyscrapers within the old city. The policy was launched by the mayor of Brussels to improve the view from the town hall balcony. It applies to 17 skyscrapers, at least two of which have already been taken down. We now cross the road behind us to look at a magnificent First World War memorial presented by the British government in gratitude to the Belgians who helped wounded Allied soldiers. The monument was unveiled in 1923 by the Prince of Wales, the future Edward VIII. It was demolished in 1956 when the new Belgian foreign office building was constructed, and many thought it was gone for good. But a minor diplomatic row blew up and the monument was eventually rebuilt on the present spot.

Our walk ends here. We can go down Rue de la Régence to the Sablon, or stroll up to Place Louise, perhaps ending with a coffee in La Crèmerie de la Vache (described on p. 167).

WALK 6

Charlotte Brontë and the royal quarter

Place Royale to the Botanique

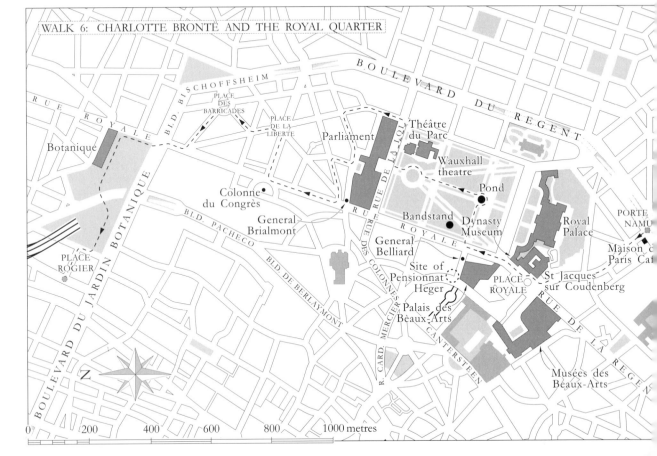

WALK 6: CHARLOTTE BRONTË AND THE ROYAL QUARTER

RUE ROYALE

BLD. BISCHOFFSHEIM

PLACE DES BARRICADES

PLACE DE LA LIBERTE

BOULEVARD DU REGENT

Botanique

BOULEVARD DU JARDIN BOTANIQUE

Parliament

Théâtre du Parc

Wauxhall theatre

Pond

Colonne du Congrès

BLD. PACHECO

General Brialmont

BLD. DE BERLAYMONT

RUE DE LA LOI

RUE ROYALE

Bandstand

Dynasty Museum

Royal Palace

PORTE NAMU

PLACE ROGIER

RUE DES COLONNES

General Belliard

Site of Pensionnat Heger

Palais des Beaux-Arts

R. CARD. MERCIER

CANTERSTEEN

PLACE ROYALE

St Jacques sur Coudenberg

Maison c Paris Cat

RUE DE LA REGEN

N

Musées des Beaux-Arts

0   200   400   600   800   1000 metres

Charlotte Brontë and the royal quarter

PLACE ROYALE TO THE BOTANIQUE

This walk takes us in the footsteps of Charlotte Brontë in search of places mentioned in her two Brussels novels. Many of the buildings have disappeared, of course, yet enough remains to justify the Brontë Society organising the occasional jaunt to Brussels. Armed with a copy of *Villette*, we can visit the park where Lucy Snowe wandered one night after taking opium, and look at a square that has changed little since Charlotte arrived there in 1842, aged twenty-six. The places with a Brontë connection take about an hour to see, but the walk can be prolonged to about three hours by continuing through the government quarter and ending at the botanical gardens.

We can do this walk at any time, though perhaps not on a rainy day as we spend all our time outside. We begin by taking the metro to the Porte de Namur and leaving by the Boulevard de Waterloo exit. This brings us to the top end of the Rue de Namur, where we can take coffee at the Maison de Paris at No. 87, unless we prefer to wait five minutes when we reach Place Royale. The short walk from the station follows in the footsteps of Charlotte and Emily, who tramped up the Rue de Namur every Sunday on their way to lunch at the Jenkins home. Mrs Jenkins, the wife of the English chaplain had recommended the Pensionnat Heger, so she was perhaps feeling slightly responsible for the girls' welfare. The Jenkins lived at the bottom of the Chaussée d'Ixelles, then a bumpy country lane beyond the former ramparts. Charlotte and Emily were escorted up this hill and down the country lane beyond the Porte de Namur by the Jenkins' two sons, but the girls barely said a word. The Sunday lunches at the Jenkins' eventually became too painful for all concerned and they were finally dropped.

I. Place Royale. The Rue de Namur runs down to Place Royale, an elegant neoclassical square designed by Barnabé Guimard in the 1770's. A hundred years ago, we could have sat out on a café terrace to admire the buildings, but all these establishments have now disappeared. We can, however, sit in Le Gresham, the new café of the Musées des Beaux-Arts at No. 3, to read about the square.

The lovely Eglise St Jacques sur Coudenberg was begun in the 1770's on the site of a demolished 12th-century chapel, the spire indicated by the letter G in the view opposite. Barnabé Guimard designed the classical front, which was embellished in the 1840's with an octagonal bell tower. The entrance is flanked by large 18th-century statues of *Moses*, carved by the French sculptor Ollivier de Marseille, and a much inferior *David*, by the Brussels sculptor François Janssens. The nave and choir were built by Louis Montoyer in a sober neoclassicism.

Charlotte Brontë knew this square well and used it in *Villette*. It was here that Lucy Snowe ended up after losing her way on her first night in Brussels. Here, she observed: 'the huge outline of more than one overbearing pile; which might be palace, or church – I could not tell.' It was probably the church behind us, which fits the description perfectly: 'Just then I passed a portico, two moustachioed men came suddenly from behind the pillars; they were smoking cigars.' This square might have seemed less threatening in daylight – one of the buildings contained Pratt and Barry's English Library, and there was a branch of the Gresham Life Insurance Company of London in the building where we are now perhaps sitting.

This square looked very different in the 15th and 16th centuries as we see in Jean van de Velde's print opposite. The great hall of the

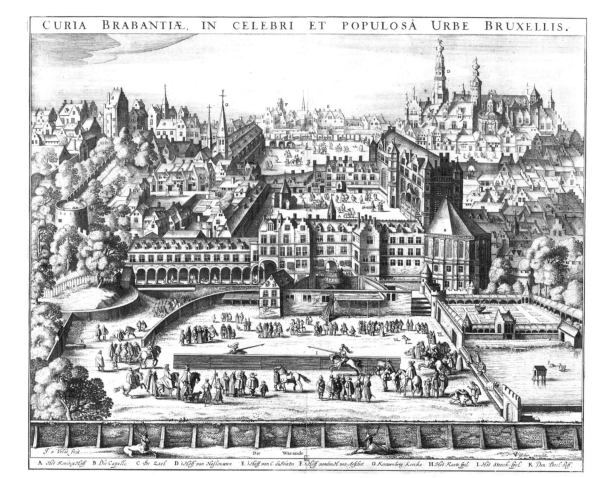

CURIA BRABANTIÆ, IN CELEBRI ET POPULOSÂ URBE BRUXELLIS.

J. v. Velde fecit.

Die Warande

... Velther excudit

A *Het Koninx Hoff* B *Die Capelle* C *De Zael* D *'s Hoff van Nassouwen* E *'s Hoff van C. de Fointes* F *'s Hoff vanden H. van Aerschot* G *Kossenbergh Kercke* H *Het Kaets spel* I *Het Steeck spel* K *Den Doel Hoff*

Palace of the Dukes of Burgundy stood on the far side of the square and the ducal chapel lay to its right. It was in the great hall, or Magna Aula, that Charles V was crowned Holy Roman Emperor in 1519. He returned here in 1555 to abdicate in favour of his son Philip II, declaring wearily that: 'For now we are indeed tired and disillusioned.'

Van de Velde showed the palace in 1645, four years after John Evelyn was a guest there during his tour of the Low Countries. Evelyn saw paintings by Bruegel and Rubens, peeped through a key-hole into the library, and noted an intriguing mural in the garden: 'painted by Rubens, being an history of the late tumults in Belgia; in the last piece, the Arch-Duchesse shuts a greate payre of Gates upon Mars, who is made comming forth out of Hel, arm'd, and in a menacing posture.' But where was this mural? The Van de Velde view shows nothing of it, nor does any other picture of the palace I have seen. We will perhaps recall from the city museum on Grand'Place that this palace was gutted by fire on 4 February 1731.

The artist F. J. de Rons, who drew the guild houses on Grand'Place in 1737, came to the ruined palace eleven years after it burnt down. Looking out of a window in the south wing in 1742, not far from where we are sitting now, he drew this view (reproduced opposite) of the ruined Hall, showing six boys playing marbles and fighting in the courtyard, while some Austrian nobles stand around in the sun. The chapel described by Evelyn as 'rarely arch'd' looks as if it has survived the blaze, but the lodgings on the right have been destroyed, and with them presumably some of the 'many excellent pieces of Rubens; old, and young Breugle, Titian, Steen-wick...' described by Evelyn and recorded by Teniers in the painting we saw earlier of *Archduke Léopold-William in his Gallery*. We can see that the building on the left had gained a clock tower some time after Van de Velde drew his view. This tower was added by Albrecht and Isabella, who may also have contributed the strange chimney cowls that survived the blaze. These charred ruins remained standing until 1774, when Barnabé Guimard

Het binnen Plein van het Hof te Brussel afgebrand den 4 Febr: 1731.

formulated a plan to turn the quarter into a formal neoclassical square modelled on Place Royale in Nancy. This involved levelling the sloping site and burying part of the Rue Isabelle and the Aula cellars below ground. We have an opportunity to visit this fascinating underground complex later on this walk.

A statue of Charles of Lorraine once stood in the middle of the square. This symbol of the old order was removed by the French revolutionaries, who put up a tree of liberty in his place. The tree later burnt down, and eventually, in 1848, the statue we see now was put up. It shows one of the greatest heroes of the middle ages, Godfrey of Bouillon, duke of Lower Lorraine, posed extravagantly on his horse. Born in the Brabant village of Baisy, Godfrey served under Emperor Henry IV before leading the First Crusade. After the capture of Jerusalem in 1099, he was proclaimed King of Jerusalem, but he renounced what seemed a vainglorious title, preferring to be called Defender of the Holy Sepulchre. He died in Jerusalem one year later.

The eight identical buildings surrounding the square were mainly financed by abbeys as town residences, though the building at No. 1, now occupied by the Musées des Beaux-Arts, was built for the administration of the Imperial Lottery. By the early 19th century, it had become the Hôtel Britannique (not to be confused with the Hôtel d'Angleterre in the Lower Town). The name, of course, was designed to attract the British, and it was here that Wellington chose to stay in 1815. Another of the hotel rooms was taken by Mrs Eaton, who watched from her window as the Highlanders marched across the square in their kilts on their route to Waterloo. 'One poor fellow, immediately under our windows, turned back again and again to bid his wife farewell, and take his baby once more in his arms. Soon afterwards the 42nd and 92nd Highland regiments marched through the Place Royale and the Parc, with their bagpipes playing before them, while the bright beams of the rising sun shone full on their polished muskets and on the dark waving plumes of their tartan bonnets.' One day after the battle, Wellington was back in his hotel room overlooking the park, talking to an officer about the events of 17 June. 'It has been a damned serious business,' he said. 'Blücher and I have lost 30,000 men. It has been the nearest run thing you ever saw in your life.'

The building at No. 10 was built by Grimbergen Abbey. It had become the Café de l'Amitié by the time the Belgian Revolution broke out in 1830. Shrapnel thudded off the walls of the building as Dutch troops fired on Belgian rebels sheltering inside the café. We can see the corner of the building in the lithograph opposite, which shows patriots manning cannons on 26 September, 1830. The rebel soldiers, including a certain 'Peg Leg' Charlier from Liège, are shown firing at Dutch troops who have taken refuge in the park.

The Hôtel Bellevue is just visible on the right of the lithograph. One of the grand hotels of the 19th century, it was a particular favourite with French visitors. Jérôme Bonaparte, a brother of Napoleon who had fought at Waterloo, stayed here in 1818. Balzac rented a room at the Bellevue in 1841, Metternich settled here with his family in 1849 after fleeing revolution in Vienna,

and Liszt and his two daughters stayed in the hotel in 1854. The Bellevue was later annexed to the royal palace by Léopold II and served as a residence for the future King Léopold III and his wife Astrid.

The former hotel now contains the Dynasty Museum, where we can find out about the family that has ruled Belgium since 1830. It's worth a visit just to climb the grand staircase, admire the Neptune Fountain on the landing and tread the polished parquet floors in the footsteps of Liszt. The museum also sells a separate ticket for visiting the underground museum below Place Royale.

We might enjoy delving in the room upstairs devoted to Léopold I, the first King of the Belgians, whose grandiose ambitions are revealed by a 19th-century map titled *Towards a Greater Belgium*. This marks the places where Belgium wanted to establish colonies, including large tracts of Africa, a small island off the coast of Australia and several settlements in the United States. We find Belgium's colonial ambitions realised in the Léopold II Room, where one old

map shows the route taken by Stanley on his 1874-77 expedition, and another indicates Léopold's Congo territories. We can also study photographs and plans of Léopold's grand projects in Brussels, Tervuren and Ostend.

Another small room is devoted to Albert I, including a drawing of a train he did as a child, the frayed rope that snapped while he was scaling a cliff in the Ardennes, and the ripped green corduroy jacket he was wearing when he fell to his death. A street in Brussels was named Rue de la Roche Fatale in memory of the tragedy.

An impressive new section in memory of King Baudouin opened recently in the ground-floor rooms. This has the king's school books, his old desk and an extraordinary mountain of mail sent to the palace after Baudouin's sudden death in 1993.

Now for the remarkable museum hidden below Place Royale, which we reach from the Bellevue Hotel by a tunnel that runs under Rue Royale. For many years, historians talked about a secret network of cellars and streets beneath Place Royale, but it was only recently that these were revealed to the public for the first time. Still one of the best kept secrets of Brussels, the underground complex contains some fascinating vestiges of the medieval town.

We start in the former crypt of the ducal chapel, lettered B on the Van de Velde view on page 195, and then wander through an extensive underground network of rooms, some with glass cases containing charred masonry, fragments of glass and rusted armour. A cobbled lane with a vaulted roof plunges down the slope in front of us. This was the Rue Isabelle – Charlotte Brontë's Rue Fossette – an ancient street created by Archduchess Isabella in 1625 to shorten the route from the ducal palace to the cathedral. The creation of this street meant cutting through an exercise ground used by the guild of crossbowmen. Being something of a crack shot herself (see pp. 144-5), Isabella did not want to offend the guild, and so offered to build them a new banqueting hall. At the time of the palace fire, the servants ran down the street carrying armfuls of illuminated manuscripts rescued from the flames and stored them in the banqueting hall.

We now go down to the bottom of Rue Isabelle and turn left. Steps lead to a restored late gothic arcade that once belonged to the Hôtel d'Hoogstraten. The open arcade on the left originally looked out on to a medieval garden, which is now roofed over.

On leaving the museum, we can turn right to look at the royal palace, which is surrounded by the most ornate lamp-posts in the city. In Charlotte Brontë's day, King Léopold I lived in a more modest palace on this site, but Léopold II's grand designs included the rebuilding of the palace in 1904 in the monumental if outdated style of Louis XVI. The palace is open to the public during the summer when the royal family is away on holiday. We can then join the queues of royalist Belgians shuffling through the sumptuous reception rooms and glittering ballrooms.

On leaving the museum, we go back to Place Royale and turn left along Rue Royale until we come to the statue of General Belliard in a little square on the left. In *Villette*, Lucy Snowe arrives in Brussels late at night, unable to speak a word of French, and is escorted through the park by a stranger. '"Now," said he, when the park was traversed, "you will go along this street till you come to some steps; two lamps will show you where they are."' Flushed with appreciation, she set off, 'hurrying fast through a magnificent street and square, with the grandest houses round.' If we look behind the statue of the general, we will come to the steps mentioned by the stranger – 'an old and worn flight', according to *Villette*. There can be no doubt that we have the right steps, for the two lamps are still there.

There is an even better description of this quarter in Charlotte Brontë's unsuccessful first Brussels novel, *The Professor*. 'I stood awhile to contemplate the statue of General Belliard and then I advanced to the top of the great staircase just beyond and I looked down into a narrow back-street which, I afterwards learnt, was called the Rue d'Isabelle. I well recollect that my eye rested on the green door of a rather large house opposite, where, on a brass plate, was inscribed "Pensionnat des desmoiselles".'

The statue of General August-Daniel Belliard

was carved by Guillaume Geefs in 1836 to commemorate a French diplomat who played a leading role in the birth of the Belgian state. He is shown here holding the 1839 treaty in which the major powers agree to respect Belgian neutrality. This is the treaty that Kaiser Wilhelm dismissed in 1914 as a 'scrap of paper'. Belliard died of apoplexy in 1832, collapsing in the park opposite. Every Belgian soldier apparently gave a day's wages to pay for the statue.

The *Pensionnat de Demoiselles* where Charlotte and Emily stayed was at the bottom of the steps we see behind the General. If we go down and stand in front of the fountain, we are not far from where it stood until its demolition in 1909. The green door would have been straight ahead of us, and the classrooms to the right, where the Fortis bank building stands. On the left, a high wall concealed an orchard. Charlotte and Emily had come here in 1842 to learn French at Madame Heger's boarding school, with the vague plan of opening their own school back at home. They slept in a dormitory on the first floor, behind the 'five casements as large as great

doors'. Lucy Snowe described her students as 'healthy, lively girls, all well dressed and some of them handsome,' just like the later generation of girls we see in this charming, if blurred photograph that still hangs in the Brontë Parsonage in Haworth. The five windows are there, and the bower, and the elderly man in the middle at the table bears an uncanny resemblance to Monsieur Heger. But disappointingly it turns out that the photograph is a red herring – or even a fake – and almost certainly does *not* show the school, which is now known not to have looked like the building here. The atmosphere cannot have been so very different, though.

The Pensionnat garden had once been that of a former convent. Its predecessor can be seen in the detail from De Tailly's map on page 122, and was originally planted with medicinal herbs. According to an old legend, a nun was buried alive in the garden for some sin she had comitted, though Charlotte Brontë dismissed the story as 'romantic rubbish'. By the time Charlotte arrived in Brussels, the grounds had been transformed into a rambling Victorian garden,

described in *Villette* as overgrown with rose bushes, fruit trees and a 'vine-draped berceau where Madame Beck sat on summer afternoons surrounded by girls sewing or reading'. This secret urban retreat inspired some of Charlotte's most memorable scenes, such as the garden party when Lucy dressed up as a man.

Charlotte and Emily were eventually invited to teach English here. They had to go to Haworth in November when news arrived that their Aunt Branwell had died, but Charlotte returned alone the following year to teach and it was then that she fell hopelessly in love with Constantin Heger, her French teacher, though he remained icily distant. He at one point tossed her love letters in the basket, where they were retrieved and read by Madame Heger.

The Pensionnat was run by the Heger's younger daughter Louise until 1909, when it was demolished, along with the rest of the street, to build the Palais des Beaux-Arts (described on page 127).

On that sad note let us go back up the steps and enter the park. If we go down the path straight ahead and turn right along the main alley, we will find several benches overlooking a round pond. We can sit down here to read the history of the park.

II. The Parc de Bruxelles. 'The trees offer us shade,' states an antiquated iron sign at one of the gates, though not the one we come through. 'Along with the plants and the flowers, they are the joy and the beauty of the country-side. Anyone who damages the trees and the plants causes damage to himself.' Despite this stern warning, the trees offer us very little shade, for they have been ruthlessly trained on trellises in the classical French style. Indeed this park may well strike us as an object lesson in geometry rather than botany. It was designed in 1787 by Barnabé Guimard, assisted by the Austrian landscape gardener Joachim Zinner, in the formal French style favoured by the Austrian governors. The straight avenues are laid out in the form of a *patte d'oie* which, seen from above, reveals various masonic emblems.

Wandering through the park in 1844, William

Thackeray complained that: 'Numbers of staues decorate the place, the very worse I ever saw. These cupids must have been erected in the time of the Dutch dynasty, as I judge from the immense posterior developments.' Thackeray was wrong about the origin of the statues, which mostly date from the Austrian period. Some of them were moved to the park from the royal castle at Tervuren. Others came from the ducal labyrinth and the gardens of the Tour et Tassis palace.

Robert Louis Stevenson was a more enthusiastic visitor, lyrically describing the pleasures of the park at night in a letter to his mother in 1872. 'If any person wants to be happy I should advise the Parc. You sit drinking iced drinks and smoking penny cigars under great old trees. The band place, covered walks, etc., are all lit up. And you can't fancy how beautiful was the contrast of the great masses of lamplit foliage and the dark sapphire night sky, with just one blue star set overhead in the middle of the largest patch. In the dark walks, too, there are crowds of people whose faces you cannot see, and here and there a colossal white statue at the corner of

an alley that gives the place a nice *artificial*, 18th century sentiment.'

The bandstand mentioned by Stevenson can still be seen, on a slight hill to the left of the alley we have just walked down. This brings us back to Charlotte Brontë, for it was here, during an Assumption Day fête, that Lucy Snowe came after taking opium. 'The swaying tide swept this way... It led me towards a Byzantine building – a sort of kiosk near the park's centre. Round about stood crowded thousands, gathered to a grand concert in the open air. What I heard was, I think, a wild Jäger chorus.' It was precisely that. The Brontë scholar Winifred Gérin found an old Brussels newspaper which listed a performance of a German Jagd Chor at this very spot on Assumption Day in 1842. 'Here were assembled ladies, looking by this light most beautiful; some of their dresses were gauzy, and some had the sheen of satin,' Lucy observed in her slightly drugged state.

Before being landscaped by Zinner, this park was a ducal hunting estate dating back to the 14th century. Charles V converted the west end into a tilting yard (the rectangular enclosure can be seen in the Van de Velde view on page 195), but the rest of the park remained wild until the Austrians made their improvements. John Evelyn strolled through the woods in the autumn of 1641, amazed that such a wild spot could be found within the city walls: 'for here is a stately Heronry; divers springs of Water and artificial Cascads, Rocks, Grotts, one whereoff being compos'd of the Extravagant roots of trees.' Guimard and Zinner did away with this natural look, but left one area untouched. A deep wooded valley survives between the pond and the royal palace, though so cunningly concealed by the trees that most people miss it altogether. An overgrown path to the left of the main alley leads us down to a dank hollow with a little spring, where we find a statue of Mary Magdalene lying in a grotto by Jérôme Duquesnoy the Younger and a bust of Tsar Peter the Great. Visiting Brussels in 1717, the Tsar came down here to drink the water from a spring and apparently fell backwards into the fountain, though the plaque put up near the spot merely mentions that he 'ennobled the fountain by drinking his wine there at three in the afternoon'.

Which brings us to the Duke of Wellington. A few weeks before the Battle of Waterloo, he was spotted by a soldier disappearing into this hollow with Lady Frances Wedderburn-Webster. They were rumours of an affair, but it was never proved. On a different occasion, not long before the battle, Wellington was strolling in the park with Thomas Creevey, who was quizzing him on his strategy for defeating Napoleon. Wellington spotted a British soldier wandering along one of the alleys, and announced, in his famous clipped manner: 'There. It all depends upon that article whether we do the business or not. Give me enough of it, and I am sure.' We will find out how well the article performed during our walk across the battlefield at Waterloo.

We now go down the main alley, away from the royal palace, until we come to another pond surrounded by banks of ivy, classical statues and the busts of twelve Roman emperors framed by pleached trees. The French once planned to erect a column in the middle of the pond in honour of the French Revolution, but they managed no more than to lay the foundation stone in 1800. According to a local legend, Byron knocked off the noses off some of the statues in the park with his walking stick. Some of the figures do, indeed, lack noses or other features, but the real culprit was allegedly Metternich, who was staying in the Bellevue Hotel and vandalised some of the statues as he rolled home drunk one night.

III. The government quarter. We now leave Charlotte Brontë's Brussels to explore the government quarter. The neoclassical building overlooking this end of the park is the Palais de la Nation, built in 1783 by Barnabé Guimard. Originally occupied by the Brabant government, it was taken over by the Belgian parliament after the 1830 revolution. The tympanum is decorated with a relief representing Justice flanked by Fidelity and Religion, while Force drives out Discord and Fanaticism.

We leave the park by the gate facing the parliament and turn right along Rue de la Loi. This brings us to the Théâtre Royal du Parc, a neoclassical building of 1782.

A lane next to the theatre leads down to an idyllic corner of the park where few people set foot. The quaint open-air theatre shown opposite is now straight ahead. Built in 1782, it was modelled on a building that stood in the Vauxhall Pleasure Gardens in London, a park laid out in 1660 on the south bank of the Thames, not a trace of which has survived. Known as the Wauxhall (Belgians have trouble with the letter v), it is now the private home of an art restorer. The building to our left with the ironwork screen is occupied by the Cercle Royal Gaulois Artistique et Littéraire, but in Byron's day it was a fashionable ballroom and café. The poet came here every day during his stay in Brussels to chat with the local dandies and eat ice cream. Long after he had gone, customers would still request the *Coupe Byron*.

Back on Rue de la Loi, we continue to Rue Ducale where a plaque on No. 51 informs us that Byron spent two weeks here in the spring of 1816. Sir Walter Scott had stayed in the same house a few weeks earlier, but his visit doesn't merit a mention. The plaque states that Byron had left his homeland, where his genius went unrecognised, and never returned. It tactfully omits to mention that he was fleeing from accusations of incest, and that he left Brussels without paying for a new coach with fitted bookshelves he had ordered from a local carriage-maker. His host, Major Pryse Gordon, gallantly footed the bill.

We turn left along Rue Ducale away from the park, past the interesting chancery of the French embassy at No. 65. Designed by the Parisian architect Georges Chédanne in 1910, it has hints of Art Nouveau. We turn left down Rue de Louvain, which brings us to the back of the Parliament. Beyond the railings is a copy of George Minne's *Fountain with Kneeling Boys* of 1906, which he created by multiplying an earlier *Kneeling Youth* statue (visible in the photograph of Van de Velde's studio on p. 303).

We now turn right along Rue de Parlement and left along Rue de la Croix de Fer, past several sandwich shops including a branch of Pain Quotidien at No. 53. We then come to a

square with a statue of General Brialmont, famous in his day for encircling Liège and Antwerp with massive fortresses which were intended to protect Belgium from invasion but proved of little use when the German army marched into the country in 1914.

We turn right along Rue Royale, past an extraordinary Art Nouveau shop at No. 13. This was originally built in 1898 by Paul Hankar for a shirt maker, but it seems far better suited to its current incarnation as Isabelle de Backer's flower shop, with its flamboyant displays, overgrown grotto and strange female mannequin hidden in the greenery.

We cross over at the next traffic lights to look at the Colonne du Congrès, built by Joseph Poelaert between 1850 and 1859 to commemorate the national congress of 1830 and the constitution of 1831. The four solemn female statues we see at the base represent the four freedoms guaranteed under the constitution. An eternal flame burns behind the tomb of the unknown soldier, which is guarded by two fierce lions. Two plaques quaintly instruct those who

pass by to raise their hats, but my favourite details are the lamp-posts, the most elaborate of which were designed by Jean-Joseph Jacquet in an unashamedly ornate style, with four children around the base, two cherubs playing on the lamp brackets and a statue of St Michael slaying the dragon. It may not be in the best taste, but it is so much more enjoyable than the bleak concrete expanse behind the column where hardly a soul ever strays.

We go back across the road and continue down Rue du Congrès to reach the seductive Place de la Liberté. This is a French-looking corner, with café terraces shaded by trees and a 19th-century statue commemorating Charles Rogier, the government minister who helped to create the Wiertz Museum we visit on our next walk. The four diagonal streets that converge on this square are named after those same pillars of the Belgian constitution (freedom of assembly, freedom of worship, freedom of education and freedom of the press).

We go down the Rue de l'Association and then right along the Rue de la Révolution. This brings us to the quiet Place des Barricades, named after the barricades erected here during the 1830 revolution, where a circle of neoclassical buildings faces a small park with a statue of Vesalius, the renaissance anatomist. Vesalius was born in the Ruelle de l'Enfer in Brussels. The inscription on the statue gives the date as 31 December 1513, but some scholars and astrologers argue that it was 1 January 1514. He grew up in the shadow of the Galgenberg, where the public gallows once stood. The story goes that he removed rotting corpses from the gibbet and hid them under his bed while he dissected them. His father sent him to study medicine at the universities of Leuven and Paris, but Vesalius found the anatomy teachers hopelessly inadequate. They tended to rely only on ancient Greek texts and considered dissections beneath their dignity, often leaving the work to the local butcher or barber. Vesalius moved to Padua, where he was appointed Professor of Surgery. It was there that he published his famous illustrated anatomy textbook *De Humani Corporis Fabrica* in 1543. Vesalius became court physi-

cian to Charles V and cured him of gout. He also spent some time on the battlefields of France tending the wounded officers. After Charles abdicated and returned to Spain, Vesalius went with him. He died in 1564 as he returned from a pilgrimage to Rome.

Victor Hugo stayed in a narrow four-floor house rented by his son at No. 4, and his long-suffering wife, Adèle, died here in 1868. He ate his meals on the ground floor and worked in a room on the first floor standing at a lectern. The young Verlaine visited Hugo here (long before he became involved with Rimbaud) and described the district as 'decorated with tolerably good tree-lined promenades, without commerce and entirely populated by the well-heeled bourgeoisie.' This was not quite true. Hugo noted in his diary a local detail at 2 Rue du Rempart du Nord: 'behind the Place des Barricades, you can get a cigar, a glass of liqueur, a cup of coffee and a woman for twenty-five centimes.'

If we turn right down the Rue de la Révolution, we will find a narrow cobbled lane running to our right, between Nos. 18 and 20. The lane is not named, but this is all that remains of the Rue du Rempart du Nord where Hugo found his prostitutes.

We leave the square by the Rue de la Sablonnière and turn right on Rue Royale to cross at the first set of lights. Here we have a good view of the Basilique Nationale on a distant summit to the north. We turn right to reach the botanical garden, or what remains of it, at No. 236. The Botanique cultural centre occupies the former neoclassical greenhouses. The complex includes a French bookshop, theatre, exhibition rooms and café.

The gardens we see below the greenhouses were laid out in 1826 during the Dutch period, but some of the greenery was torn up to construct the rail tunnel linking Nord and Midi stations, and further land was sacrificed to widen the ring road. Most of the uprooted plants and trees were moved to the botanical gardens at Meise, a few kilometres north of Brussels. All that remains here is a romantic pond and a few benches overlooking clipped box hedges, though an impressive collection of statues by Constantin Meunier and other 19th-century sculptors has survived.

We might end our walk in the café of the cultural centre or perhaps sitting on the terrace outside. We can take the metro from Botanique station, or catch one of the trams that run along Rue Royale, or walk down through the gardens to reach Place Rogier.

WALK 7

The Cinquantenaire Museums and the European Quarter
FROM PLACE DU LUXEMBOURG TO THE MUSÉE DU CINQUANTENAIRE

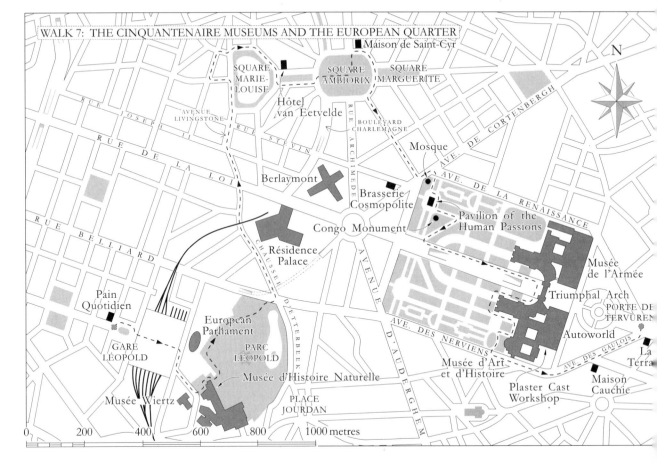

WALK 7: THE CINQUANTENAIRE MUSEUMS AND THE EUROPEAN QUARTER

Maison de Saint-Cyr

SQUARE MARIE-LOUISE

SQUARE AMBIORIX

SQUARE MARGUERITE

N

RUE JOSEPH II

AVENUE LIVINGSTONE

RUE STEVIN

Hôtel van Eetvelde

RUE ARCHIMEDE

BOULEVARD CHARLEMAGNE

AVE. DE CORTENBERGH

RUE DE LA LOI

Berlaymont

Mosque

AVE. DE LA RENAISSANCE

Brasserie Cosmopolite

RUE BELLIARD

Congo Monument

Pavilion of the Human Passions

CHAUSSEE D'ETTERBEEK

Résidence Palace

AVENUE D'AUDERGHEM

Musée de l'Armée

Pain Quotidien

Triumphal Arch

PORTE DE TERVUREN

European Parliament

PARC LÉOPOLD

Autoworld

GARE LÉOPOLD

AVE. DES NERVIENS

AVE. DES GAULOIS

La Terra

Musée d'Art et d'Histoire

Musée d'Histoire Naturelle

Maison Cauchie

Musée Wiertz

PLACE JOURDAN

Plaster Cast Workshop

0   200   400   600   800   1000 metres

WALK 7

The Cinquantenaire Museums and the European Quarter

FROM PLACE DU LUXEMBOURG TO THE MUSÉE DU CINQUANTENAIRE

Our next walk takes us into a fascinating quarter where the grandeur of Léopold II's architecture stands alongside the anarchic spread of the European Union buildings. This walk takes in three museums, all of which are closed on Monday, so we should choose another day and set off, if possible, bright and early. We spend the morning exploring the Musée Wiertz and a district of splendid Art Nouveau architecture, then head off in the afternoon to look at two museums in the Parc du Cinquantenaire. We can look forward to eating lunch in the European quarter and ending our day in a traditional Belgian tavern.

I. The Léopold Quarter. First of all, let us drink a coffee on the 19th-century Place du Luxembourg (reached on foot from Trône metro station or by buses 38 or 60). Here we find a branch of Pain Quotidien on the corner of the square, at Rue du Luxembourg 68, which has, along with the familiar refectory table and pots of jam, an interesting view of the elegant neoclassical Gare de Luxembourg designed in 1855 by Gustave Saintenoy and the modern glass architecture of the European Parliament rising behind. Note that the architect of the Parliament has copied the outline of the station clock in the curved glass roof of the new building. More about the Parliament later, but first we have a museum to visit. It opens at ten, so we need not rush.

On leaving Pain Quotidien, we cross the square, pausing to admire the statue of John Cockerill, the son of a Lancashire industrialist who settled in Belgium. The Cockerill we see here – inevitably with a pigeon perched on his head – established massive engineering works at Seraing where the first locomotives on the Continent were built in 1835. We now take the footbridge to the left of the station, following the signs pointing to the European Parliament. This brings us out on a concrete promenade that has a striking view of the new buildings designed to accommodate the European Members of Parliament when they meet in Brussels. Built partly on the site of an old brewery, the Parliament (reached through a grand arch) has been dubbed the Caprice des Dieux because of its oval plan, said to resemble the cardboard carton in which a well-known French cheese is sold. It is typical of the Belgians to be thinking of food when they should be thinking about politics.

Now for the curious Musée Wiertz, which we reach by going to the right of the Caprice and up the hill. Concealed behind an iron gate at No. 62, this museum is one of the secret delights of the city and a source of ghastly inspiration for artists; Delvaux admired Wiertz's nudes and Ensor relished the morbidity on view.

Built on a summit, the Wiertz house looks almost like an artist's villa in Rome. This is quite fitting, for Antoine Wiertz, like his hero Rubens, had spent some years in Rome, where he developed a fondness for Italian art. Three small rooms of the museum contain delightful little studies by Wiertz of festive Italian scenes. But the paintings that prompted Thomas Hardy to write in *Tess of the D'Urbervilles* of 'the staring and ghastly attitudes of a Wiertz Museum' are found in the huge atelier adjoining the house. On the back of the door is written a definition, of modesty as 'a mask that flatters the vanity of others to draw praise to oneself'. Antoine Wiertz suffered no such modesty, for his paintings are among the largest in the world. *The Revolt of Heaven Against Hell*, the largest work in the museum, is over eleven metres high and almost eight metres wide. The canvas has been tilted forward to improve visibility, and the cleaning staff, irreverently, use the space behind to store their mops and brooms.

The Musée Wiertz is perhaps not a museum for a dark winter's day, since many of the paintings are deeply pessimistic, such as *The Suicide* in which Wiertz captures the terrible moment when a depressed man, with a book titled *Matérialisme* lying on the table, blows out his brains. Reproduced overleaf is another gruesome work, *Premature Burial*, in which we see a man's blind panic as he tries to escape from a coffin.

Born in Dinant in 1806, Wiertz studied art in Antwerp where he spent hours in the baroque churches copying works by Rubens. After studying in Rome and Paris, he began work on his first masterpiece, which measured eight metres long by five metres high. He submitted this to the Paris Salon of 1839, hoping that it would win instant acclaim. To his horror, he found that it had been hung out of sight near a skylight. Wiertz left Paris in a foul temper, vowing never to return. Back at his mother's home in Dinant, he began to plot his revenge on the Parisian élite. The following year, he submitted under

his own name several drawings by Rubens, which were unanimously rejected by the jury. Now fully vindicated, Wiertz began to work in an abandoned Liège church on another enormous painting called *The Triumph of Death*. His mother died while he was working on this canvas and he locked himself away in the gloomy church for a year, until a friend eventually persuaded him to move to Brussels. He found an abandoned factory there and began work on *The Triumph of Christ*.

Baudelaire described Wiertz as a 'charlatan, idiot and thief', yet he enjoyed immense popularity in mid-19th-century Belgium. By 1850, he had managed to solve the obviously difficult problem of storing his gigantic paintings by persuading the government to build this house and studio for him. Under the terms of this peculiar agreement, all the paintings Wiertz completed after 1850 became the property of the state, on condition that they remained attached to the walls for ever. This struck Baudelaire as an absurd arrangement: 'What is Brussels going to do with all that?' he grumbled. Yet

Brussels has kept its side of the bargain, even though Wiertz is now relegated to the second rank of Belgian artists. The house has changed remarkably little since Wiertz worked here – its studio is still lit by natural light and the paintings are protected by brass railings, though one intriguing feature described in Baedeker's 1905 guide has unfortunately disappeared. 'In the corners of the room are wooden screens, through peep-holes in which paintings hung behind them are seen. The effect is curiously realistic.' As we leave, we might be amused to read a large manifesto hung in the corridor, in which Wiertz outlines his plan to turn Brussels into the capital of Europe and reduce Paris to the status of a provincial town. Oddly enough, his proposal has been realised, as the next few hours will prove.

The Museum of Natural History at the top of the hill contains an outstanding collection of fossils, stuffed animals, shells and insects. Anyone with an interest in natural history should allow a couple of hours to visit the museum. The modern block we see here dates from the 1960's,

but there is an older and more picturesque building at the back, which was designed by Emile Janlet and opened by King Léopold II in 1891. The collection was begun in 1772 during the Austrian period, but its fame rests on the extraordinary iguanodon skeletons discovered in 1878 in a coal mine at Bernissart in southern Belgium. The Belgian palaeontologist Louis Dollo laboured for several years to fit the pieces together, assembing nine skeletons in the Nassau Chapel on the Mont des Arts. Dollo concluded that the dinosaurs had perished together in a bog during the Jurassic Age, though the cause of the disaster remains a mystery. Once the new museum was built, the dinosaurs were moved to a special prehistoric hall decorated with ornate iron columns and elegant balconies. This remains the most striking department in the museum, with a lifesize reconstruction of the skeletons as they were found lying in the coal seam. The collection has now been enhanced by animated models of dinosaurs that growl and blink with disarming realism.

While we are in the prehistoric department, we

should look out for the skeleton of a Nean-
derthal man found two years after the
iguanodons near the village of Spy in southern
Belgium. Other departments in the museum
have been restored after years of neglect, such
as the collection of 5,000 butterflies and beetles,
the exotic shells, and the room of whale bones.

Back down the hill, a gate on the right at No.
41 leads into the Parc Léopold, a romantic spot
originally mapped out as a zoo in 1851. The
rolling site was landscaped by the architect
Alphonse Balat (who later built the royal greenhouses) with advice from the Prussian landscape
designer Louis Fuchs. The animals have long
gone, leaving a wistful pond surrounded by old
trees. By the turn of the century, Ernest Solvay
had his eye on the park for a centre of scientific
research. Five institutions were established here
between 1892 and 1914, covering anatomy,
hygiene, sociology, trade and physiology. We
pass some of these splendid buildings as we
descend the meandering footpaths to the foot of
the hill.

Now we come to an area which has changed
enormously in recent years. The busy Rue
Belliard has been tamed and an attractive square
with 24 fountains has been created on former
wasteland. Ahead of us, we can see the remains
of the Résidence Palace rising on the right.
Built in 1925, this Art Deco apartment building
promised to bring the glamour of Manhattan to
this quarter. Part of the complex has been
demolished, but it still has its private swimming
pool, Art Deco theatre and railway station.

The red-brick convent of the Dames de l'Adoration Perpétuelle on the left was built here in
1908, but its history goes back many centuries.
It replaces a medieval convent which stood near
the Hôtel Ravenstein on the site of an ancient
synagogue. After the convent was expropriated
in 1907 for a road building project, a substitute
was built here in the style of the original. The
building includes two chapels – the smaller is a
copy of a neo-classical building of 1735 while the
larger reproduces a neo-gothic chapel of 1856.
But the road project was never carried out and
the original convent was left standing until 1955.
For almost half a century, there were effectively

two sets of identical chapels in the city. To add to the confusion, the original 18th century chapel was used as a garage for many years. The 1908 replica eventually fell into ruin, but the red-brick convent has now been sensitively restored to accommodate the European Commission's library, while the small neo-classical chapel is used for services.

Our route goes straight ahead along the Chaussée d'Etterbeek and under the railway bridge. This dingy street connects the European Commision buildings on Rue de la Loi with the European Parliament. In an attempt to improve the image of the quarter, Brussels Region recently launched a plan to create a 'European walk' along this route. The winning design was produced by Luc Schuiten, a visionary Brussels architect with a fondness for hanging gardens. The plan seemed to have been abandoned, like so many in Brussels, but a small park with a waterfall was recently created just beyond the Maelbeek metro station. And that is not all that is new. The Charlemagne building, which we see rising behind the park, was once a dull 1968 office block. But the German architect Helmut Jahn has created a thrilling new architectural style by enclosing the old building with a glass curtain wall.

We continue straight ahead along Avenue Livingstone to reach one of the most romantic spots in the city. As we enter Square Marie-Louise a neo-renaissance plaque on the corner building on the right (No. 33) tells us that this group of six houses was created in 1895 by A. Gellé and J. Prémont. If we now cross over to the lake we come to an odd statue of *The Birth of the Nation* in which a couple cradles a child representing the young Belgian state. We should find a bench near here where we can sit down to read about this district.

II. The Squares. We are about to stroll through a handsome district planned by Gédéon Bordiau in 1875. Faced with a difficult sloping site, Bordiau created a striking series of landscaped squares and terraced gardens, decorated with ornamental ponds, fountains and statues. The original residents of this exclusive district added to its allure by building fanciful houses between 1890 and 1914. This was, until the 1960's, a stable, bourgeois district with large family houses on quiet streets, but the arrival of the European institutions has damaged the elegant residential harmony. Many of the old town houses, some of them wonderfully picturesque, have been replaced by oversize office blocks and apartment buildings. Yet we can still find some splendid neoclassical and Art Nouveau houses, especially on Avenue Palmerston and the forgotten Square Gutenberg.

We are now on Square Marie-Louise, where Bordiau achieved his most romantic effect by designing a pond surrounded by weeping willows and artificial grottos. The fake rock in the middle of the pond occasionally spouts water, and the abandoned grotto on the opposite side was where the 19th-century park keeper liked to pose for photographs.

We can take a brief detour along the right side of the lake to look at the house dated 1896 at No. 70 where W. H. Auden and Christopher Isherwood shared an apartment in 1939, imag-

ining themselves as modern-day versions of Rimbaud and Verlaine. 'Brussels is raffish and shabby, with dark monkeyish errand boys and great slow Flamands with faces like bits of raw meat,' Isherwood wrote in a letter to Stephen Spender.

Our walk takes us along the left side of the lake, until we come to a statue of a girl carrying a lute. This is signed by Emile Namur and titled, improbably, *The Cicada*.

Here, we leave the lake on a brief detour that takes us left along Rue Ortélius, then right along Rue Philippe-le-Bon, where we cross to the side with the even numbers. A row of three Art Nouveau houses at Nos. 51 to 55 are being restored. The solid neoclassical mansion at No. 68 was built in 1902 by Guillaume Löw, who added his signature on a stone on the right. The striking Art Nouveau corner house at No. 70 was built in 1899 by Victor Taelemans, who preferred his work to remain anonymous.

We now come to an unexpected little square, Square Gutenberg, which has kept its late 19th-century look intact, though perhaps not for much longer. Notice the splendid Art Nouveau house at No. 5, with its undulating door handle, rusty bell-pull and graceful boot scraper. This was designed by Armand van Waesberghe in 1898, as was No. 8, where we can read his signature to the left of the window. We might indeed have guessed it was the same architect from the similarities, such as the ground-floor windows and the three dormer windows, though No. 8 is a more elegant design, with floral motifs etched into the plasterwork above the windows and an expressive bay window. No. 19 is another Van Waesberghe house, though less recognisably so: it was built in 1898, but substantially modified in 1906, which robbed it of much of its Art Nouveau character.

We leave the square on the side bordering the lake, crossing over to where a statue of General Bernheim gazes in our direction. We now turn left, keeping to the water's edge. At the top of the slope, we climb Avenue Palmerston, stopping to look at Nos. 2 to 4 on the left side. We won't find any architect's signature on this Art Nouveau building, but a plaque informs us that this is the Hôtel van Eetvelde, built by Victor Horta from 1895-1901. It is, even from the outside, a remarkable building, totally unlike anything else in the neighbourhood. From the moment Horta met Edmond van Eetvelde, who made his wealth as a Congo administrator, he realised that he had found the perfect client. 'I presented him with the most ambitious plan I had ever drawn up,' Horta wrote in his autobiography. The house at No. 4, begun in 1895, is particularly inventive, with its projecting iron façade decorated with small brown mosaic tiles laid in swirling Art Nouveau patterns. Even the iron boot scraper is a miniature masterpiece of Art Nouveau design. Mme. Eetvelde was sniffy about all this iron: 'très peuple', she said, in a snide reference to the Maison du Peuple that Horta was building at the same time. No. 4 was completed in 1897, the year of Léopold's great Congo Exhibition, when Van Eetvelde was involved in commissioning a series of Art Nouveau interiors for the Congo Pavilion in Tervuren. The house at No. 2 was begun in 1898 as a combined extension (to the right of the

door) and rental property (facing the Square Marie-Louise). The city authorites had little patience with Art Nouveau, and Van Eetvelde – by then a Baron – had to use all his political influence to persuade them to accept the plan. The photograph here shows the remarkable octagonal hall.

If we cross to the other side of Avenue Palmerston, we can look at another house by Horta at No. 3. The Hôtel Deprez was built in 1896 as a weekend residence for Georges Deprez, the director of the Val Saint-Lambert glassworks in Seraing. It was reconstructed in 1910 by Horta and later modified again by one of his students. Though no longer the original house, it is still recognisably a Horta building with its alternating bands of grey and yellow sandstone, elaborate chimney, and slender columns bursting out at the top in Art Nouveau flourishes.

Now we climb Avenue Palmerston, a virtually intact 19th-century street. No. 14, signed by Léon Govaerts in 1900, has vaguely Moorish windows, and the romantic Villa Germaine on the left at No. 24 is a striking house with bands of glinting tiles that catch any afternoon sun. It was built in 1897 by a couple who named the house after their daughter. We cross the road to enter the landscaped gardens in the middle of Square Ambiorix, with their old chestnut trees and wooden benches enclosed by ornamental hedges. Proceeding up the central alley, we pass a string of defunct ponds and a statue of Max Waller carved by Victor Rousseau. Waller established the artistic movement *La Jeune Belgique* in 1881, bringing together symbolists such as Fernand Khnopff and Georges Rodenbach. Just beyond the statue, we turn left along the broad alley to look at one of the most extraordinary Art Nouveau houses in Brussels. The exceptionally narrow Maison de Saint-Cyr at No. 11 was built by Gustave Strauven in 1903 for the painter Georges de Saint-Cyr. The façade is a delirious riot of carved stone and wrought iron, ending with an eccentric wrought iron pinnacle. The ornate wrought-iron fence we see here was almost torn down by the city authorities, but Saint-Cyr saved his costly ornament by convincing the bureaucrats that it embellished the

neighbourhood. As it does.

Strauven had worked in Horta's studio, assisting him with the design of the Van Eetvelde house we have just seen. His style closely followed Horta's, though his clients tended to be less well off and so could only afford narrow plots of land. Strauven consequently became adept at designing tall, slender houses, such as this one and another, even more bizarre, just off our route at Boulevard Clovis 85. He gave up architecture in 1906 and turned his mind to developing inventions such as a glass brick, a central heating system and a unicycle.

We now turn right up the hill, passing a neo-renaissance house at No. 13 signed by Henri van Massenhove in 1895. At the end of the square, we pass one of the modern apartment blocks that have invaded this district, at No. 22. A mysterious head of Margaret of York, minus her nose, sits in the garden of this building. Its partner, the head of Ambiorix, who defeated the Romans at Tongeren in 54 BC, stands in the garden opposite (at No. 23). These two weather-beaten relics were rescued from a house that

stood on this corner until 1969.

We leave the square just beyond here, and turn down Avenue Michelange, where a 19th-century art admirer chose to decorate his house at No. 60 with a replica of Michelangelo's pensive statue of Lorenzo the Magnificent, placed in a niche at the top. Our walk continues through the park straight ahead, but we might want lunch before we visit the last two museums. We can eat at the traditional Italian restaurant Rosticceria Fiorentina at Rue Archimède 43 (described on page 392), the Vietnamese Le Rocher Fleuri at Rue Franklin 19, or, for Irish food and draught Guinness, Kitty O'Shea's at Boulevard Charlemagne 42. But if we are short of time, the restaurant of the Musée du Cinquantenaire offers good food and a fine setting.

III. The Parc du Cinquantenaire. Now for the park, which we enter from Avenue de Cortenberg. The round building in the corner, now a mosque, was built in 1880 to display a large panoramic painting of Cairo. Panoramas such as this one were popular for a brief period in the late 19th century, providing visitors with realistic scenes of battles or views of exotic cities. Several workshops in Brussels specialised in these circular paintings, which were displayed in large rotundas built for the purpose. Only three have survived intact in Europe – one of them conveniently nearby at Waterloo (described on page 319).

We go around the left side of the mosque, past a small playground. This brings us to a neoclassical temple behind the mosque, inscribed *Les Passions Humaines par Jef Lambeau*. The Pavilion of the Human Passions was built in 1889 by the young Victor Horta to display Jef Lambeau's giant sculpted frieze of *The Human Passions*. The work covers the entire back wall of the pavilion, and is lit from above by a glass roof. Not that we are likely to see anything of the work. Lambeau's fleshy nude figures proved too erotic for the delicate sensibilities of the time. People were outraged and, just four days after the opening ceremony, the city had to close the building to the public. The arcade was permanently bricked

up, and has remained so ever since, apart from the occasional open day when long queues form for a glimpse of the forbidden sculpture. We can peer through the keyhole at the work or, if that seems too shifty, examine the small bronze version which the Musée des Beaux-Arts recently dared to exhibit in its new 19th-century rooms (see page 151).

Now for a monument that lies forgotten in a clump of trees to our left. The Congo Monument was carved by Thomas Vincotte in 1901 and repaired in 1921. A large curving frieze illustrates Belgian explorers and missionaries battling through the jungle to bring civilisation to the Congo basin. 'I have undertaken the Congo project for the benefit of civilisation and the well-being of Belgium,' reads the inscription taken from a speech made by Léopold II in 1906. A reclining African representing the Congo river is badly weathered and the basin is now dry. The last repair done to the monument was when the inscription below the figures on the left was altered to read: 'Belgian military heroism defeats the *Arab* slave trader.' I have never managed to

find out what the original inscription said.

We continue beyond the monument to reach the main alley, where we turn left and look for a bench among the trees on our right. It is time to read about this park.

Originally a military parade ground, the Parc du Cinquantenaire was created in 1880 for the Belgian Exhibition, held to celebrate fifty years of independence. Two large iron-and-glass halls were built by Gédéon Bordiau at the far end of the park, as we see in the photograph here, which was taken from one of the houses opposite the park on a damp day before the exhibition opened. The buildings look ready, but the arch linking the two halls was far from finished. The money had run out, forcing the architect to construct a temporary arch out of wood and stucco. This makeshift structure had still not been replaced when a second exhibiton was held here in 1897. Léopold was deeply hurt by this shambolic episode. 'I am the king of a small country of small-minded people,' he complained. He had hoped that the 1897 exhibition would promote the development of the Congo, but

visitors seem to have spent more time in the section of the park devoted to the Bruxelles Kermesse. Here, they could wander through a mock Flemish village crammed with old-fashioned taverns, including an English one called 'Here is Ye Cherry Blossom'.

Eight years after Ye Cherry Blossom had been dismantled, Léopold finally found the money to build his triumphal arch. He had to look for a new architect, though, as Bordiau had died in 1904, and he approached Charles Girault, who had designed two vast exhibition halls – the Petit Palais and Grand Palais – for the 1900 Paris Exhibition.

Now let us look at the triumphal arch, which was finally completed by Girault in 1905 to celebrate seventy-five years of Belgian independence. As we approach, we will see four large female statues at the base carved with the names of Belgian provinces. A romantic figure of Antwerp holds a ship in her hand as her cloak blows in the wind, while a wild-looking woman representing Namur is accompanied by a deer. A further four figures on the other side of the arch represent four more Belgian provinces. The two women depicting East and West Flanders were carved by Jef Lambeau, though here he adopted a more cautious style than his Pavilion of the Human Passions. But where is the ninth Belgian province? We have to peer up at the top of the arch, where Brabant is riding in triumph on a chariot pulled by four horses. We will seem more of Brabant later, but first we might explore the museum on the left side of the esplanade.

IV. The Musée de l'Armée. Even if guns are not our passion, we should spend a short time in this outstanding military museum, if only to look at the oldest stuffed horses in the world and survey the city from the terrace above the triumphal arch. As we enter the museum, we pass a row of field guns and cannons, several of which were cast in Liège, including two large weapons inscribed *Luik 1818* which date from the Dutch period, when Liège was briefly known by its Dutch name. Another large gun manufactured by Krupp in 1888 may have been left by the Germans at the end of the First World War.

The army museum has a likeable old-fashioned air. Wooden cabinets are crammed with rusty horseshoes and worn saddles, cannon that pounded Flemish cities in the middle ages, and dented Spanish armour. The entrance hall is filled with weapons from the battlefield at Waterloo (which we tramp across on walk 12). Many of these relics were brought here from a museum established on the battlefield by Sergeant Cotton, a soldier in Wellington's army who had spent the night before the battle sleeping in a waterlogged ditch. Cotton settled in Waterloo after 1815, guiding visitors over the site and building up a sizeable collection of relics. Several cabinets in the entrance hall contain objects found on the battlefield, including rusted horseshoes, Prussian sabres, coins, buttons, guns and a portrait of an unidentified soldier. We can see a cannon cast in The Hague, another in Britain in 1813 and a third, improbably named *La Baleine* (the whale), made that same year for Napoleon in Douai. One of the oddest relics is a fragment of shrapnel that served Victor Hugo as a paperweight, but perhaps the most evocative exhibit is Napoleon's satchel (or at least what remains of it after a fire in Madame Tussaud's in London, where it was on display) which was discovered by Prussian troops in Napoleon's carriage, along with his hat and sword.

The 19th-century rooms may seem impossibly antiquated and cluttered, but they contain some remarkable exhibits. We might enjoy the flamboyant 19th-century uniforms worn by the Second Cavalry Regiment of the French army (room 8, cabinet 8), whose troops trotted into battle with sabres drawn and helmets glinting. The Belgian army was no less immune to the exigencies of military fashion. The rebels in the 1830 Revolution (room 2) sported a pale blue smock and a twelve-inch stove-pipe hat topped with a red pompom. For the ill-fated Mexican campaign (room 8, cabinets 34 and 35), they adopted a fetching dark-blue jacket with green trim, charcoal grey plus-fours and their favourite stove-pipe hat, topped this time with a clutch of feathers.

The dusty relics of the Mexican Expedition (in cabinets 34 and 35) recall the tragic episode in the 1860's when the European powers estab-lished Archduke Ferdinand Joseph Maximilian of Austria as Emperor of Mexico. Maximilian had married Léopold II's sister Charlotte, seen as a child on page 34. The couple might have lived the rest of their life in the Castello di Miramare, Maximilian's Italian retreat near Trieste, had it not been for Napoleon III's dream of colonial expansion in America. Mexico's failure to pay a debt was a pretext for sending a French army to depose the republican government of Benito Juarez and establish some reactionary puppets. Searching for a suitable monarch, Napoleon offered the crown to Maximilian in 1864. Maximilian is said to have wavered, but Charlotte persuaded him to accept, and the couple sailed to Veracruz that year, settling into a lavish palace in the cool hills at Chapultepec. For several years, they lived grandly among the cactuses and Aztec ruins, Maximilian reading and collecting exotic butterflies, while Charlotte (now calling herself Carlotta) organised dazzling balls.

The colonial adventure came to a tragic conclusion in 1867. Keen to enforce the Monroe

Doctrine (which was aimed at halting such colonial adventures), Abraham Lincoln wrote a stiff letter to Napoleon and Maximilian ordering them to leave Mexico alone. Sensing that the game was up, Napoleon withdrew his troops, leaving poor Maximilian stranded as the Mexican rebels led by Juarez recaptured their country. Charlotte sailed back to Europe in a desperate attempt to find someone willing to rescue their tottering Empire, but neither the Pope nor anyone else was prepared to help such a lost cause. Maximilian made a brave stand at Querétaro, but he was finally forced to surrender, and was shot. The execution inspired Manet's famously unceremonious painting of 1867 in which he shows the Emperor and two aides facing the firing squad in a courtyard as Mexican peasants peer over the walls to watch. (The painting was destroyed, but Manet's made a print of a version of his composition, reproduced opposite.)

A hasty sketch of the execution lies gathering dust in case 35. Made by the French photographer François Aubert, this reveals that Manet took some liberties in his painting. Aubert shows Maximilian and his two companions standing alone on a bare hillside as a grey mass of Mexican soldiers prepare to fire. Aubert had arrived in Mexico in the 1860's, and soon began to take splendid photographs of Belgian generals with muttonchop moustaches, officers' wives dressed in long heavy gowns and, in complete contrast, a series of astonishing portraits of Mexican peasants. Aubert was later appointed as official photographer to the Imperial Court. He travelled with the Belgian troops during their campaigns against the Mexicans, and ended up, by pure chance, in Querétaro on the day of Maximilian's execution. He took several extraordinary photographs after the execution, including one of Maximilian's white shirt riddled with bullets, and another showing his lavishly-decorated bedroom. But the most haunting is the photograph shown overleaf, of Maximilian lying in an open coffin, dressed in his long shiny boots and buttoned-up tunic.

Aubert seems to have sided with the Mexican peasants, for he stayed on in Mexico after the

revolution, taking a photograph later that year of the crowds gathered at the unveiling of the monument to the revolution. He abandoned his camera on returning to France in 1869, though his brief career in Mexico earned him recognition as one of the finest pioneers of documentary photography. Thanks to Aubert and Manet, Maximilian's execution became one of the great romantic tragedies of the 19th century. Madame Tussaud's in London displayed several items used by Maximilian while he was being held in prison before his execution, including his pillow case, his last pair of socks and the remains of a loaf of bread that he left on his plate after eating his last meal. Yet the story of Maximilian is now almost forgotten, apart from the paintings in Stuttgart and London and the dusty relics in these two glass cases.

Another cabinet contains memorabilia of Léopold II, including his umbrella, hat box and dumb-bells, while his British-made tricycle stands nearby. Perhaps it is fortunate that Léopold died before the outbreak of the First World War, for this conflict shattered forever his innocent belief

WALK 7: THE CINQUANTENAIRE

in progress. It was Léopold's son Albert who found himself in the unhappy role of defending a small corner of Belgium from the German army, while his wife Elisabeth cared for the wounded in a hospital in De Panne. The museum owns an extraordinary collection of relics from this appalling conflict – stretchers stained with blood, battered howitzers, mud-stained uniforms, first aid kits, torn maps, fragments of crashed aircraft and wreckage from sunk ships. This collection used to be utterly chaotic, as if it had only recently been dredged from the mud of Flanders, but it has been more systematically arranged. An interesting new section in the 19th-century Bordiau Hall illustrates daily life in Belgium during the German Occupation. It includes a reconstructed street, the interior of a house, and video interviews with concentration camp survivors.

Another vast hall built in 1880 contains a collection of about 130 aircraft, ranging from flimsy biplanes that dropped bombs on the Ypres Salient to a streamlined Lockheed Starfighter. Several salvaged relics of aircraft are also displayed, including the battered wing of an American B-17 bomber shot down in Liège province and used until recently by a local farmer to enclose a chicken run. A flea market devoted to ephemera is held in the air museum every first Saturday of the month from 9 to 2. Wizened dealers brave the freezing cold to lay out their stock amid the fighter aircraft. Rummaging among the stands, we might find an interesting old guide to Bruges, a stack of German banknotes from the period when a wheelbarrow of Deutschmarks bought one egg, a 1934 *Good Housekeeping* magazine with a recipe for suet pudding, or perhaps a copy of the 1962 Aeroflot timetable. Several dealers bring along shoe boxes filled with ancient postcards, which sometimes bear touching messages. The collectors retire to pore over their latest finds in the café, which offers beer, boiled sausages and a blast of heat.

Back in the entrance hall, we now follow the sign to the Arcades, which leads us to a room filled with gleaming medieval armour and artillery, including a battering ram which had quite literally a bronze ram's head on the end. As well as hefty pieces of jousting equipment, we can admire a miniature suit of armour made for the young Joseph-Ferdinand of Bavaria. But we might be more struck by the large glass case containing the two mouldering stuffed horses. Archduke Albert rode into Brussels in 1599 on the slightly better preserved beast on the left. This horse was later wounded during the siege of Ostend in 1601-4. His wife Isabella rode on the other.

But we are not here only for the horses. A small sign next to Isabella's points to Titeca-Arcades. Though few people follow this route, it leads to one of the secret delights of Brussels. A lift and a winding stair takes us up to a room at the top of Léopold's triumphal arch, where we find a bust of Georges Louis Titeca, a Belgian banker who donated a collection of military relics spanning the period 1787 to 1914. Titeca collected medals, scarlet tunics, swords, braid and old photographs, but his real passion, as we can see, was military helmets.

If we go up a few more stairs, we can step out onto the roof terrace, just below the bronze figure of Brabant. Looking east towards the forest, we will see the broad tree-lined Avenue de Tervuren built by Léopold II in 1897 to connect the Cinquantenaire with the Congo Exhibition in Tervuren (which we explore further on walk 13). Turning to face the other way, we can see the European quarter sliced through by the Rue de la Loi, with the glass arch of the European Parliament rising above the roofs of the Léopold quarter, the shiny steel spheres of the Atomium glinting in the distance, and the Berlaymont building straight ahead of us, still unoccupied at the time of writing. This star-shaped modernist building was put up in 1963 on the site of a 19th-century boarding school; it was used for many years as the headquarters of the European Union. Though unloved by most of the 3,000 people who once worked there, the Berlaymont is being renovated by the Belgian government in the firm conviction that the building has become an irreplaceable landmark worth preserving at all costs.

On leaving the museum, we will see another

WALK 7: THE CINQUANTENAIRE

19th-century exhibition hall opposite. This contains Autoworld, an outstanding collection of several hundred vintage cars, including Léon Bollée's *voiturette* which first bumped along the country roads of France in 1896, several splendid Minervas built by a Belgian firm that went bankrupt decades ago, and the 1956 Cadillac that carried John F. Kennedy through the streets of West Berlin in 1963 to deliver the rousing speech that began, 'Ich bin ein Berliner.' Autoworld also displays a collection of 19th-century carriages from the Musée du Cinquantenaire. To reach the entrance, we go back through the arch and turn left along the front of the building, following signs to the Albert-Elisabeth door.

V. The Musée du Cinquantenaire. This sprawling museum occupies a sober late Art Deco building put up after Bordiau's original south hall burnt down in 1946, and an older wing constructed by Bordiau in 1902-12. The museum owns an enormous and fascinating collection of decorative art from all parts of the world – a Belgian version of the Victoria and Albert Museum – yet the rooms are often completely deserted, apart perhaps from the occasional scholar seeking the Egyptian collection (which is superb) or a tourist wandering lost among the relics of Carthage. A few years ago, the museum tried to improve its dusty image by opening some fifty new rooms where hidden treasures from the reserve collection could be shown for the first time in years. The Treasury was moved to a splendid rotunda in the Bordiau wing and the café redecorated. It finally seems as if this museum might be on the road to recovery, though it still suffers from a staff shortage, which means that rooms are occasionally roped off without warning. The staff at the information desk can usually escort you into a closed-off department, though this often involves considerable fuss as they hunt for keys, rouse a guard and then waste ten minutes trying to locate the light switch.

The door to the left of the information desk leads to the Art Deco wing, where antiquities are kept. We might begin by looking at the Egyptian collection (Room 123-139), where school

classes file into the reconstructed Mastaba of Neferirtenef, a tomb from Sakkara decorated inside with hieroglyphics showing scenes of everyday life in about 2400 BC. We may also find a school group peering over a balcony at a superb scale model of Rome (Room 20). Built by a Belgian architect, this detailed model shows the city in the 4th century BC. Much of the museum's Roman collection was brought back by Belgian archaeologists from Apamea, the capital of Roman Syria. We can wander through the Great Colonnade which once lined the main street (Room 122) and look over another balcony at a mosaic from the governor's residence showing Romans on horseback hunting lions (Room 25). Other mosaics come from the Great Colonnade and the Synagogue in Apamea, suggesting that there cannot be much left of Apamea *in situ*.

Some of the best parts of the collection take some effort to track down. A door behind the bookshop leads to the Wolfers Room (No. 50), a reconstructed interior from the Art Nouveau department store designed by Victor Horta in

1912 at Rue d'Arenberg 11, which we passed on walk 2. The cabinets now contain *fin-de-siècle* objects including two silver candlesticks designed by Henry van de Velde (opposite).

Other rooms nearby (Nos. 45-49) contain reconstructed interiors salvaged from Belgian mansions. A rococo room comes from a house in Verviers and an interior from Bruges contains a series of paintings representing the five senses. A clavichord in Room 45 is decorated with views of Belgian cities under siege and Room 49 contains a set of eight gilded chairs designed in the fashionable Egyptian style popularised by Napoleon's adventure.

Back to the entrance hall to reach the rooms in the older wing, which have an exceptional collection of Flemish art. The Great Tapestry Hall in the depths of the building (No. 53) contains a series of large Flemish tapestries illustrating the Life of Jacob. The eight tapestries here, together with another two that have been lost, were ordered in 1520 by Cardinal Lorenzo Cambeggi to decorate his palace in Bologna. The surviving tapestries were recently returned to Belgium and superbly restored in the De Wit tapestry workshop in Mechelen; notice the glowing red cheeks of the figures in this story from Genesis. Based on cartoons by Bernard van Orley, the tapestries were woven by Willem de Kempeneer in 1550-60. One scene shows Jacob and Laban dividing the flock, another has a wonderfully sinister Rebecca and Jacob. The letters B. B. in the margin signify that the tapestries were woven in Brussels, Brabant.

A small room off the hall (No. 52) contains the curious Musée du Cœur Boyadjian. An obsessive heart surgeon amassed this collection of objects related to the heart, including love tokens, saints with arrows piercing their heart, and a whimsical Valentine card illustrating *Le Langage de la Moustache*. A portrait of Dr Boyadjian shows him standing in front of a bookcase which contains volumes such as *Bedside Cardiology*.

We now cross the hall to enter a neo-gothic cloister (No. 71) filled with stone sculptures, stained glass and aristocratic tombs salvaged from Belgian churches, including a wonderful incised tomb slab of Enghelbert d'Anghien looking very like Ned Kelly – in the Sidney Nolan paintings – all helmet. Looking across the garden, we will see a replica of the late gothic Nassau chapel, which we passed when we climbed the Mont des Arts on walk 3.

We return to the great hall, hoping that the door into Room 54 is open. If not, we will have to ask one of the guards to let us look at the locked rooms, for we cannot leave without a glimpse of the delightful Rhineland tapestry of 1425 showing men playing various games such as backgammon. A side room known as the Ypres Room (No. 55) is furnished in late medieval style rather like the interior of the Master of Flémalle's Annunciation reproduced on page 129. The tapestry hanging on the wall was woven in about 1425 in Tournai. It shows a shepherd shearing sheep in a forest while his companion, with a wooden spoon stuck in his hat, hacks off a slice of bread and offers it to a woman.

The next rooms contain elaborate retables carved and painted in Brussels, Antwerp and Mechelen. One of the most impressive is the Passion Retable of Claudio Villa and Gentina Solaro, constructed in Brussels about 1470. We have to picture it hanging in a family chapel with the gilt details (most of which have flaked off) glinting in the flickering candlelight. The two kneeling figures represent the donors, Claudio Villa, in armour, and his wife Gentina Solaro, wearing a lovely red brocade dress.

Grisly martyrdom scenes decorate the St George's Retable, carved in Brussels in 1493 by the sculptor Jan Borreman. This long wooden retable originally hung behind the altar in a Leuven church, no doubt striking fear into the congregation with its gruesome scenes of martyrdom, including a man sitting calmly as his head is split in two with a saw, and another victim who is being roasted alive inside an ox. By the 16th century, when the Maria Retable of Pailhe was carved, the designs had become less morbid. The exotic costumes and foreign faces we see here reflect the cosmopolitan spirit of Antwerp. The huge Passion Retable of Oplinter was carved in Antwerp in about 1530, but though the figures wear renaissance costumes, they pose like figures painted by a Flemish Primitive. It is only with the Judgement of Solomon Retable carved in Mechelen in the late 16th century that we see the full impact of the renaissance reaching the retable workshops.

Now we come into a room (No. 62) hung with three large tapestries woven in Brussels. European aristocrats were prepared to pay enormous sums for tapestries marked with the letters B. B. One such order was placed with Jean Baudouyn's workshop in 1546 for a series of eight tapestries to decorate the palace of Ferrante Gonzaga, Duke of Guastalla. As Charles V's commander in chief, Guastalla chose the bellicose theme of *The Fruits of War*, based on a series of paintings by an Italian renaissance artist. The tapesty we see hanging here, illustrating *The Triumphal Procession of the General*, is the only one of the eight to have survived intact. Another tapestry hung in this room depicts the *Legend of Notre Dame du Sablon*, a theme we have met in the city museum on Grand'Place (page 73).

The gilded oak cradle in the middle of Room 62 is known as Charles V's Cradle, though it is far from certain that it was ever occupied by

the infant Charles. If it was, the cradle was probably second-hand or even third-hand by then. It is thought to have been carved in 1476 in anticipation of the birth of Philip the Fair or perhaps three years later for his sister Margaret of Austria. By the time Charles was born in 1500, it was certainly not new.

A renaissance door leads us into a room filled with various old furnishings, including a grand wooden staircase rescued from a demolished house in Brussels, and a floor covered with majolica tiles saved from an Italian family chapel. The curious Nassau chapel we saw earlier is just beyond here (Room 73). Recently restored and reopened, it contains a collection of copper objects from Dinant. Continuing our tour, we find the Mérode Door in Room 66 carved in the renaissance style of Cornelis Floris and painted with the gilt initials P. P. and B. B. We may notice that it is dated 1540 on two panels and 1626 on a third. It was carved in 1540 for Westerlo Castle and moved in 1626 to the church of St Dympna in Geel.

Back in the Great Tapestry Hall, we now go downstairs to the Treasury (open 10-12 and 1-4), where the museum's collection of Mosan art is superbly displayed in a rotunda with rugged Doric columns supporting an iron architrave. Modelled on the treasuries of the great medieval abbeys and churches, the dimly-lit rotunda creates a vague sense of religious awe. The retables encrusted with jewels seem to prefigure the miniature perfection of the Flemish Primitives. One of the most fascinating works is the Portable Altar of Stavelot, carried by a 12th-century traveller on his journeys. If we look closely, we can see that the seated figures of the Four Evangelists form the feet of the altar. Each of the figures is writing the opening words of his gospel using quill pens and delightful little ink wells. Notice the figure of St John leaning pensively on one elbow after inscribing the words *In principio*.

An older Mosan ivory shows the Crucifixion and again the Four Evangelists at the corners holding ink pots. This work was carved in the 11th century in an abbey near Liège. There is much left to see in the museum, including a massive and melancholy Easter Island figure in

Room 38, a collection of Belgian archaeological finds in Room 1 and a room of 18th-century sledges once owned by Belgian aristocrats, including one decorated with a lion chasing a startled chicken and another fitted with a snug pair of fur slippers for the driver (in the hall beyond the bookshop). If time permits, we should also glance in the rooms devoted to America, if only to peer inside a forgotten room in the Pre-Columbian department furnished like a cabinet of curiosities (Room 32).

On leaving the museum we turn left, past the rotunda where the Treasury is located, and left again down a cobbled lane that runs beside the museum. This brings us to the plaster cast workshop (open Monday to Friday), where one of the largest collections of 19th-century casts is stored. We can wander inside to watch workmen producing casts to order, admire a hall of finished statues, and perhaps order a bust of Lorenzo de' Medici for the mantelpiece. In the days before photography, and when learning from the past was encouraged, such cast workshops were a vital part of the educational

process. All the great museums and art schools had displays of casts taken from the greatest works of art; now only the one in the V&A in London survives intact. But they no longer make casts.

On leaving the workshop, we should cross the Avenue des Nerviens and turn left, pausing before we cross the Rue des Francs to look at the Maison Cauchie at No. 5. This was designed in 1905 by Paul Cauchie – though this hardly needs to be spelled out, since the architect advertised himself on the two carved plaques on either side of the entrance. The façade has echoes of Charles Rennie Mackintosh's Glasgow style, and the large sgraffito panel showing the nine muses could almost be a work of the Pre-Raphaelites. The interior, which still has wonderful murals by Cauchie, is open on the first weekend of every month, 11-2 and 2-6.

This is the end of our walk. Turning right along the Avenue des Gaulois brings us to the Avenue de Tervuren where we will find the café La Terrace at No. 11. This traditional Belgian tavern has changed little since it opened on this corner one hundred years ago. Its Art Nouveau partitions and iron coat hooks recall the comforts of Léopold II's Belgium. Let us settle into one of the welcoming banquettes to savour the atmosphere. We can catch the metro from the Mérode stop nearby.

WALK 8

Art Nouveau Architecture
FROM AVENUE LOUISE TO THE PARC TENBOSCH

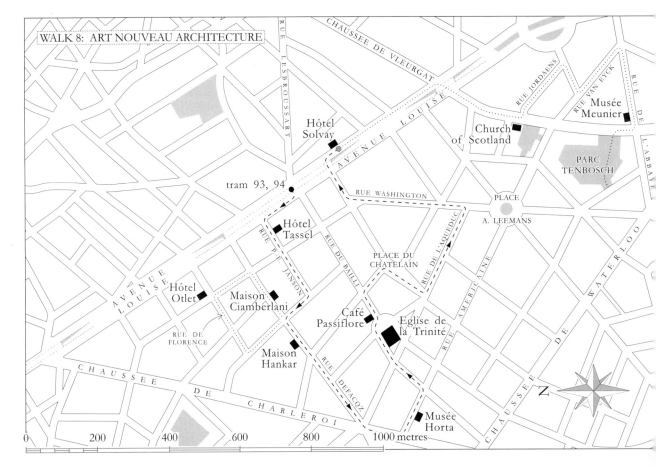

WALK 8: ART NOUVEAU ARCHITECTURE

RUE LESBROUSSART

CHAUSSEE DE VLEURGAT

RUE JORDAENS

RUE VAN EYCK

RUE DE L'ABBAYE

Musée Meunier

Church of Scotland

PARC TENBOSCH

Hôtel Solvay

AVENUE LOUISE

tram 93, 94

RUE WASHINGTON

PLACE A. LEEMANS

Hôtel Tassel

RUE P.-E. JANSON

RUE DU BAILLI

PLACE DU CHATELAIN

RUE DE L'AQUEDUC

RUE AMERICAINE

CHAUSSEE DE WATERLOO

AVENUE LOUISE

Hôtel Otlet

Maison Ciambérlani

RUE DE FLORENCE

Café Passiflore

Eglise de la Trinité

Maison Hankar

RUE DEFACQZ

CHAUSSEE DE CHARLEROI

Musée Horta

N

0   200   400   600   800   1000 metres

Art Nouveau Architecture

FROM AVENUE LOUISE TO THE PARC TENBOSCH

This walk takes us into a quarter of Ixelles where several Belgian architects launched a new style of architecture in the 1890's. More than a century later, the Art Nouveau buildings still catch our eye with their tendrils of wrought iron and curvaceous stonework. The highlight of the walk is a visit to a house designed by Victor Horta in 1899 as his studio and home. This is only open from 2-5.30 (and not on Mondays), so the walk is best done in the afternoon.

We therefore need to eat lunch somewhere. My advice is to take tram 93 or 94 to the Lesbroussart halt. The Fresh Company at Rue Lebroussart 216 is run by an Irish cook who concocts delicious dishes (open for lunch from Monday to Friday). If that is full, we can eat a Japanese lunch at Kushi-Tei next door (No. 118) or try one of the sandwich bars in Rue du Bailli, on the other side of Avenue Louise.

While we are eating lunch, we might familiarise ourselves with the Art Nouveau style we are about to encounter on our walk. Most of the houses were built in a period of about ten years at the turn of the 19th century. The style emerged at a time when Belgium was one of the richest countries in Europe. The wealthy clients often wanted a modern house to reflect their progressive ideals. They found the answer in Victor Horta, who built his first Art Nouveau house – the Tassel House – not far from here in 1893. One of the distinctive features of Horta's style is a curvaceous line – the whiplash – which

he borrowed from English Pre-Raphaelite design.

Horta's closest rival was Paul Hankar, who built his first Art Nouveau house in the same year, and indeed in the same neighbourhood, as Horta's Tassel House. Hankar studied under Henri Beyaert, an architect who specialised in fanciful wrought iron designs, such as the railings around the Place du Petit Sablon we saw on walk 4. His houses tend to have elaborate ironwork on the façade, but rather conventional interiors.

I. The Horta House. Let us now look at some of the buildings that have survived from this extraordinary period. To do so, we return to Avenue Louise and after crossing to the other side, turn right.

The house that started Horta on his career is in Rue Paul-Emile Janson, the first street on the left, at No. 6. Most of the building plots on this street were still empty when Horta built the Tassel House in 1893 for an engineer employed by Ernest Solvay. Most of its neighbours were designed in traditional Belgian neo-baroque style, with square bay windows projecting over the pavement like huge wardrobes. Horta introduced motifs here that would inspire a generation of architects – iron columns, curvaceous stonework and elaborate doorways. But the most striking feature is the staircase that lies behind the high bay window, seen in this photograph taken soon after the house was built. 'The day will arrive when people make a pilgrimage to this house,' the art critic Sander Pierron forecast in 1924.

Continuing down this street, we will see a house at the end built by Albert Rosenboom in 1900. The site at Rue Faider 83 was clearly chosen because it can be seen from Avenue Louise. The façade is particularly striking in the early morning when the sun glints on the gilded details, illuminating a sgraffito frieze. Rosenboom was an eclectic Dutch architect who worked as a draughtsman in Horta's firm in 1896. He flirted briefly with Art Nouveau before turning to other styles. Horta's influence can be seen in the ornate boot scraper by the door,

the organic wooden door frame and the beautiful letter box (overleaf) that looks almost like a detail from a medieval illuminated manuscript. The house next door, No. 85, was built in the same year by Armand van Waesberghe, but in a duller Art Nouveau style.

We now turn right and walk to the end of the street. It is worth taking a brief detour here to look at two houses by Paul Hankar. We cross the road and turn right to admire the Maison Ciamberlani, at 48 Rue Defacqz, built by Hankar in 1897 for the Symbolist painter Albert Ciamberlani. The artist worked in the studio on the upper floor where there is a row of windows facing north. Most of the façade was covered with elaborate sgraffito decorations designed by Ciamberlani and executed by Adolphe Crespin, but the harsh northern weather has taken its toll on the Mediterranean painting so that we can now barely make out the sunflowers, peacocks or couple with a child.

The house next door, at No. 50, was built by Hankar one year later for the painter René Janssens in a less flamboyant style.

WALK 8: ART NOUVEAU

While we are here, we might want to look at two other houses in the neighbourhood designed by Octave van Rysselberghe, brother of the Impressionist painter Theo. The houses are in the Rue de Livourne, which is the next street to cross Rue Defacqz. The architect's own house is just on the left at No. 83. Built in 1905 when van Rysselberghe was at the height of his career, it has a circular stair tower which gives the house something of the appearance of a Scottish baronial castle.

The earlier and more impressive house is on the other side of Rue Defacqz, at No. 48. It has a Tuscan roof, bay windows and a striking entrance at 13 Rue de Florence. Van Rysselberghe worked on it from 1894 to 1898 for Paul Otlet, the son of a Belgian industrialist who had made his fortune constructing railways in China. Paul Otlet, like many an heir to a large fortune, was a romantic dreamer, who spent most of his time pursuing eccentric and unrealistic projects. Obsessed with the idea of amassing all human knowlege in one building, he invented a decimal classification system for use

in libraries, and he also published dozens of books, arguing for an international currency and 'the end of war and the establishment of a world charter'. To achieve his lofty aims, he proposed setting up various institutions with names like the Mundaneum, Urbaneum, Brussellaneum and, not surprisingly, Otletaneum. Otlet's optimistic faith in progress was shattered by the Second World War, and he died in 1944 leaving a vast collection of miscellaneous posters, postcards and newspapers from all over the world. The Mundaneum was one of the few plans to be realised. This enormous collection of documents was stored for a time in a building in the Léopold Park, then moved to a gloomy underground museum below Place Rogier. When that closed down some years ago, it might have seemed that Otlet's dream was at an end, but the Mundaneum has been reconstructed in a former department store in Mons. It is an extraordinary place with walls lined with index files and cabinets filled with a miscellany of strange objects.

We will never, however, see the beach resort financed by Otlet in 1903. Built by the same

253

architect as the house we are looking at now, this development of sixty villas in the coastal resort of Westende was destroyed in the First World War, leaving only the crumbling Bellevue Hotel as a last vestige of the project.

Van Rysselberghe later worked with Henry van de Velde on a house on the Riviera for the French painter Paul Signac. He also designed stations for the Trans-Siberian Railway and several buildings in Peking. Sadly, he is now almost forgotten.

We now go along Rue de Florence, away from Avenue Louise, until we come to Rue Faider. If we turn right here, we can look at an example at No. 10 of the heavy neoclassical style that was being built at about the same time as Horta and Hankar's Art Nouveau houses. This house was designed by Octave van Rysselberghe for Count Goblet d'Alviella, a well-travelled academic who taught religious history at the Free University of Brussels. The house was one of the architect's earliest works, completed in 1882 in a style that clearly shows the influence of his stay in Florence. The rusticated stonework and the

classical arcade at the top look decidedly odd in Brussels. The round medallion carries a relief of Pallas Athene; the frieze above, now attacked by pollution, shows Neptune amid a stormy sea.

We now go back along Rue Faider, past an extraordinary neo-gothic house with a turret and loggia at No. 37, built by a minor architect called Buisseret; the date, 1880, is on the iron wall anchors to the left of the bay window.

Back on Rue Defacqz, we turn right to look at the house and studio Paul Hankar built himself at No. 71. Signed and dated like a painting, this house was completed in the same year as Horta's Tassel House. It is basically a conventional Brussels house with square projecting balconies, like the houses we saw in the street with the Tassel House, but Hankar embellished it with flamboyant wrought-iron and stained glass. The artist Adolphe Crespin added sgraffito panels to the balconies showing cats treading along the iron railings. Crespin also decorated the upper frieze with a cock to symbolise dawn, a dove for day, a swallow to represent evening and a bat for night. Two years after the house was built, the

Parisian architect Hector Guimard made a study trip to Brussels to sketch the façade, borrowing some of the ideas for the Art Nouveau houses and metro station entrances he went on to build in Paris.

Now for the Horta House, which we find by walking to the end of Rue Defacqz and then turning left down Chaussée de Charleroi. We go down the first street on the left, Rue Américaine, keeping on the left side. No. 27 is an eccentric Moorish house of 1900, built by Jules Brunfaut, but more interesting are the two houses on the adjoining plots, Nos. 25 and 26, built at much the same date. Horta was at the height of his career when he designed this house and studio for himself in 1898-1901. If we stand opposite the house, we can see the wonderful butterfly balcony on the top floor of the family house, and the large glass windows of the studio on the right. When we cross over, we discover more of the details lovingly dreamed up by Horta, such as the doorbell, letterbox and carved house number.

Yet we have to go inside to discover the true

genius of Horta, which is expressed in the twisted door handles, the disguised water pipe in the entrance hall and the bench concealing a radiator behind the cash desk. The house is full of evocative photographs of Horta houses, fragments of demolished buildings and a scale model of the Hôtel Aubecq. We will also see iron balconies in the garden salvaged from the Maison du Peuple and a plaster cast of a letter box from the Hôtel Frison at Rue Lebeau 37 (the building, though not the box, is still there). Despite the exuberant décor, Horta's house seems at first rather cold, with tiled walls and chilly mosaic floors in the dining room. But it warms up as we ascend the stairs, culminating in the golden glow of the attic, where there is a wonderful feature I will leave as a surprise. Horta lived here from 1901 until the outbreak of war in 1914, when he left Belgium and moved first to London and later to America. On his return in 1919, he sold this house and moved into a traditional bourgeois town house.

II. The Trinité district. On leaving Horta's

house, perhaps with a few Art Nouveau postcards to send to friends, we turn right and then left down Rue Africaine, past an Art Deco corner house at Rue Américaine 42 signed by F. van Meulecom in 1923. If we keep to the left side of the church we can admire No. 92, where Benjamin de Lestré de Fabribeckers built a curious house in 1905 in which a neo-baroque bay window is combined with geometrical motifs inspired by the Vienna Secession.

The Eglise de la Trinité has a strange history. The baroque façade comes from the 17th-century chapel of an Augustinian priory that once stood in the Lower Town. Francis Coghlan described it in his 1837 guide as 'a fine piece of architecture', mentioning that the church had been used as a hospital after the Battle of Waterloo and again fifteen years later during the Belgian Revolution. Already closed in Coghlan's day, the church was eventually demolished in 1893 when Place de Brouckère was created on the site, but the façade was later rebuilt here to form the east front of the church, while the pulpit was moved to the Eglise Notre-Dame du Sablon.

The church is now, as we can see from the metal girders supporting the walls, in dire need of renovation.

Opposite the front of the church, we find a striking corner building at Parvis de la Trinité 6 faced with ceramic tile pictures showing swallows in flight. The café Passiflore on the ground floor has an exotic interior of fake gilt chairs and plump purple cushions. We can stop here for a coffee while we consider our next move.

III. The Châtelain district. If there is time to spare, we can look at another cluster of Art Nouveau houses in the streets around the Place du Châtelain. On leaving Passiflore, we stroll down Rue du Bailli, following the route of tram 81, then turn down the first street on the right, Rue Simonis. A strange white house with stained glass windows at No. 64 was built in 1891 by Paul Hankar for a local sculptor. Even at that early date, Hankar is showing hints of a modern geometric style in details such as the tall windows. Traces of the Vienna Secession can be spotted in the stone consoles supporting the iron

beams of No. 66, which is signed F. Seeldrayers. We now reach Place du Châtelain, an attractive square surrounded by traditional neoclassical Belgian town houses built at the time Horta was developing his new style. The Place du Châtelain is best seen on a Wednesday afternoon when market stalls fill the square with the smell of Italian olives and ripe melons.

We cross to the other side of the square and turn right, then left down Rue de l'Aqueduc, where Victor Horta built No. 157 in 1909 for Sander Pierron. He was the art critic who predicted that Horta's houses would one day become shrines, though his own house seems rather forgotten. At the end of the street we go left along Rue Washington, until we come to a small roundabout. Here, we can take a short detour down Rue du Magistrat to look at an Art Nouveau house built by Léon Delune, brother of the more prolific Ernest, at No. 45. But we must then go back to the roundabout and continue down Rue Washington, where we pass a neo-renaissance house at No. 66 decorated with putti and friezes, and a former blacksmith's workshop at No. 64 which still has its elaborate wrought iron sign hanging above the entrance, though the building is now occupied by a local joiner. The most interesting house in the street is No. 50, built by Ernest Blérot in 1898 in a flamboyant Art Nouveau style. The frieze in the attic, now dilapidated, is a typical Blérot touch, as is the elaborate signature chiselled on a stone to the left of the door. Further along, we pass a pair of neoclassical buildings at No. 28-30, built as an artist's studio by H. van Dievoet in 1889. At the end of the street, we turn right along Rue du Châtelain to return to Avenue Louise.

We will find the Solvay House on the opposite side at No. 224. This impressive house, with the number 224 carved in Art Nouveau numerals, was built by Victor Horta between 1894 and 1898 for Armand Solvay, son of the Belgian soda manufacturer Ernest Solvay, who invented a technique known as the Solvay process for manufacturing sodium carbonate. Used in glass-making and the production of chemicals, the process turned Solvay into one of the world's largest chemical companies.

The new industrialist style still had not been named when Armand Solvay showed Horta a wide plot of land he had bought on Avenue Louise. Horta later wrote in his *Memoirs* that: 'in choosing me, he showed himself to be as courageous as the Solvay brothers were when they invented soda.' Standing outside the house, we can admire the results of this courageous (and no doubt costly) decision to employ Horta. A decade ago, we might have been the only people to do so, but the house is now a regular stop on cultural tours of the city.

The main details visible from the street are the extraordinary wrought iron window frames, the sensually-curved balconies and the stonework that seems to swell under the weight of the building. If we look more closely, we can see Horta's painstaking attention to detail in the letterbox design and the way the lower wall gently curves out to meet the pavement. Horta also designed the ash and mahogany bed for the Solvays' bedroom, along with their wardrobes, tables, chairs, towel rails and even fire tongs.

The mansion remained in the hands of the Solvay family for almost sixty years. The last to live here was Armand's son, named Ernest after his grandfather. One of the great Belgian philanthropists, he bequeathed the family estate at La Hulpe to the Belgian state. He also offered in 1955 to leave his house to the nation as a museum, but the government was uninterested, being at that time obsessed with tearing down old buildings to construct modern apartment blocks, like the ones that now loom over the Horta mansion. If Ernest's offer had been taken up, we would now be able to go through that handsome carriage entrance, turn right once we were inside, and climb the grand Art Nouveau staircase to reach the landing where Theo van Rysselberghe's mural *Reading in the Park* has glowed since the house was completed.

We can end our walk here and take a tram back to the centre. Or we can continue for about another hour to look at an interesting 19th-century quarter around the Parc Tenbosch. If we opt for the longer walk, we continue down Avenue Louise to the next crossroads, pausing a moment to admire the apartment block at No. 244, an Art Deco building with a boldly curved corner. A glance inside the shiny lobby with its polished brass letter boxes helps us to appreciate the allure of this Modernist style. The signature of Jacques Saintenoy and the date 1938 are at the far right, in modern brass letters. A more recent attempt to create a round corner building, rather less successful, stands further along at No. 250, and a more romantic neoclassical example, still with its graceful balcony, faces it at No. 262. The neo-baroque mansion with lions' heads at No. 280 is signed, but the signature is now hidden by a tangle of wires, leaving visible only the year 1914. A sadder sight is the Pharmacie Stouffs at No. 288, with its windows boarded up and facing stones falling off. Yet it still has two modernist lamps above the door and a modest plaque on the right attributing it to C. de Lestré, 1937.

IV. The Tenbosch district. We cross to the other side of Avenue Louise at the traffic lights, and go along the Chaussée de Vleurgat, keeping to the left side. We turn left opposite the Scottish Church, built in 1925 by Waddel and Young of Glasgow, and surrounded by railings decorated with thistles. We now walk down Rue Jordaens, a handsome street that retains most of its turn-of-the-century architecture. Crossing to the side with odd numbers, we can admire No. 6, a large brick mansion in the style of a Venetian *palazzo* and with a frieze incorporating ten heads and a vaguely crenellated parapet. A grand house with an Arabic inscription at the top at No. 22 was designed by Jean Maelschalck,

and No. 24 is lightly inscribed with the name of the architect Tilley, but Nos. 28-30 perhaps interest us more because of their sgraffitto friezes, which are not signed, but only dated 1902. The building occupied by Sotheby's at No. 32 was put up one year earlier, as we know from the four iron wall anchors at the top, but it looks, at least to judge from the dormer window, as if it might be 17th century – an impossibility since this quarter was then open countryside. The Maison de Brouckère on the corner at No. 34 was built in 1896 by the Art Nouveau architect Octave van Rysselberghe, whose brother painted the mural in the Solvay House.

We turn right now up Rue de Crayer, left on Rue Van Eyck, and right up the tree-lined Rue de l'Abbaye. The Constantin Meunier Museum at No. 59 occupies the solid bourgeois home of Belgium's greatest 19th-century sculptor. If we ring the bell, we can look inside at the collection of sketches of steel furnaces, paintings of tobacco girls in Seville and displays of grubby paint brushes and sculpting tools. We can also enter the lofty studio where Meunier worked on his massive bronze figures of reapers and dock workers. Not many people come here, yet this little museum introduces us to one of the great Belgian realists of the 19th century.

Two doors down, No. 63 was built by Octave van Rysselberghe for his brother Theo, who in 1884 invited Whistler to show with Les Vingt in Brussels. This avant-garde exhibition group was dissolved in the year this house was built, 1893. It was also the year of Horta's more radical Tassel House; here the bay windows and porch illustrate the Van Rysselberghe brothers' lingering fondness for the English Arts and Crafts style.

Back on the Chaussée de Vleurgat, we turn right and a few yards down on the other side, go through the gate next to No. 217. This leads into the romantic Tenbosch park, with its winding paths, landscaped ponds and ruined brick walls covered in ivy. A gate at the bottom end brings us out on Square Henri Michaux, where we turn right down Rue Washington to reach Place Leemans. Here we can catch bus 60 back to the centre. Or we can remain in this neighbourhood for dinner, choosing between La Quincaillerie, Le Fils de Jules, or Thoumieux (all described in the restaurant section on pages 386-393).

WALK 9

The Ixelles Ponds and the Abbaye de la Cambre
FROM AVENUE LOUISE TO THE BOIS DE LA CAMBRE

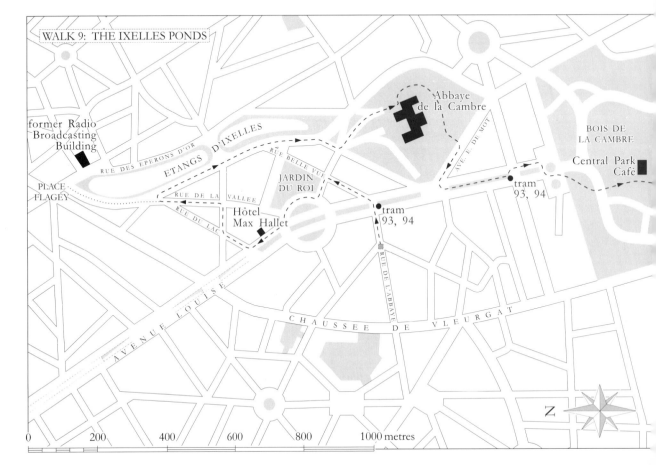

WALK 9: THE IXELLES PONDS

former Radio
Broadcasting
Building

RUE DES EPERONS D'OR

ETANGS D'IXELLES

RUE BELLE VUE

PLACE
FLAGEY

RUE DE LA VALLEE

RUE DU LAC

JARDIN
DU ROI

Hôtel
Max Hallet

Abbaye
de la Cambre

AVE. E. DE MOT

BOIS DE
LA CAMBRE

Central Park
Café

tram
93, 94

RUE DE L'ABBAYE

tram
93, 94

AVENUE LOUISE

CHAUSSEE DE VLEURGAT

Z

0   200   400   600   800   1000 metres

The Ixelles Ponds and the Abbaye de la Cambre

FROM AVENUE LOUISE TO THE BOIS DE LA CAMBRE

This walk takes us into another 19th-century district where Art Nouveau architecture briefly flourished in the 1890's and 1910's. The houses were built on the slopes to the west of the Maelbeek Valley, where a string of ponds is all that remains of the Maelbeek stream. Known as the Etangs d'Ixelles, the narrow ponds were landscaped in a romantic 19th-century style.

Many of the Art Nouveau houses we pass on this walk were designed by Ernest Blérot, a neglected architect who designed homes for less wealthy families in districts not quite so fashionable as Horta's customers could afford. The plan of the typical Blérot house remained strictly conventional, which kept down the costs, while the façades were decorated with a hectic display of Art Nouveau wrought iron and Arts and Crafts bay windows. We can easily track down Blérot houses and follow the development of his style, since he usually carved his signature and the date of construction on the building in the flourishing calligraphy we saw on p. 258. His houses have other distinctive features, too, such as triangular bay windows and small pointed gables.

We can do this walk any day, though the café at the start of the walk is closed at weekends. We begin by taking tram 93 or 94 down Avenue Louise to the Abbaye stop. As we wait for the tram, we might read the following brief history of Avenue Louise.

xelles. — Avenue Louise.

I. Avenue Louise. Named after Léopold II's eldest daughter, Avenue Louise was created in 1864 to link the Upper Town with the Bois de la Cambre, which had been landscaped two years before. Planted with four rows of Léopold II's favourite chestnut trees, the broad avenue soon became a popular place to stroll and ride in open carriages. Some of the grandest houses in Brussels were built here in the late 19th century, including the occasional Art Nouveau mansion. The Belgian passion for apartment life in the 1930's and 1940's led to the destruction of many of the old houses, but far worse damage was done in the 1950's when a highway was created down the central lanes to speed traffic to the 1958 World Fair. Old photographs such as this one taken in about 1900 show the avenue in its prime. Yet some improvements have recently been made, which we might spot from the tram, such as the grand entrance created at Place Stéphanie by the two office blocks designed by André Jacqmain in a vaguely Art Deco style.

Just beyond, on the right, we can see the Conrad Brussels Hotel at No. 71-83, another project by Jacqmain which incorporates the elegant neo-baroque façade of the old Wiltcher's Carlton Hotel. The original five-floor hotel with its sweeping frontage has been preserved, but with extra floors inserted above the parapet and four squat towers added to the roofline. Several old mansions have also been restored next to the hotel, such as No. 77, which was designed by Henri Beyaert in 1874, and No. 79A built a few years earlier by Emile Janlet in 1871.

The first Art Nouveau house of the day is on the right at No. 81. The façade is costly pale-yellow sandstone, decorated with elaborate iron details that twist like creepers. This was designed by Paul Saintenoy about a year after the Old England department store we saw on walk 3.

On leaving the tram, we keep to the right side of the avenue. A brief detour down Rue de l'Abbaye brings us to Le Pain de l'Abbaye on the corner at 2 Rue St Georges (open Monday to Friday from 7.30 am to 3.30 pm). This friendly café is a popular place for a coffee and croissant.

Café Max on the opposite side of the road is open on Saturdays, but both are shut on Sunday.

II. The Ixelles Ponds. After a coffee, we cross over to the side with Max and go back to Avenue Louise. The corner building on the opposite side of Rue de l'Abbaye (at 413 Avenue Louise) was designed by Marc Poons in 1990. The curious peeling façade reveals an older style of architecture beneath – a reminder that other buildings have stood on this site. A series of four panels on the side wall show the predecessors: an Art Nouveau building of 1911, a Modernist block of 1941 and a postwar modern building from the booming 1960's.

We cross Avenue Louise and go straight ahead down the steep Rue de Belle-Vue. We should stop to admire the row of three houses signed *Ernest Blérot 1899* at Nos. 42 to 46. The first, No. 46, has been well cared for over the years. It has a lovely Art Nouveau door, a tall stained glass window and a striking sgraffito flower frieze at the top. The middle house has a curious bay window and a fine door, though the

267

sgraffito panels are almost worn away. No. 42, has had a new door and windows installed, but here too the sgraffito panels are now almost too decayed to see the peacocks and flowers.

There are two more Blérot houses further down the hill at Nos. 30 and 32. Notice the wonderful curved lines of the door frame on No. 30 with its tiny swans' heads and delightful whiplash flourish above the boot scraper.

Now comes to a little park called the Jardin du Roi with a statue of King Léopold. We return to Avenue Louise up the Rue du Monastère, keeping the park to our right. Olivier Strebelle designed the sculpture straight ahead on a grassy knoll. It is called *Phoenix 44* and commemorates the liberation of Belgium in 1944. We turn right and follow the crescent to look at a statue of *La Mort d'Ompdraille* which was considered worthy of a star in old editions of Baedeker's guidebook. *En souvenir de Léon Cladel, créateur d'Ompdrailles*, the French inscription says. The Dutch translation, added at a later date in brass letters, omits any reference to Ompdrailles, the hero of a novel by Cladel. The bronze figures were designed in 1892 by Charles van der Stappen, and the granite plinth was carved (and signed) by *Baron* Horta.

Further along Avenue Louise we come to the Maison Max Hallet at No. 346. Victor Horta built this elegant town house in 1903 for a prominent socialist politician. It is a sober façade, almost Louis XV, and we might easily walk past without noticing the wispy curves of the Art Nouveau window ledges or the convoluted wrought iron in the door. Horta seems to have been forced to temper his style by Hallet's wife and her rich, conservative parents. Yet one feature is quite astonishing. If we go through the coach door at No. 344 (now Rick's restaurant), we can walk through to the back garden and look over the wall. We will then see the extraordinary conservatory with three glass domes resting on slender iron pillars. Horta designed this for Madame Hallet, who sat here working on flower arrangements.

Turning right just beyond Rick's down the Rue du Lac, we then go down Rue Vilain XIIII, named after a 19th-century politician whose ancestor was given the odd title of XIIII by

Louis XIV after he had successfully saved Namur from attack. Blérot's signature will be spotted on the apartment building on the right side at No. 31. Originally a four-floor block, it was later given two extra floors. There is a more recognisably Blérot house on the street that crosses Vilain XIIII – the Rue de la Vallée – at No. 40. Dated 1903, it has a romantic pointed gable and an unusual Art Nouveau garage with tendrils of iron curling across the door.

Further down the right side of the lovely Rue de la Vallée, there is an almost unbroken row of houses signed by Ernest Delune, whose two brothers were also architects. Delune's signature is more sober than Blérot's and his houses, too, are rather restrained. Yet there are a few details that catch the eye, like the elegant vertical lines reminiscent of the Vienna Secession that flank the entrance to No. 28 and the curious Moorish window on No. 32.

On reaching the pond, a brief detour up the street to our left – the Rue du Lac – brings us to this door, which belongs to No. 6. This eccentric home was built in 1904 by Léon Delune, brother

of Ernest, for a stained-glass craftsman who worked in the room at the top with the wooden bay window facing the northern light. It is worth timing a visit here after dark to get a glimpse the wonderful floral details on the stained glass windows lit from inside.

Back to the pond, we see on the far side the round Art Deco tower of the former Belgian radio broadcasting house on Place Flagey, designed in 1935-8 by Joseph Diongre. The glinting interior, with its grand staircases evoking luxury liners, has been lovingly restored as a new arts centre, Le Flagey, with several concert halls, a cinema and a large café. The church to the right is the Eglise Sainte-Croix. It was built in 1863 in neo-gothic style, but modified in the 1940's, when the strange spire was added. It contains unusual modernist confessionals and a 16th-century painting of the *Virgin with an Apple* that once hung in the Abbaye de la Cambre.

A short detour left along the waterfront brings us to a statue at the end of the pond. *Till Eulenspiegel* commemorates a popular 19th-century novel by Charles de Coster. Designed in 1894 by

Charles Samuel, it is an appealing classical monument that shows a weary bronze Till and a flirtatious Nell whispering in his ear. Some of the symbols allude to Till's alternative name of 'Owl Glass', but what the cat, the cauldron and the dog asleep under the spinning wheel signify is more obscure.

Our route continues away from Place Flagey along Avenue du Général de Gaulle, where Blérot built two adjoining houses in 1904, at Nos. 38 and 39. His signature is above the door of No. 39, though we might have guessed it was he from the little pointed dormer window. This house has wonderful wrought iron work on the balconies and stairs. Notice that some of the railings around the garden have tiny birds' heads etched into the iron tips.

Continuing along the water's edge, we come to the romantic Ixelles war memorial showing two fallen soldiers being comforted by young women. A very short detour up Rue Vilain XIIII brings us to two houses (Nos. 9 and 11) signed by Ernest Blérot in 1902. The splendid door pictured here is that of No. 11. We can identify the architect

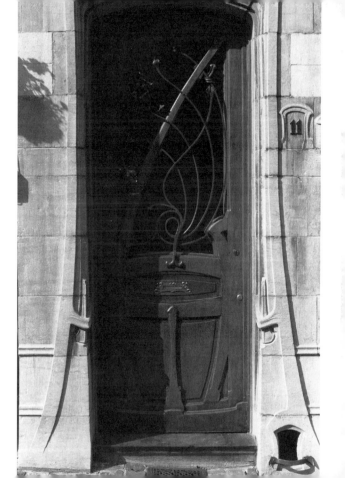

straight away from the bay windows, Art Nouveau doors and florid wrought iron railings.

We now go back down the hill, past a handsome neoclassical bay window at No. 7 built by the architect Frans Tilley. On the opposite side of the street, a solemn neoclassical house at Nos. 2-4 was built and signed by O. Francotte in 1908. Blérot built himself an Art Nouveau mansion in 1901-8 on the corner opposite with a large bay window overlooking the two ponds, but it was demolished in 1965 – the same year that Horta's Maison du Peuple was torn down. Blérot died in 1957 in the West Flanders village of Voormezele, where he had built himself the strange concrete castle of Elzenwalle (left, and still standing).

We now continue along the edge of the lake, past an eerie house signed by Paul Jaspar at No. 44. Jaspar borrowed various renaissance motifs such as the satyrs carved on wooden beams, but he created his own bizarre style by adding a half-timbered bay window that could almost have come from an English cottage. A short distance further along, we pass the Jardin du Roi once again. We press on, straight ahead, to reach one of Brussels' most romantic corners.

III. The Abbaye de la Cambre. We should stand at the end of Avenue Général de Gaulle next to the post box. This is close to the spot where an artist drew the view (overleaf) of the *Abbatia Beatae Mariae de Camera* for the second edition of the Sanderus atlas. From our vantage point, we can see a baroque gateway, the abbey church and a baroque wing with a clock in the pediment. The gardens had only recently been planted when the engraving was published in 1726. Tall Art Deco apartment blocks now stand on the tree-lined ridge we see in the Sanderus view, but the abbey grounds remain untouched.

If we had stood on this spot in 1910, we would have seen Rodin's bronze statue of the *Burghers of Calais* on the lawn at the end of the lake. It was put here for the 1910 Exhibition, and offered for sale to the *commune* afterwards. The local authority was not interested, and the bronze group ended up on the lawn next to the Houses of Parliament in London.

We now go down the hill and enter the abbey through the coach entrance on the left. The building we pass through does not appear in the engraving overleaf as it was put up in 1728 as a brewery and coach house. It is now occupied by the Belgian cartographical institute (open Monday to Friday 9-5), where we can pick up a detailed map of the Forêt de Soignes or a reproduction of Mercator's wonderful 16th-century map of Flanders to take home as a souvenir.

Crossing the courtyard, we enter the abbey church (closed 12-2). The 12th-century Cistercian abbey was founded by an aristocratic woman known simply as Gisèle, who lived in Brussels at the time of Duke Henry I of Brabant. It was called the Abbaye de la Cambre, or Terkamerenabdij, after the room or *chambre* in Nazareth where Mary lived. After Count Egmont was beheaded on Grand'Place in 1568, his widow and eleven children fled here. Most of the abbey buildings were burnt by the Spanish in 1581 to prevent the Dutch rebels from turning it into a military stronghold, though the archdukes Albert and Isabella paid for the reconstruction of the church seventeen years later.

ABBATIA BEATÆ MARIÆ
DE CAMERA
ORDINIS CISTERCIENSIS
IUXTA BRUXELLAS

The abbey was ransacked several times in the 17th century by the armies of Louis XIV and the nuns were finally expelled in 1796 by the French revolutionaries. The abandoned building became in turn a sugar refinery, a cotton factory, a hospital, a refuge for beggars, a boarding school and a military academy. Finally, in 1921, a Society of Friends of the Abbey was set up to save the crumbling ruin. Five years later, La Cambre art school was set up in the former infirmary. Henry van de Velde, who had founded the Weimar School of Arts and Crafts in 1907, was persuaded to return to Brussels as La Cambre's first director.

The abbey church, begun in about 1400, is more ornate than most Cistercian buildings. A small shrine in the north transept contains the relics of Saint Boniface, a 13th-century bishop of Lausanne who spent his last years at La Cambre. A door in the south transept leads into the cloisters, which were rebuilt in the 17th century in baroque style. The stained glass windows are decorated with the coats of arms of former abbesses, including Mary Scott of Buccleuch. On leaving the church, we walk around the choir, past the art school and carp pond, to reach the gardens which rise on our right. The slope was terraced and planted with topiary trees in 1725 under the Abbess Louise Deliano y Velasco. The gardens were restored to their original appearance in the 1930's by a landscape gardener who used our engraving as inspiration. The curious pyramid-shaped trees, the broad walk and the square parterres are all there, though not the star-shaped enclosure which was torn up in 1910 to allow the broad Avenue Emile Demot to be created as a sweeping entry to the 1910 Exhibition site.

The woods are not far, but we have to cross a busy road before we get to them. If we climb to the top of the gardens by the stone steps and turn right, we can cross the avenue at the lights. We now find ourselves back on Avenue Louise, where we keep to the side with the even numbers. Oscar Simon signed his name in a flourishing chiselled script on the building at No. 518-520 in 1889. He was right to be proud of this picturesque corner building with its neo-gothic window arches and wooden dormer window. The style must have seemed old-fashioned to the Horta school of architects, though they might have been pleased to notice the exposed iron columns, which were considered the ultimate mark of the modern spirit. A building by Horta, the Hôtel Aubecq, did indeed stand here, but it was demolished in 1950 to build the apartment block at No. 522. One of Horta's students saved the outside fabric, amounting to 640 stones, 36 windows and 15 sections of wrought iron. Two of the stained glass windows are now incorporated in the Horta metro station while the rest remains in storage. A plan was once mooted to rebuild the Maison Aubecq as a residence for the President of the European Commission. More recently, the Musée du Cinquantenaire was proposed as a possible site. We live in hope.

IV. The Bois de la Cambre. We now cross the road and walk to the end of the Avenue Louise. The two 19th-century neo-classical toll houses opposite were moved in 1863 from the Porte de Namur, to the entrance of the Bois de la Cambre. 'The alleys in this park are thronged with fashionable equipages,' Karl Baedeker informed his readers one hundred years ago. Now they are thronged with traffic, fashionable dogs and red-faced joggers, though something of the former elegance has survived. Once part of the Forêt de Soignes, the Bois was landscaped in 1862 by Edouard Keilig in the rustic romantic style popular in France and Germany. If we explore the meandering footpaths, avoiding those set aside for horses, we will find old street lamps, rusticated iron benches and an artificial lake with a wooded island reached by a creaky mechanical ferry. People could once eat lunch in the Châlet Robinson on the island, but the building burnt down in 1991, depriving us of the romantic scene we see in the postcard from the early years of the century opposite. (It may be rebuilt in 2004, in a style similar to the original.) We can end the walk in one of the cafés near the entrance to the woods. The Jardins du Bois, with a children's playground, has survived intact from 1870. The nearby Central Park café, next

BRUXELLES — Lac & Châlet Robinson.

to an open-air roller skating rink, is particularly romantic in winter when the fire is lit. The lawn nearby, known as the Pelouse des Anglais, was once believed to be the site of a cricket match played by British officers on the eve of Waterloo. The story seems unlikely since the site was still thick woodland in 1815. Yet a commemorative plaque has been screwed to a mock tree stump in defiance of historical evidence.

When it is time to leave, we go back to Avenue Louise to pick up tram 93 or 94.

Saint Gilles

FROM THE PORTE DE HAL TO PLACE BRUGMANN

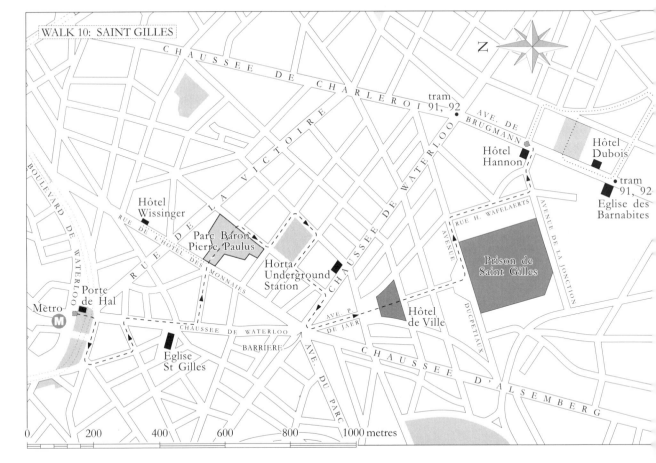

WALK 10: SAINT GILLES

CHAUSSÉE DE CHARLEROI

tram 91, 92

AVE. DE BRUGMANN

Hôtel Dubois

Hôtel Hannon

tram 91, 92

Eglise des Barnabites

RUE H. WAFELAERTS

AVENUE

AVENUE DE LA JONCTION

Hôtel Wissinger

RUE DE L'HÔTEL DES MONNAIES

RUE DE LA VICTOIRE

Parc Baron Pierre Paulus

Horta Underground Station

CHAUSSÉE DE WATERLOO

Prison de Saint Gilles

DUCPÉTIAUX

BOULEVARD DE WATERLOO

Porte de Hal

Métro M

CHAUSSÉE DE WATERLOO

BARRIÈRE

Eglise St Gilles

AVE. P. DE JAER

Hôtel de Ville

AVE. DU PARC

CHAUSSÉE D'ALSEMBERG

Z

0   200   400   600   800   1000 metres

Saint Gilles

FROM THE PORTE DE HAL TO PLACE BRUGMANN

We are now going to head off the beaten track, into the 19th-century commune of Saint Gilles. This dense urban district grew rapidly in the 19th century, changing from a scattered village of some four thousand inhabitants in 1846 to a booming industrial district with a population of sixty thousand by the end of the century. Much of the population worked in the factories near the station, but better-off lawyers, artists and sculptors settled in the upper district near the town hall. In the 1950's, people began to move from Saint Gilles to the leafy suburbs, yet this district is gradually becoming fashionable again, as artists and Europeans do up dilapidated mansions. During this walk, we will see flamboyant Art Nouveau houses, romantic parks and

one of the most spectacular town halls in the country (the inside of which is well worth seeing, so the walk should be done on a weekday). The walk should take about three hours.

I. The Porte de Hal. We take the metro to Porte de Hal, or walk from the old town along Rue Haute. The metro trip allows us to glimpse a strange art installation in the Porte de Hal station, where the comic strip artist François Schuiten has created an imaginary city complete with Brussels trams. If we leave by exit 2, we emerge near the spot where the 19th-century photograph overleaf was taken, probably from an upstairs window of the Hospice des Aveugles behind us. The curious brick tower we see was

originally a city gate, the Porte de Hal, built in 1381. Bruegel left the city by this gate in the 16th century when he tramped out to the Flemish villages of the Pajottenland to prepare works such as *The Blind Leading the Blind*. At that time, the tower was being used by the Spanish as a prison. It later went through various uses – a barn, a Lutheran church and an archive depot – before being turned into a prison once again after the city walls were torn down in the 1780's.

If we turn up Boulevard du Midi to the end of Rue Haute we can can stand on the spot where Vitzhumb drew this view on 11 May 1826. The houses we see in the drawing have all been torn down, including the old inn on the right known as Le Cornet with the carriage outside and the date 1627. The Porte de Hal was transformed in 1868 by Henri Beyaert, who also designed the lovely gardens on the Petit Sablon. The French architect Viollet-le-Duc, an expert on restoring medieval buildings, made a special trip to Brussels to advise Beyaert. But was it good advice? The old Porte de Hal is unrecognisable now. The windows look as if they belong on a church.

Vue de la Porte de Halle, de l'intérieur de la Ville

11 Mai 1836 pub. Jeet

A large stair tower blocks the original gateway and the top is a fanciful collection of turrets, machicolations, beaver-tail roof and wrought iron balustrade. The rugged city gate has been turned into something out of a children's fairy tale.

Now an outpost of the Musée du Cinquantenaire, the Porte de Hal has been closed for several years. It will be worth a visit when it does reopen, if only to see the remains of the portcullis on the ground floor, and to climb Beyaert's fanciful neo-gothic staircase. This takes one into a vaulted upper room where the enemies of Alva were once imprisoned, and to the roof for a fine view of the boulevards below.

We turn left to walk around the gate, past an ancient siege mortar abandoned in the long grass. Looking back, we can see the original pointed gothic gateway and the remains of two overgrown walls. We now cross the boulevard and turn right, then left up Avenue Jean Volders, a grand 19th-century street bristling with civic pride. The *commune* of Saint Gilles strictly controlled the façades and height of the buildings,

producing a solid and, it must be said, somewhat overbearing architecture. We can clearly see the effect of these municipal rules on Ernest Blérot, who built and signed the building at No. 44 in 1902. The house dates from the same period as the lovely row of three houses we saw in Rue Vilain XIIII, yet the Saint Gilles regulations forced Blérot to adopt a heavy, even severe design. The building contains ten apartments, as we can tell from the letterboxes inserted in the Art Nouveau door.

The corner building next door is another Blérot design – we can spot the signature under the sign to the left of the door. The café on the ground floor was once cluttered with tin signs advertising Martini and Stella Artois, but has now been restored and renamed La Porteuse d'Eau. Admittedly the Art Nouveau interior is no more authentic than the turrets on the Porte de Hal, yet it is a pleasant spot for a coffee, and the door handles, if nothing else, are original. On leaving, we turn left along Rue Vanderschrick, where we find a row of seventeen houses built by Blérot in 1900. This was the largest project Blérot ever undertook – perhaps the most ambitious Art Nouveau housing development in the country. We need to cross the street, for only then can we see the sgraffito birds and flowers on No. 19, the floral ironwork on No. 21's door, and the ornamental balcony, now sadly rusted, of No. 9. When these houses were new and the paint gleamed, this street must have seemed quite extraordinary. A modest restoration would bring it back to life.

The shop front on No. 3 seems to have been added to an older building, and vaguely evokes the style of the Vienna Secession, which gained a foothold in Saint Gilles in the early 20th century. We now turn right up the Chaussée de Waterloo, a busy road lined with Portuguese restaurants and noisy Belgian cafés. A short climb brings us to the Parvis Saint Gilles, another expression of bourgeois pride. The splendid collection of lofty apartment buildings and solid shops, included the Art Deco Triperie Saint Gilloise at No. 19 which still has a splendid tiled interior, though it is now occupied by a driving school, and Ægidium at No. 18, where

a former cinema auditorium in exotic Moorish style is now used as a second-hand furniture store (open on Saturday mornings). The Parvis is one of the liveliest squares in Brussels, especially when the morning market is being held and the café terraces spill out onto the pavements.

Leaving the square on the side opposite the church, we cross the dusty little park on the right to reach the Rue de l'Hôtel des Monnaies. Here we can make a brief detour to look at the Hôtel Wissinger at No. 66 which was built by Victor Horta in 1894. Notice the undulating door handle and other odd details like the iron ventilation grille. The stained glass windows are decorated with the initials LB, standing for Lion Belgique, an insurance company founded in 1899. An antique shop next door sells rusty metal irons, tin tram signs and old Brussels street signs.

We go back up the Rue de l'Hôtel des Monnaies and turn left at No. 122, next to the metro station. This brings us into the Parc Baron Pierre Paulus, where we find an unexpected romantic landscape composed of rocky crags, cascades, and three classical columns suggesting a ruined temple.

Once we have circled the lake and watched the overweight ducks, we climb up the hill on the far side to Rue de Parme where we find the strange Maison Pelgrims perched above the crags. We now turn right and then left into Place Louis Morichar where a sumptuous house at No. 14 was designed in the Horta style and decorated with sgrafitto panels symbolising the art of music and painting. The next house on our tour is on the far side of the square, but before we go there, we might wonder about the story behind the plaque on No. 18 which records that Charles Plisnier lived here from 1923 to 1937: 'writing Marriages and False Passports'. The plaque refers to two novels by Plisnier, a Communist writer awarded the Goncourt Prize.

Now for the house at No. 41. Its splendid mosaics catch our eye, especially if we are here early in the morning when the sunlight is striking the gilded rising sun, though it can be just as impressive in the evening when the ground-floor stained-glass windows are lit from within. This spectacular Art Nouveau house was built in 1899 by Ernest Blérot, as we might have guessed from the oriel and the mosaics. The house next door at No. 42-43 was once equally striking, though the gilt mosaic lettering has faded until it is now almost illegible.

We now walk down the hill and turn left along Rue du Lycée, past a school named after Horta. On reaching the Chaussée de Waterloo, we will see the entrance to the metro station Horta where several fragments of Horta's Maison du Peuple (pictured on page 182) are preserved. A Brussels architect saved most of the ironwork and masonry when the Maison du Peuple was demolished, hoping that the building might one day be reconstructed. The fragments lay for years in Saint Gilles cemetery, where the iron rusted and the stone eroded in the rain. Some of the ironwork was spirited away by scrap dealers, and the remaining relics were recently incorporated into the interior of a new café in Antwerp, called Horta.

The stained glass windows above the station

platform were saved from another Horta house, the Hôtel Aubecq, which was demolished in 1950. Once again, the masonry and ironwork were piously saved and stored away. There are now vague plans to rebuild this house, but until then, all we can see are these fragments of stained glass (and that only if we have a stamped metro ticket).

If we take the escalator back to the street and turn right down the Chaussée de Waterloo we come to the Barrière de Saint Gilles, a busy crossroads with a fountain in the middle. This junction looked much grander when it had a massive lamp-post in the centre designed by Alban Chambon, architect of the Métropole Hotel. The lamp-post has been moved to the Avenue du Parc, but a copy of the figure on top has been placed here. Known as *La Porteuse d'Eau*, it was carved by Julien Dillens in 1898. He is said to have modelled the water-carrier on a girl he saw near his studio in the Rue Saint Bernard, who was carrying buckets of water to the horses that drew the trams.

II. The Hôtel de Ville. The original statue is now in the town hall, visible now on the slope in front of us. Directions are hardly necessary, for Saint Gilles has one of the largest town halls in the country, built between 1900 and 1904 and given a belfry decorated with gilded angels. We reach it along the impressive Avenue Paul de Jaer, where Paul Hankar was refused permission in 1898 to build a house at No. 10 because the planning committee considered it 'too simple for this important avenue'. He made a second attempt, which was passed by the committee. Gustave Strauven's Art Nouveau house opposite, at No. 9, seems, if anything, too ornate, but that presumably was considered entirely appropriate for this grand approach. Built in 1902, it combines red and white brick, grey stone and wrought iron. The splendid flourish of curving stone and iron at the top may remind us of Strauven's Maison de Saint Cyr, which we saw on walk 7.

An old butcher's shop front at No. 16 still has its gold sign advertising the Charcuterie Ardennaise. The wooden counter is decorated with a tile frieze, though it can hardly be seen for all the dusty bell jars and antique chandeliers stored inside. Perhaps it can still be saved, like the two shop fronts at Nos. 20 and 22. The first, signed by A. van Roose, has become a chic bar-restaurant called Y'a Pas de Miracle, filled with sofas, gilt columns and chandeliers. The shop next door is now a fashionable hairdresser with yet more chandeliers.

The street ends with a grand architectural flourish. The corner building on the right, No. 37, was built and signed by Pierre Meewis in 1907. Opposite, No. 35 was designed in 1903 by the French architect Louis Margerie as a home for the director of a French insurance company. And now, we are at the town hall. It was designed by Albert Dumont in the style of a French renaissance château; the statue in front was carved by Jef Lambeau, the sculptor whose *Human Passions* relief remains locked away in the Cinquantenaire Park. The naked woman we see here represents the *Goddess of the River Bocq*. She was commissioned by the local water company in 1894 to adorn a memorial fountain, but once

again proved too sensual for delicate Belgian sensibilities. The statue was stored in the basement of a local school until 1976, when the authorities finally allowed it to be put on public display, though half buried in a clump of municipal shrubs for the sake of decency.

If it is a weekday, we can now go inside to admire the vast town hall, which is decorated with rare marbles, polished woods, statues, frescos and gilt lamps. The *commune* seems positively to encourage visitors, for it has several entrances which are normally open to the public. We can even go through the carriage gateway under the main staircase, which brings us into a cobbled yard where horses were once tied up. This is now empty, apart from the occasional parked car and the three giants of Saint Gilles gathering dust in a corner. We go through a glass door and climb the main staircase, pausing on the landing to admire the original *Porteuse d'Eau*.

We can also see a bronze self-portrait by Jef Lambeau, who looks positively worn out as he sits on a chair with his head resting on his hand. That the Belgians were shocked by his nude figures seems more astonishing when we look up at the ceiling above us, which is decorated with an erotic fresco celebrating *Freedom arriving in the world and bringing joy to Humanity*. The artist, Omer Dierickx, has included various nude figures without any fear of censorship. The side walls are also decorated with large panels showing naked men and women. These were painted by Albert Ciamberlani, whose Art Nouveau home on the Rue Defacqz caught our attention on an earlier walk (page 251).

If we go through the door on the right at the top of the stairs, we come to a small museum where porcelain and local paintings are displayed. An extraordinary work by Henri Gervex and Alfred Stevens illustrates the *Entry of Napoleon into Paris*. This is a fragment of a large panorama painting displayed at the 1889 Paris Exhibition. The panorama was cut into sections after the exhibition and sold to various collectors. The fragment we see here shows Napoleon riding at the head of the army, followed by Marshal Ney and other generals who would fight a few months later at Waterloo.

III. The St Gilles Prison. We now go back down the main staircase, and leave the town hall by the back door. The elegant Avenue Jef Lambeaux leads to the Saint Gilles prison. Undeterred by the penal institution, well-off families settled in this quarter in the late 19th century. The architect Victor Boelens built a strange Art Nouveau house in 1899 at No. 11, and Georges Peereboom built another, equally curious, for his brother at No. 12. But the most striking house in the street is the corner house at No. 25, built by Paul Hamesse in 1910 as his private home. Hamesse had by then abandoned the curvaceous Art Nouveau style for a more sober eclectic neoclassicism, evident from the slender pilasters that frame the door.

We now come to Saint Gilles prison, a model 19th-century institution built on this summit between 1874 to 1884, and thus well established by the time Hamesse moved here. Its turrets and battlements were clearly inspired by English mock gothic architecture, which adds a poignant touch to the fact that Edith Cavell was held here in 1915 along with several Belgians who had helped Allied soldiers to escape. The American chaplain in Brussels came to the prison after she had been sentenced to death. Her famous words were spoken to him inside these walls: 'I know now that patriotism is not enough. I must have no hatred or bitterness towards anyone.'

We now reach Place Antoine Delporte, where we find a house in the style of Charles Rennie Mackintosh at No. 17 and a possible homage to another Glaswegian, Alexander 'Greek' Thomson, at No. 2. We continue left along Avenue Ducpétiaux, pausing to admire the corner house built by Valère Dumortier in 1885 at No. 90. Dumortier founded the influential periodical *L'Emulation* in 1874, and ran a highly successful firm designing eclectic houses such as this one, which has carved dolphins, angels and a curious figure of an architect at the corner. Turning right down Rue Henri Wafelaerts, we pass the Maison de Madame Geubel at No. 25 built by Louis Couprie in 1909 (the signature is to the right of the garage door) in a geometrical Art Nouveau style akin to Hankar's style. No. 37 is a plain townhouse with two mosaics made by Joseph Godchoul, who had his workshop here. The house opposite, at Rue Delhasse 2-4, is a striking Art Deco apartment block. Designed in 1926 by Marcel Simon, this is one of the most picturesque apartment buildings in the city, with carved flowers tumbling down the walls, blue tiles glinting in the sun and a Mediterranean-looking loggia at the top. We continue to No. 53, where Antoine Pompe built a pioneering example of modernism in 1910, signing it in solid letters to the left of the door. The building was designed as an orthopaedic clinic for a Dr Maurice van Neck. Its three oriel windows look as if they too might have been inspired by Mackintosh. A sign to the left of the door, now hidden by a brass plaque, reads *Institut du Docteur Maurice van Neck, Orthopedie Chirurgie des Enfants, Radiographie*. The tinkling xylophone tunes we may hear as we stand here come from the percussion school now based in Dr Van Neck's clinic. The house next door at No. 55 was built in 1923 by Jean de Ligne for Mademoiselle Mullier in a style that is modern but defies precise definition.

Continuing to the end of the street, we pass a modernist corner building with exposed iron beams at Avenue de la Jonction 23. L. Bochums signed this building one year after Dr. van Neck's clinic was built. We now go left along Avenue de la Jonction, past a striking Art Deco house signed *Paul Hamesse et Frères* at No. 14 and an adjoining house at No. 12 signed by Paul Hamesse alone in 1909. The more interesting of the two, on the left, has elongated geometrical panels in the style of the Vienna Secession. Here we might take a brief detour left down Rue Félix Delhasse opposite, where Nos. 28 and 30 are signed, though we have to look closely to see the name Paul Picquet carved in Art Nouveau letters to the left of the basement windows. Another Art Nouveau house at No. 24 was built in 1905 and signed by Emile Lambot, a professor at the Royal Academy of Fine Arts in Brussels. Lambot had studied in Horta's Rue Américaine studio, as we can probably tell from the undulating façade and the convoluted door handles. Nos. 11 and 13 were built by Paul Hamesse in 1905 and signed in an unusual Art Nouveau script. Hamesse

worked for Hankar in his Rue Defacqz studio, learning to master this geometrical Art Nouveau style.

IV. The Hôtel Hannon. Back on Avenue de la Jonction, a much more distinguished example of Art Nouveau stands opposite at No. 2. The Hôtel Hannon was designed in 1903 by Jules Brunfaut. Brunfaut was a successful architect who was versatile in various styles. The Hôtel Hannon was in fact the only Art Nouveau house he ever built (his own house at 228 Chaussée de Charleroi is Louis XVI). The reliefs at the top – a woman spinning, a dog and a rising sun – are by Victor Rousseau.

The owner of this splendid mansion was Edouard Hannon, an engineer who worked for Ernest Solvay in various factories in Russia and America. Hannon took advantage of his foreign trips to pursue a serious interest in photography. His home is now occupied by the Contretype photography gallery, which organises exhibitions of contemporary photography as well as displaying a few of Hannon's photographs of

Russian factories and American cities. If the entrance at Avenue de la Jonction 1 is open, we should take the opportunity to go inside this exquisite house, which only narrowly escaped demolition in the 1970's. We buy a ticket in the former smoking room, where Paul-Albert Baudouin, a Rouen artist, painted a rich red Art Nouveau fresco. Among the other pleasures are an exotic conservatory with a sweeping stained glass window, a swirling mosaic floor in the entrance hall and a curving staircase decorated with a fresco painted by Baudouin.

On leaving the Hannon House we cross Avenue Brugmann for a good view of two neo-renaissance houses opposite at Nos. 49 and 51. These were built in the 1880's when this antiquated style represented the Flemish bourgeois ideal. We are more interested in the house at No. 55 built by Edouard Pelseneer in 1895. Two owls perched on the gable, and two more above the door, give this house its romantic name *Les Hiboux*.

We now go straight ahead down the Avenue du Haut Pont and turn right along Rue Frans

Merjay. The white house we pass at Nos. 55-57 was built by D. Willaert in a geometrical Art Deco, while No. 69 has Moorish arches above the windows and a whiplash design on the door. The Art Nouveau house at No. 93 was built in 1907 by Paul Vizzavona, whose signature is just legible to the left of the door. Vizzavona worked in Horta's studio, where he learned the art of designing features such as the boot scraper, door handle and bell. Perhaps the most interesting house is on the far side of the little garden, next to a flower shop, at Rue Emile Bouillot 14. Victor Boelens built it in 1906, adding an angular signature on the left. The signature and the windows are more evidence of the impact of the Glasgow School, probably via Vienna, where Mackintosh had such an influence that the Austrians took to calling the style 'Mackintoshismus'.

We have a choice of routes to end our walk. The shorter version goes up the gently curving Rue Emile Bouillot to Place Georges Brugmann, while the slightly longer route takes us back to Avenue Brugmann to look at a Horta house. If we opt for the longer version, we should cross to the other side of the garden and go through the gate next to No. 79. This brings us into the Parc Abbé Froidure (open from 8-6), a formal garden with tall hedges, blue metal pergolas overgrown with clematis, and water trickling along a stone course. The park is named after a priest who created parks in Brussels for disadvantaged children, saved Jewish children from the Nazis and himself spent several years in a concentration camp.

We come out on Avenue Brugmann, a handsome tree-lined avenue built in 1875 to link the new districts of Saint Gilles with the rural settlement of Le Chat. Georges Brugmann, a wealthy banker provided the financing for this major project. The avenue was designed according to the aesthetic ideals of the day, with a double row of trees and handsome street lights. Avenue Brugmann soon attracted wealthy families who built houses in a variety of fanciful styles, as we will see even along the short stretch we cover today.

The large house at No. 80 was designed by Victor Horta in 1901-6 for the sculptor Fernand

Dubois. The lovely doorbell is an Art Nouveau detail telling us, even without a signature, that this is a Horta house.

The Eglise des Pères Barnabites is on the opposite side at No. 121. If it looks open, we should cross over to look at the neo-gothic columns, curious Art Deco confessionals (each with an electric doorbell) and, quite unexpectedly, two slender iron columns supporting the organ loft.

Our route takes us left down Rue Darwin, a well-preserved *fin-de-siècle* street with a spectacular pair of Art Nouveau houses on the right side. No. 15 was designed in 1902 by Ernest Blérot for the painter Louise de Hem. Two sgraffito panels show swallows flying in a blue sky and a cock crowing, while the stone under the bay window is carved with a large sunflower. The studio at No. 17 with its enormous arched windows was added in 1904. The unfinished sgraffito panel shows a woman with Pre-Raphaelite looks – Louise de Hem we must assume – painting a landscape.

We continue to Place Georges Brugmann, a handsome square with a French bookshop at No. 2 and a café at No. 3 where we can stop for coffee and cake. The restaurant Aux Beaumes de Venise is conveniently close at 62 Rue Darwin (described on page 389). When it is time to return to the centre, we can either take bus 60 from Place Brugmann or catch one of the trams on Avenue Brugmann.

WALK II

Uccle

FROM AVENUE BRUGMANN TO NOTRE-DAME DU BON-SECOURS

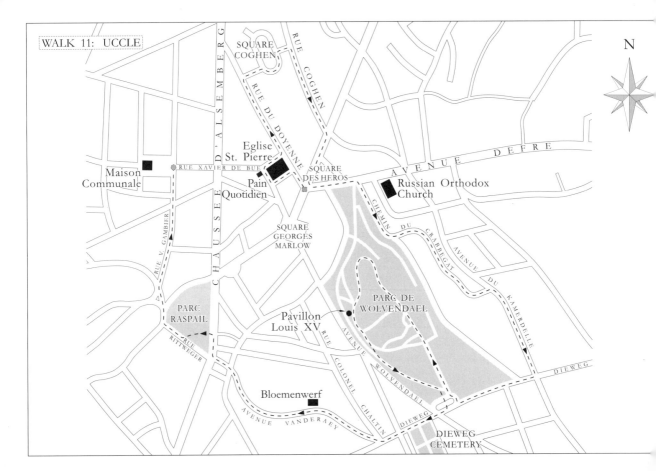

WALK 11: UCCLE

SQUARE COGHEN

RUE COGHEN

RUE DU DOYENNE

RUE DE BUE

SQUARE COGHEN

CHAUSSEE D'ALSEMBERG

RUE XAVIER DE BUE

Maison Communale

Eglise St. Pierre

Pain Quotidien

SQUARE DES HEROS

AVENUE DEFRE

Russian Orthodox Church

RUE V. GAMBIER

SQUARE GEORGES MARLOW

CHEMIN DU CRABBEGAT

AVENUE DU KAMERDELLE

PARC RASPAIL

PARC DE WOLVENDAEL

Pavillon Louis XV

RUE RITTWEGER

AVENUE COLONEL CHALTIN

AVENUE WOLVENDAEL

DIEWEG

Bloemenwerf

AVENUE VANDERAEY

DIEWEG

DIEWEG CEMETERY

N

Uccle

FROM AVENUE BRUGMANN TO NOTRE-DAME DU BON-SECOURS

Uccle is the most rural of the city's 19 *communes*, its quiet suburban streets gradually melting into the forest, as tarmac gives way to cobblestones, and lanes turn into muddy tracks. There are no major museums in Uccle, yet its bucolic charms are hard to resist. We will walk down cobbled lanes, pass whimsical suburban villas, and delve into ancient country inns where Bruegel might have stopped. This is a walk for a summer afternoon when we feel like escaping the crowded centre and sipping a beer in a garden shaded by old trees.

I. Avenue Brugmann. We will probably need to take a tram to get out to Uccle. The 91 and 92 take us to Square des Héros from Place Louise or Place Royale. If we look out of the left side going down Avenue Brugmann, we can see a house designed by Victor Horta at No. 80. Further on, we might catch a glimpse of two splendid Art Nouveau houses designed by one of Horta's followers at Nos. 176 and 178. The architect was Paul Vizzavona, as we can see from the tram now that the masonry has been cleaned. On leaving the tram at Square des Héros, we see a curious war memorial on the left decorated on the base with crabs and frogs. We cross to the other side of Avenue Brugmann and turn left, past a strange, wistful house at No. 519 signed by J. B. Dewin in 1910 and decorated with tile friezes in the style of the Vienna Secession. If we turn right along Rue du Doyenné, and left at the church, we can stop for coffee in Pain Quotidien at Parvis Saint-Pierre 16 (open every day from 7 am). On leaving here, we follow a circuitous route back to Square des Héros. After crossing the road we turn right along the Parvis Saint-Pierre, then left up Rue du Doyenné. If we then turn right just beyond No. 54, we enter Square Coghen, an idyllic enclave of modernist houses now smothered with ivy and clematis. After walking through a passage, we turn left past houses with hints of the Modern Movement, though nothing too extreme, a rounded corner or porthole window being enough to establish your modernist credentials in Uccle. The gardens are strangely overgrown for Brussels, where formality is otherwise the rule. We find more traditional gardens on leaving the square (strictly speaking an oval) and turning right down Avenue Coghen. Some extraordinary houses can be found on this sweeping avenue, such as a gabled Belgian version of an English country house at No. 177, a sombre English Tudorbethan house at No. 189 and a flamboyant Flemish baroque building at No. 193. Most of the styles are histor-ical, but the house at No. 266 has a hint of Art Nouveau, and its neighbour, though more reticent, has a fanciful iron railing at the top.

Back at Square des Héros, we turn left along Avenue de Fré. A sign here points to the Hôpital Deux Alices, which was founded by a Belgian politician in 1877 and named in memory of his dead daughter and grand-daughter, both named Alice. We continue along this road, past the entrance to Parc Wolvendael. The country house we glimpse through the trees dates from 1765. We will explore the park later, but first we should look at the curious Russian Orthodox Church further along the Avenue de Fré next to No. 21, which was built by Russian exiles who fled the 1917 Revolution. Modelled on a 16th-century chapel at Ostrov, near Moscow, the church is filled with glinting icons and memorials to the victims of the Revolution.

We now retrace our steps to the cobbled lane called Crabbegat, where we see an old brick inn with walls painted pink. Dating back to 1570, this originally had the Dutch name 't Hoff 'ten Horen, but is now the Auberge du Vieux Cornet.

We can see the *cornet* in question on an old façade stone embedded in the tower. This inn was popular in the 19th century with Brussels writers and artists, such as Charles de Coster who, we are told by a plaque on the opposite wall, set an episode of his picaresque *Légende d'Uilenspiegel* in the tavern. (The novel had a tremendous impact; reproduced here is one of the less decadent illustrations produced for it by Félicien Rops.)

If we are wearing stout shoes, and the ground is not too muddy, we can go up the cobbled lane on our left, past an ancient door with the name *Ulenspiegel* painted above. The easier route is to go back to the park and climb the hill, in which case we can ignore the next two paragraphs. We now plunge into the cool, damp woods, following an old sunken lane overgrown with ivy and tree roots. It doesn't go very far, of course, but is still a wonderful road to find, untouched for centuries apart from the derelict lamp-posts along the way. We soon come to a fork, where we take the left path (the right being blocked by a dilapidated bridge propped up

BON BUVEUR VIDANT LES POTS RIEN QU'EN LES REGARDANT.

Félicien Rops imp. del. et sculp. Brux

with scaffolding). At the end of this lane, we turn right up Kamerdelle, another cobbled lane though this one used by the occasional vehicle. Wandering past the rambling villas, we can begin to appreciate why an address in Uccle is so coveted.

On reaching Dieweg, we turn right past gardens planted with hollyhocks, rhododendrons and other hints of English-style gardening. We may be amused to notice the electricity substation next to No. 178, which has been designed to resemble a baroque wayside chapel, though with an 11,000-volt transformer instead of a statue of the Virgin. Soon after this, we turn right into Parc Wolvendael, the rambling park that once belonged to the country house we saw earlier. No clipped hedges or neat borders here; Wolvendael has been left to grow wild. Keen gardeners are sometimes upset by the unkempt appearance, but I think it is rather in keeping with the rustic temperament of Uccle to leave it as wild woodland. We follow the straight avenue on the right side, passing a café called La Guinguette. The name harks back to the 19th-century pleasure

gardens that once drew city dwellers out to Uccle. This *guinguette* may not be quite the same thing, though it does have an old-fashioned playground and a café terrace.

We now head down the hill, following the path as its curves across the lawn. Here, we might spot some tables under the trees on the left. These belong to the Louis XV, an elegant restaurant located in an 18th-century rococo pavilion. This flamboyant building once stood in a back garden in Amsterdam's Jewish Quarter. It was bought in 1909 by the owner of the Wolvendael estate and rebuilt as a summer house. If we are here at the right time, we can drink a coffee or a beer at one of the tables under the trees.

II. Dieweg Cemetery. We now head back up the hill, leaving the park by the entrance on Dieweg. After crossing the road, we turn right to reach the entrance of Dieweg Cemetery (open 9 am-4 pm). Closed many years ago, the cemetery has been preserved as another deliberate wilderness, with shattered tombs overgrown with ivy, broken statues of cherubs and dented metal photographs of the departed. Death should be like this, not neatly tended as it is in other Belgian cemeteries. The Dieweg cemetery is a popular spot with botanists, who have identified a dozen types of ivy, 60 varieties of wild flowers, 200 plant species, and a host of rare lichens clinging to the mouldering tombs.

The main avenue is lined with crumbling 19th-century tombs of former burgomasters and generals, whose names probably mean nothing to us, though we may recognise Paul Hankar, whose Art Nouveau home we passed on walk 8. Hankar died in 1901 at the age of 42, and is buried under a plain marble stone on the right. If we strike off down the side alleys, we will find the tombs of other people we have met on our walks in Brussels, including the architect Jean-Pierre Cluysenaer, who designed the Galeries Saint Hubert we strolled through on walk 3.

Some of the tombs are quite splendid, such as the mock-gothic chapel of the Fumière family, the sphinx that adorns the Sermon family's tomb, and a curvaceous Art Nouveau tomb designed by Victor Horta for the Stern family. Lurking in the tangled wilderness to the right of the main alley is the grave of Georges Rémi, the creator of Tintin, who lived with his wife on the Dieweg. Hergé, as he signed himself, died in 1983, and was buried in this old cemetery even though it was officially closed. A little metal sign points to the tomb, but anyone hoping for a statue of Tintin or Snowy will be disappointed by the sober slab.

On leaving the cemetery, we turn left along the Dieweg, then right down the steep Avenue Vanderaey, where we can perhaps glimpse the blue and white striped gables of Bloemenwerf through the trees at No. 102. Henry van de Velde built this country house in 1895 for himself and his wife Maria Sèthe. Van de Velde was then a painter, at the forefront of modernism and experimenting with a pointillist style based on Seurat, but taking on symbolist ambitions too. The house was his first attempt at architecture, and the trouble he then had in furnishing it in a way he thought appropriate persuaded him to

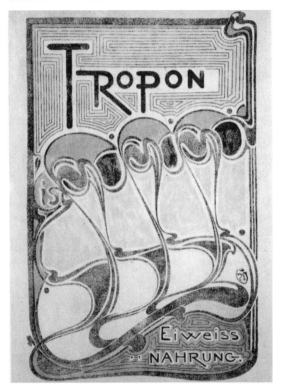

design his own. (In this he was much influenced by William Morris, and indeed Van de Velde's irrepressible energy and knack of turning his hand to all arts are reminiscent of Morris.) We saw some of Van de Velde's candlesticks in the Cinquantenaire museum (page 240). It was the beginning of a brilliant career that lasted until the Second World War. Shortly after he finished the house he was approached by a German industrialist with the task of designing a marketing campaign for a patent drink called Tropon. Van de Velde's name was quickly made in Germany and demand for his designs was so great that in 1900 he moved to Berlin. In 1907 he founded the pioneering Weimar School of Arts and Crafts, which under his successor Walter Gropius became the Bauhaus.

We see Van de Velde and his wife in this photograph taken in the studio on the first floor on a sunny day in about 1898. The statue in the corner is George Minne's *Kneeling Youth* of 1896, which we may remember from walk 6.

We continue down the hill past an abandoned park, then follow the cobbled Rue Rittweger to

reach the chapel of Notre-Dame du Bon-Secours, just to the left along Rue de Stalle. This rare relic of Brabant gothic architecture dates back to the 14th century and is still visited by pilgrims hoping to be cured of various ailments. We now cross Rue de Stalle to enter Parc Raspail opposite, named after the French chemist and educationalist François Raspail who lived here in exile from 1857 to 1862. Raspail fled to Belgium to escape Napoleon III, settling in a white mansion above this park. The house has gone, but we can wander in the former garden with its dank pond and overgrown rhododen-drons. Victor Hugo and Alexandre Dumas made their way to this remote house to visit Raspail, who earned a comfortable living selling a patent elixir in the shops of Brussels.

We leave the park at the top end, where the house once stood, and turn right along the cobbled Rue Victor Gambier. We follow this street until we see the town hall on our left, then turn right down Rue Xavier de Bue, a lively shopping street that leads back to Square des Héros. Here, we can take tram 91 or 92 back into town, or go back to Parc Wolvendael to sit on that seductive café terrace we passed earlier.

WALK 12

Waterloo

FROM THE WELLINGTON MUSEUM TO THE LION MOUND

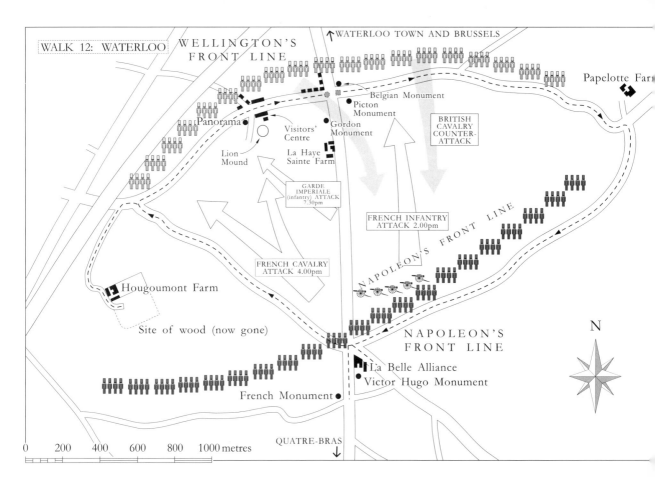

WALK 12: WATERLOO

WELLINGTON'S FRONT LINE

↑ WATERLOO TOWN AND BRUSSELS

Papelotte Far

Belgian Monument

Picton Monument

Panorama

Gordon Monument

BRITISH CAVALRY COUNTER-ATTACK

Visitors' Centre

Lion Mound

La Haye Sainte Farm

GARDE IMPERIALE (infantry) ATTACK 7.30pm

FRENCH INFANTRY ATTACK 2.00pm

NAPOLEON'S FRONT LINE

FRENCH CAVALRY ATTACK 4.00pm

Hougoumont Farm

Site of wood (now gone)

NAPOLEON'S FRONT LINE

La Belle Alliance

Victor Hugo Monument

French Monument ●

N

0   200   400   600   800   1000 metres

QUATRE-BRAS
↓

Waterloo

jWe have already seen relics of Waterloo in the Musée de l'Armée, and perhaps stood on the lawn in the Bois de la Cambre where the English might have played cricket on the eve of the battle. But we have still to visit the battlefield itself, which lies in open countryside some 18 kilometres south of Brussels. Getting out there is not that easy; indeed, it was simpler in the late 19th century when a coach left from Place Royale every day. We now have to take a local bus, join a guided tour or, possibly, rent a car for the day (the various options are described on page 377).

The artist Robert Hills wasted no time getting to Waterloo; one month after the battle, he packed his sketch book and water-colours, and set off for the Low Countries. Arriving in Ostend harbour, he saw his first wounded soldiers heading home. 'We passed amidst several large transports filled with wounded men from Waterloo, and saw numerous flights of wild fowl,' he wrote in his *Sketches in Flanders and Holland*. Several thousand casualties were still being treated in Brussels when Hills arrived. 'Brussels… bore the aspect of an extensive hospital,' he observed. The wounded were everywhere, wandering dazed in the street and parks, with bandaged heads, arms in slings and stumps where their legs had been sawn off. The city's hospitals could not cope with the sheer number of casualties. 'In every street were doors and windows with paper labels, intimating that 'wounded' were within.'

The poet Robert Southey followed in Hills' footsteps about a month later, describing his impressions in his *Journal of a Tour in the Netherlands in the Autumn of 1815*. Southey had not particularly wanted to join the masses trekking out to Waterloo, but as Poet Laureate he was under a certain obligation to pen some lines on the battle. He set off in early October with his wife and daughter, carrying a letter from the anxious parents of Richard Carbonell, who was one of the 25,000 wounded soldiers hospitalised in Brussels.

By the time Southey tracked down the hospital where Carbonell had been taken, the young soldier had become another one of the 40,000 dead. The sight of so many wounded, including French soldiers, made a deep impression on the poet. 'I saw some waggons full of wounded men, who had been taken out for air – a most melancholy sight. Some were lying upon straw, pale, emaciated, and with the utmost languor and listlessness in their appearance.' Even the Hôtel de Flandre, where Southey had booked a room, was full of wounded officers. One of them,

Lieutenant Colonel Millar, had been shot near La Haye Sainte farm. 'His thigh was broken by a grape-shot, and splinters and the rags which were driven into the flesh prevent the wound from healing.'

Southey dutifully set off for Waterloo, where a Belgian guide led him through the fields to Hougoumont farm, pointing out a bloodstained wall, the footprints of soldiers in the mud, and a mound of earth where six hundred French soldiers were buried. Yet already the scars of the battle were disappearing; even the trees in the orchard, where some of the fiercest fighting had occurred, were bearing autumn fruit.

The apples in Hougoumont orchard had fallen by the time the British writer Henry Smithers arrived in Ostend in the late autumn. He was bound, like everyone else, for Waterloo. Smithers visited the church in Waterloo, noting the shiny marble memorial to William Livingstone Rolse, who, the inscription read, 'fell nobly at Waterloo, aged 24'. Smithers was already too late to find much evidence of the battle. Most of the wounded had limped home, the battlefield was virtually stripped of relics, and the muddy foot-prints at Hougoumont had been washed away by the rains. 'The heroes who fell on that day have mouldered into dust, but the valour which inspired them holds its fixed residence in the hearts of Britons,' Smithers mused, as if he was talking about an episode of the Trojan Wars.

It was not until the following summer that Byron made a brief detour to Waterloo, buying souvenirs for his children and galloping across the battlefield singing a Turkish cavalry song. He included some verses on Waterloo in his epic poem *Childe Harold's Pilgrimage*. Forty-five years later, in 1861, Victor Hugo stayed five weeks in the Hôtel des Colonnes, writing in his hotel room in the morning, and strolling around the village in the afternoon, occasionally pointing tourists in the direction of the battlefield. The result was a poem that tolls in French like a funeral bell: 'Waterloo! Waterloo! Waterloo! morne plaine!' as Hugo meditated the bitter 'flight of those before whom the world took flight'. Charles Baudelaire followed Hugo three years later, though all we know of his visit is that

he ordered three eggs swimming in butter from a local innkeeper and proceeded to eat them with his fingers. In the late summer of 1926, James Joyce took a bus out to Waterloo, chatting incessantly with the driver as they drove through the forest. He mentions the 'Willingdone Musey-room' at Waterloo in the opening chapter of *Finnegan's Wake* and describes Wellington for some obscure reason as a Ghentleman.

The battlefield has changed dramatically since Roberts Hills produced his sketches in 1815. The Dutch destroyed the rolling contours when they constructed the Lion Mound in honour of the Prince of Orange, and the gnarled elm by the roadside where Wellington is said to have rallied his generals fell prey to souvenir hunters. We might be disappointed at first, as Wellington was when he returned here in 1821, complaining that: 'They have spoilt my battlefield.' Yet a surprising area of the landscape has survived, thanks to the Waterloo Preservation Act passed by the Belgian government in 1915. We only need to turn off the main road and wander down the country lanes to find ourselves on the edge of the sloping fields of rye where the Imperial Guard galloped on that wet June afternoon, about to lose its reputation for invincibility.

Our first stop is Waterloo town centre, which we reach by taking the Chaussée de Waterloo out of Brussels, following the same route that the British soldiers marched down in 1815 (the instructions that follow assume we are driving). Much has changed along the way, yet we still pass the occasional house or inn that has survived, such as the building at No. 901 dated 1731. Fanny Burney, who had fled to Brussels from Paris as Napoleon advanced on the city, described the Belgians who lined the road to Waterloo. 'Placidly, indeed, they saw the warriors pass; no kind greeting welcomed their arrival; no warm wishes followed them to combat... Even while standing there in the midst of them, an unheeded, yet observant stranger, it was not possible for me to discern, with any solidity of conviction, whether the Belgians were, at heart Bourbonists or Bonapartists.'

We may ask the same question. The souvenir shops on the battlefield seem to be in the hands of the Bonapartists, for they are full of Napoleonic souvenirs. The town of Waterloo, though, would appear to be solidly Bourbonist, for it has a cinema, shopping arcade and museum named in honour of Wellington. The museum is our first stop. We should see it on the left as we drive into town, though we will probably have to look for somewhere to park behind the church on the right. Before we go into the museum, we might stop for coffee and croissants in La Brioche at Chaussée de Bruxelles 161.

Waterloo's one claim to fame is the battlefield. Oddly enough, we won't find the battlefield marked on the town maps, as the site in fact lies in the adjoining communes of Braine l'Alleud, Genappe and Plancenoit. Wellington chose to call it Waterloo after the village where he established his campaign headquarters on 17th June. Southey, among others, would have preferred a different name. 'Call it Hougoumont, call it La Belle Alliance, or La Haye Sainte, or Papelot, or Mont St Jean – anything but Waterloo.' Despite Southey's plea, and the occasional moves by Braine l'Alleud to rename the battle, it remains Waterloo, giving London its Waterloo bridge and station, and providing the English language with a quaint phrase to denote a crushing defeat. Only the Prussians refused to talk of Waterloo. They refer to it as the Battle of Belle Alliance, adopting the name of the inn to the south where Wellington and Blücher met after the battle. A Berlin square was renamed Belle-Alliance-Platz after the victory, though, being Berlin, the name was later changed to Mehring-platz.

I. The Wellington Museum. The outstanding Wellington Museum at Chaussée de Bruxelles 147 occupies an old 18th-century coaching inn where Wellington spent two nights on 17th and 18th June. The building has been carefully preserved as it looked in 1815, down to its ancient tiled floors and creaky oak doors. The former bedrooms are now devoted to the different nations that fought here – most of the countries of northern Europe, in fact. Among the relics, we find rusty swords, pistols, military maps, letters, newspaper cuttings, prints and models of the battle. One sad room at the back (No. 4) contains the wooden bed where Alexander Gordon died. An almost illegible label stuck to the headboard tells us that: 'Major General Lord Gordon was brought to this bed when mortally wounded on the 18th of June 1815.' This room also contains Lord Uxbridge's wooden leg, though we must wait until we go out into the garden to look at the tomb where Uxbridge, in a whimsical episode endlessly retold around 19th-century English dining tables, buried his amputated limb.

Wellington clearly had the best room in the inn (now No. 6), looking out on the church where memorials would be placed after the battle. We can still see the rickety card table where he wrote his dispatches on the night after his victory and a browned copy of *The Times* dated 22 June 1815 containing a report of 'the great and glorious result of those masterly movements by which the Hero of Britain met and frustrated the audacious attempt of the rebel Chief.' One wonders how the news of the victory affected audiences at the advertised exhibition of musical automata made by Monsieur de la Roche of Paris, among which was 'a mechanical canary bird which sings ten different tunes.'

But back to more serious matters. A glass case in the Dutch Room (room 7) allows us to examine the contents of General de Constant Rebecque's travelling trunk, which included four pewter goblets, two silver candlesticks, four silver egg cups, tweezers, nail file and a perfume bottle. In another room we find photographs of some of the Duke of Wellington's illustrious descendants, including two who were less fortunate in war – a brother of the 5th Duke who died at Ypres in 1914, and the 6th Duke, killed in the Salerno landings of 1943.

The museum devotes four rooms to local history, documenting Waterloo's navvies who laid many of the cobbled country roads in Belgium and displaying some old photographs of the hotel where Victor Hugo stayed, before it was torn down in the 1960's. The final room contains a world map pinpointing the many other towns named Waterloo.

We now go out into the garden where we find a curious brick chapel. This is the tomb of Lord Uxbridge's amputated leg. The worn inscription, in French, translates: 'Here lies the leg of His Majesty's illustrious, brave and valiant General the Earl of Uxbridge, Commander in Chief of the English, Belgian and Dutch cavalry, wounded on the 18th June at the memorable Battle of Waterloo.' Etc. Etc. Karl Baedeker was quite sniffy about this tomb in his 1905 guidebook to Belgium and Holland: 'The garden of a peasant (a few paces to the north of the church) contains an absurd monument to the leg of Lord Uxbridge,' he wrote.

The tomb used to stand, as the old Baedeker reveals, in a garden across the road. We can go there now, crossing the road at the lights and turning right. The derelict house behind the iron railings at Chaussée de Bruxelles 214 (it is is still there) was known as the Château Tremblant in 1815. It was here that Lord Uxbridge's leg was amputated on the dining room table. The leg was buried in the garden and a weeping willow planted on the spot by the owner of the house, Hyacinthe Paris. Visitors began to call here to look at the spot where the leg was buried, and Hyacinthe realised that money could be made from this eccentric British pilgrimage. He built the marble tomb we have just seen in 1825 and charged visiors to look at the tomb, the boot from the severed leg and various other curiosities.

A minor diplomatic row flared up in 1878 when George Paget, son of Lord Uxbridge, visited Waterloo in search of the family tomb, as it were. He discovered to his consternation that the descendants of Paris intended to sell the house – complete with his father's leg. The Uxbridge family demanded the return of the leg, but the Belgian courts, after carefully pondering the issue, ruled that it had to be reburied in its old location. Another dispute arose recently when a road-widening plan threatened to destroy the house. The tomb was moved to this garden, but minus the bones, which had probably been discarded by the Paris family as long ago as 1934.

The Chapelle Royale opposite the museum looks as if it might have been put up by the British as a memorial, but the Latin inscription on the pediment reveals that it was built in honour of Charles II of Spain (the sickly king whose head decorates the Maison du Roi d'Es-pagne on Grand'Place). The foundation stone was laid in 1690 by François Antoine Augusto, Marquis of Castanaga. The interior is now filled with memorials of Waterloo, commemorating British regiments and generals who had served under Wellington in Spain, Portugal and France. One plaque was put up by the brothers and sisters of Alexander Hay of Nunraw, a trumpeter who was only eighteen when he died. Let us now look at the battlefield where Alexander Hay died on a wet June afternoon.

The road south of Waterloo is now an ugly strip of car showrooms, hamburger restaurants and furniture shops, making it hard to believe that this could be the same route that John Wilson Croker rode down a few weeks after the battle. Sent by the British government to report on the aftermath of the battle, he wrote back that the road was still 'strewed with soldiers' hats and caps, broken arms, bones of horses'.

Poking around the battlefield, he found more melancholy evidence: 'cartridges and waddings of the cannon, letters which had been torn out of the pockets of the killed and wounded... torn remains of hats, caps and helmets.'

We reach the battlefield soon after passing Mont Saint Jean, a white-walled Brabant farmhouse on the left side of the road used as a British field hospital in 1815. On arriving at the crossroads on the ridge, we should ignore the sign pointing to the Lion Mound and turn left, taking the road to La Marache. With any luck, we should be able to find a parking space near the crossroads where we can read about the battle.

After escaping from Elba and marching north towards Brussels, Napoleon hoped to crush Wellington's army of British, Belgians and Dutch while they were separated from Blücher's Prussian troops. After fighting the Prussians at Ligny, and defeating the Dutch and Belgians at Quatre Bras, Napoleon's superior army faced Wellington's in the fields south of Waterloo village on 18 June. It had rained all night and Napoleon lost valuable time waiting for the ground to dry; battle did not begin until 11.30 am, with a fierce French attack on Hougoumont farm on Wellington's right flank, where the defenders stood firm. In the early afternoon, after a heavy barrage the French infantry attacked Wellington's left, forcing the Dutch and Belgians to fall back, but the situation was saved by a cavalry charge led by Lord Picton. The French then attacked the farmhouse of La Haye Sainte, finally capturing the building at about 6 pm, although they were driven out soon afterwards. The British centre was attacked by Marshal Ney's cavalry at about 4 pm, but they failed to break through the infantry, which was drawn up in squares. Meanwhile, to the east, Blücher's Prussians finally arrived at Plancenoit, where they were driven back by a force of 30,000 troops led by Grouchy. Napoleon made his last attempt at about 7.30 in the evening, ordering the Imperial Guard, led by Ney, to attack Wellington's centre once again. The British infantry lay hidden until the last minute, when they fired a devastating volley, followed by a bayonet charge. At about the same time, Blücher's troops finally pushed Grouchy aside and arrived on the battlefield. The French troops fled in confusion, pursued by the Prussians, and shortly after 9 pm the victorious leaders Wellington and Blücher met at the Belle Alliance inn on the Charleroi road.

Looking over the gentle rolling fields, it's not too difficult to imagine the scene on that wet June morning when 68,000 Allied troops huddled along the ridge we are now standing on, facing 72,000 soldiers of Napoleon's army on the distant ridge. The fields in front of us were planted with tall rye in 1815 and the lane we see here was sunk below the fields, with high hedges on both banks. We have to imagine 1,200 cavalry gathered in the fields behind us, the horses snorting and rearing as the French artillery bombarded the lines. It was about two in the afternoon when the French, led by Count Drouet d'Erlons, marched up the slope we see in front of us. One of the first casualties was Lord Picton, who is commemorated by a small stone on the spot where he fell leading his men against the first French attack.

Much grander monuments have been erected at the crossroads nearby. On the far side of the main road, a stone column commemorates Major General Lord Gordon, who, Byron wrote, 'rushed into the field, and, foremost fighting, fell'. Gordon later died in the bed we saw in the Wellington Museum. His family paid for this classical column with its lengthy inscription, ending on the words: 'In testimony of feelings which no language can express, a disconsolate sister and five surviving brothers have erected this simple memorial to the object of their tenderest affection.' Later inscriptions record that Gordon's brother repaired the monument in 1837 and 1863, and his great-nephew paid for later work in 1871 and 1885, since when the family seems to have abandoned its illustrious ancestor.

Another monument at the crossroads was put up one year later to commemorate the Hanoverian officers killed defending the farmhouse of La Haye-Sainte. A short walk down the busy Brussels to Charleroi road brings us to this whitewashed farmhouse where a plaque tells us that this building was taken by the French at about 6.30 in the evening, after 'heroic assaults' led by Marshal Ney. Smithers was told a story of an old Belgian woman living in the farmhouse who refused to leave during the battle. 'Let them fight it out,' she said. 'It's nothing to do with me.' Entering the courtyard four weeks later, Robert Hills was struck by the chaos: 'The straw-yard was literally covered with wrecks of shoes, boots, foraging-caps, hats, cockades, knapsacks, canteens, oilskins, broken cartouche boxes, stocks of muskets, scabbards, gaiters, leaves of music, playing-cards, leathern straps, rags that had stanched the blood of the wounded, and tatters of every description.' Even now, the green barn door bears the scars of French bullets.

II. A walk across the battlefield. We now go back to the lane known as the Rue de la Croix and head across the fields, watching out for the occasional car. After a few minutes, we come to a fork in the road, where we turn right down Rue du Dimont. We continue along the ridge, pausing to look across the fields to a distant column on the main road, which marks the ridge where the French army stood. The fields we see in front of us, now empty, were filled on the day with 140,000 men – fighting, dying and confused. Fanny Burney was one of the first to visit the battlefield after the fighting ended. 'Piles of dead! Heaps, masses, hills of dead, bestrewed the plains!' she wrote.

The road we are walking down soon becomes a sunken lane, with trees on either side, giving us the one chance we have to appreciate the appearance of the Allies' front line in 1815. At the foot of the hill, we turn left along the Chemin des Cosaques, but only as far as the little chapel dedicated to St Roch. A private lane on the left leads up the hill to the Papelotte farm, the scene of bitter fighting in 1815. The farm was attacked and taken by the French at about four in the afternoon, though they were driven out in the early evening. The original farmhouse was destroyed in the fighting; this strange brick building with its octagonal tower was built in 1858.

Ignoring the lane to the farm, we instead turn

right up a rough farm track where an old dented sign indicates the route of the Promenade de la Belle Alliance. A sunken lane, its steep banks overgrown with ivy, leads to a fork, where we take the right track. This brings us out in the open countryside, where we can see the Lion Mound in the distance and perhaps the traffic lights at the crossroads where we parked. We are now walking along the high ridge that formed the French front line. It was along this route that General Blücher arrived in the early evening with his Prussian troops, just in time according to some historians to save Wellington from defeat. On reaching the road to Plancenoit, we turn left and follow the road a short distance until we see some steps on the right leading to the top of a low embankment. This is signposted as Napoleon's observation post, though the Emperor only came here at about four in the afternoon, and probably saw little of the battle, which was being fought in the hidden valleys to the north.

We now go back down the road to the cross-roads and turn left along the main road, where there is a whitewashed building on the corner. A plaque above the door that tells us that this was the Belle Alliance tavern where Wellington and Blücher met after the battle. In fact, the meeting probably took place outside an inn called the Maison du Roi, a short distance away, but the name Belle-Alliance, even if a mistake, sounds so much better. Despite their decision to name the battle Belle-Alliance, the Prussians have not made much of this site, choosing instead to build a monument at Plancenoit.

The main monument near here stands a short distance down the road towards Charleroi. A tall Doric column honouring Victor Hugo was begun in 1912, but remained unfinished when German soldiers poured across the frontier in 1914. It was still being built when another generation of German soldiers passed this way in 1940. Finally, in 1956, almost a century after Hugo came to Waterloo, the monument was formally unveiled. As the trucks hurtle past, we can read Hugo's description of Waterloo as a 'mournful plain'.

The only other sight here is the French

monument on the other side of the road, next to a night club. Enclosed by iron railings decorated with Napoleonic N's, it depicts an eagle with a pierced wing holding a torn flag. A gardener is still employed to clip a little box hedge in the shape of an N, suggesting that there may be some closet Bonapartists around even now.

Walking back to the Belle Alliance crossroads, we pass a local café called Le Petit Galop which once served as Marshal Ney's headquarters. Beyond the bus stop, we turn left down a farm track which takes us across the main battlefield. The French cavalry galloped across the fields to our right at about four in the afternoon, heading for the ridge where a fence now runs. Earlier in the day, French troops had marched through the fields on the left making for the farm of Hougoumont, where the fighting went on all day. We can see the red tiled roof and the stone wall of the farmhouse near a clump of trees on the left. It is worth making a short detour to look at the farm, which is one of the most evocative spots on the battlefield. On reaching the ridge, we turn left along a quiet road, following it round to the left. This old Brabant farmhouse bore the brunt of Napoleon's first attack at about 11.30 in the morning. An eye witness described the ruined building a few weeks after the battle: 'Burnt and battered with shot, the trees around it cut to pieces... the fields around it broken up with graves.' Cows now graze peacefully in the fields around the farm where some 6,000 men were buried in mass graves. One of the trees, miraculously, is still standing.

Back on the ridge, we now head for the Lion Mound, passing a memorial to Lieutenant Augustin Demulder, one of the French cavalry officers who galloped through the fields we have just crossed. Demulder was born just a few kilometres south of here, in the Brabant town of Nivelles and, like many Walloons, supported the Napoleonic cause. The lane we are on leads to a cluster of cafés where the owners seem to share Demulder's fondness for Napoleon. But before we stop in one, we have to climb the 226 steps of the Lion Mound.

III. The Lion Mound. This earth pyramid, now slightly sagging, was constructed by the Dutch on the spot where the Prince of Orange was wounded in the shoulder. Some people see the lion on top as a symbol of British imperialism; others take it to be the Belgian lion, but it is actually a Dutch lion, resting its paw on a cannonball and growling in the direction of Paris. This rather vain project was carried out in 1824-26 by piling up thirty-two thousand cubic metres of earth dug from the battlefield; a massive project that destroyed the sunken lanes and the rolling topography in this area of the battlefield. We can buy a ticket, then climb the steps to the top for a view of the battlefield.

We might be tempted to visit some of the other tourist attractions here which attempt, with varying success, to recreate the battle. The oldest exhibition is the Waxworks Museum, which was created by Sergeant Edward Cotton, a veteran of the battle who had spent the night of June 17 huddled in the open fields as the rain drenched everything. He settled in Waterloo after the battle, guiding visitors around the fields

and finally employing experts from the Musée Grévin in Paris to create lifelike figures of the protagonists. We can perhaps give this dusty collection a miss, and visit instead the Panorama of Waterloo, which occupies a white neoclassical rotunda next to the Lion Mound. After climbing a creaking staircase, we reach a round platform surrounded by a circular painting lit from above by natural light.

Panoramas such as this one drew thousands of visitors at the end of the 19th century, offering strangely realistic views of battles or exotic places. The Waterloo Parorama was painted by Louis Dumoulin, a French artist who specialised in these large canvases. He also painted the Cairo Panorama which was shown in the building in the Cinquantenaire Park now used as a mosque. Dumoulin was clearly a Bonapartist, choosing to depict moments in the battle when the French had the upper hand. The first thing we see on reaching the top of the stairs is the detail reproduced overleaf showing Marshal Ney galloping towards us through the trodden rye, his helmet already fallen on the ground.

We meet the heroic Ney again in a second scene where he is leading an attack on the British squares, but we have to look hard to find any hint of the Allies' ultimate victory.

The latest attraction is the Visitor's Centre, which has a moderately interesting *son et lumière* show and a short film that appeals to children. Once we have seen this, we can sit in one of the cafés at the foot of the Lion Mound, such as the old-fashioned Le Cambronne. As we sip our coffee, perhaps sitting on the terrace under the wing of a French Imperial eagle, we might find ourselves wondering what would have happened if the Allies had failed to hold the ridge we are on. The French cavalry would have galloped into Brussels that night, causing panic in the Richmond household and the Hôtel d'Angleterre. By the next day, they might have been in Ostend, threatening the Channel. It did not work out that way. By 19 June, Napoleon was fleeing without his hat or sword, and Wellington had returned to Brussels to complete his dispatches. It was, as he said, a close run thing.

Back in Brussels, we might be wondering if

anything survives of the house where the Duchess of Richmond held her famous ball on 15 June, two days before the battle of Waterloo. Byron immortalised the event in *The Eve of Waterloo*: 'There was a sound of revelry by night, /And Belgium's Capital had gathered then/Her beauty and her Chivalry.'

The ball was a carefully planned ruse to trick Napoleon into thinking that Wellington was frittering away precious time. Yet the trick almost backfired, for while the officers danced (and Wellington flirted with Lady Frances Wedderburn-Webster), Napoleon was rapidly advancing up the road from Charleroi. As dinner was being served, news arrived that Napoleon had reached Quatre Bras, the crossroads where Wellington had originally planned to confront the French army. 'Has anyone a good map?' Wellington is said to have asked at this moment. In the event it was a Dutch-Belgian army that resisted Napoleon at this point, giving Wellington precious time to regroup his forces for the main encounter at Waterloo.

The house stood on the corner of Rue des Cendres and Rue de la Blanchisserie, near Place Rogier. Old guidebooks mention a plaque on the wall, but this has vanished, leaving nothing to recall the ball.

WALK 13

Tervuren and the Africa Museum
FROM THE CONGO PAVILION TO TERVUREN PARK

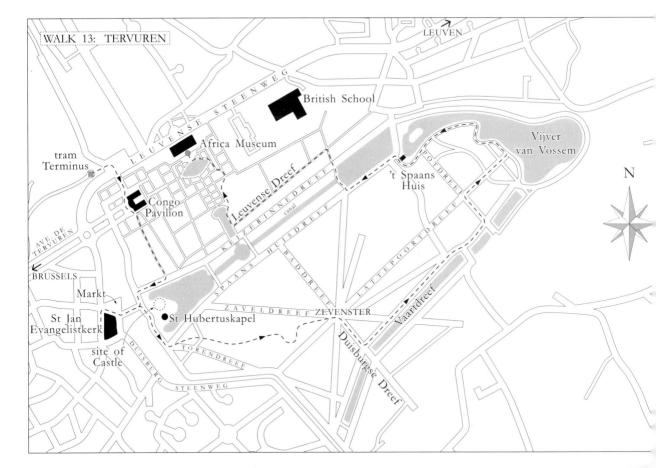

WALK 13: TERVUREN

LEUVEN

British School

Africa Museum

tram
Terminus

LEUVENSE STEENWEG

Vijver
van Vossem

Congo
Pavilion

Leuvense Dreef

't Spaans
Huis

canal

KEIZERINNEDREEF

POTDREEF

AVE. DE
TERVUREN

SPAANS HUISDREEF

BADDREEF

LATTEPOORTDREEF

N

BRUSSELS

Vaartdreef

Markt

ZAVELDREEF ZEVENSTER

St Jan
Evangelistkerk

St Hubertuskapel

Duisburgse Dreef

site of
Castle

DUISBURG

TORENDREEF

STEENWEG

Tervuren and the Africa Museum

FROM THE CONGO PAVILION TO TERVUREN PARK

We are going out of town again, this time to the Flemish village of Tervuren where Léopold II built a Congo Museum in the early 20th century. But there is much more to Tervuren than Léopold II's grand schemes. In the course of this walk, we will discover the ruins of a ducal palace, the spot where St Hubert died and Dr Livingstone's battered suitcase. We can easily do this trip in a half day but, if the weather is good, we might want to devote a whole day to the expedition, and spend the afternoon walking in the woods nearby. It is worth remembering that Tervuren is in Dutch-speaking Flanders; most locals would rather speak English than French.

Getting out to Tervuren is simple thanks to Léopold II, who financed the construction of the Avenue de Tervuren in 1897 to connect the Parc du Cinquantenaire with the Congo Pavilion in Tervuren. We first take the metro or tram to Montgomery, then change to tram 44 which leaves from an underground platform. The trip to Tervuren takes us outside the urban transport zone, so we a ticket must be bought from the tram driver.

As we wait for the tram to leave, we can familiarise ourselves with the remarkable history of the town we are about to visit, which has been an aristocratic retreat since the early 13th century. It was Henry I, Duke of Brabant, who built the first castle at Tervuren on the edge of a lake. Expanded in the 14th century, it was

then abandoned for a long period by the Dukes of Burgundy, who preferred the urban sophistication of Brussels. Archdukes Albert and Isabella restored the castle in the 17th century, adding new baroque buildings and landscaping the estate. Further embellishments were made by Charles of Lorraine, the Austrian governor, who was fond of idling away his days at Tervuren, sailing on a Dutch-style canal in his private gondola and visiting his lakeside porcelain factory. The view opposite, drawn in 1763, hints at the graceful country life enjoyed by Charles of Lorraine and his court; that same year the historian Mansaert described Tervuren as 'the most dazzling residence in the Brussels countryside'.

Charles of Lorraine died in Tervuren Castle in 1780, bringing an end to this golden age. The Emperor Joseph II, who succeeded Maria Theresa in Vienna that same year, had little time for frivolities in his northern lands, and ordered that Tervuren be torn down. A new castle that was being built for Charles at the time of his death, the Karelkasteel, was also destroyed. The site, near the tram terminus, was later used by the Dutch in the early 19th century, when they built a country house for William Frederik, Prince of Orange, who had led the Dutch forces at the Battle of Waterloo, receiving a wound on the spot where the Lion Mound was later constructed.

If Coghlan's 1837 *Belgium* is to be believed, the Prince of Orange's residence was 'surpassed by few palaces in Europe in the magnificence of its internal decorations.' Adorned with rich damask, Italian marble fireplaces and wainscoting, this became the home of Léopold II's unfortunate sister, Charlotte, seen at the age of eight in the portrait on page 34. As we found out in the Army Museum, Charlotte married Maximilian of Austria, and thus became Empress of Mexico. She enjoyed a charmed life for a few years, until Mexican rebels stormed the royal palace and executed Maximilian. Charlotte never recovered from the shock. She settled here, in Tervuren Castle, spending her days talking to empty chairs, claiming to be an officer in the French army, and signing her sad letters 'Charles'. A further disaster struck her life in

327

1879 when fire swept through Tervuren Castle, destroying the precious interiors that had so impressed Coghlan. Charlotte was moved to Bouchout Castle, north of Brussels, where she died in 1927, still convinced that she was a soldier in the French army.

Perhaps the tram has set off by now. Soon after the stop Père Damien, we pass the Palais Stocklet on the right at No. 281, pictured opposite. This was designed by the Austrian architect Josef Hoffman in 1905 for the rich Belgian industrialist Mons Stocklet. The pure geometric lines of the building reflect the principles of the Wiener Werkstätte movement, which Hoffman had founded with Koloman Moser in 1903. 'We will use ornament where appropriate,' they declared, 'but without compulsion and not just for its own sake.' In other words, Art Nouveau was out. As we can see in the photograph, even the trees in front of the Palais Stocklet have been trimmed into neat geometric shapes. The palatial interior is decorated with murals by Gustav Klimt, but the house remains firmly closed to the public.

The tram now rumbles past the gently rolling Parc de Woluwé, another of Léopold's creations. If we are tempted to stretch our legs, we should leave at the stop curiously named Chien Vert, though Tervuren offers us even better walks. We soon leave the city behind and plunge into the Forêt de Soignes, a wonderfully wild beech forest which skirts the southern edge of the city from Tervuren to Waterloo.

I. The Congo Pavilion. On arriving at Tervuren's rustic tram terminus, we will see the former Congo Pavilion on the opposite side of the main road. Built in 1897 on the site of Charlotte's ruined castle, this neoclassical pavilion formed the centrepiece of Léopold's Congo Exhibition. Financed largely by the King, the exhibition was intended to convince prospective investors of the vast untapped resources of the Congo. The pavilion was built by Ernest Acker, a minor Brussels architect, in Léopold's favourite Louis XVI style, while the interior contained an astonishing series of Art Nouveau rooms commissioned by Edmond van Eetvelde,

secretary-general of the Free Congo State. We saw Van Eetvelde's house on walk 6, built by Victor Horta and nearing completion at the time. Clearly an admirer of the new style (unlike the conservative Léopold), Van Eetvelde commissioned some of the most important Art Nouveau architects to design the exhibition halls. Henry van de Velde, looking much as he did in the 1898 photograph on page 293, created the exporters' room; Gustave Serrurier-Bovy designed the importers' room, and Paul Hankar, working in his Rue Defacqz studio, produced an extraordinary interior to display the ethnography collection, blending Art Nouveau and Congolese influences into a style that became known as *le style Congo*.

Surrounded by mouldering iron statues cast in Paris, the neoclassical pavilion is now used for the occasional banquet. Nothing at all remains of the palace where Charlotte lived, nor have any of the extraordinary Art Nouveau interiors survived, apart from a curious wooden frame at the back of the building, which few people ever find. Designed by Georges Hobé, this structure built using exotic wood shipped from Africa originally stood in a room devoted to Congolese exports such as coffee and cocoa. The Congo Pavilion soon became overcrowded with masks, weapons, jewellery and geological specimens, not to mention various stuffed animals. Still awash with money, Léopold commissioned his favourite French architect, Charles Girault, to plan a new Congo Museum in the style of the Petit Palais which Girault had built for the 1900 Paris Exhibition. The new museum was begun in 1904 but not finally opened until 1910, one year after Léopold's death. Let us cross the park to look at the extraordinary building that Léopold never saw completed.

II. The Africa Museum. The museum displays the limitless riches of the Belgian Congo within its vast marble halls, including outstanding collections of insects, mineral samples, stuffed animals and African art. As we approach, we can see linked letter Ls decorating the architrave, a reminder that this building was begun by Léopold. The double Ls even appear on the lapels of the guard's uniforms, to remind visitors of Léopold's contribution to this world-famous institution.

On entering the Rotunda, we see several statues dating from the 1897 Exhibition, including one with the title *Belgium Brings Prosperity to the Congo*. Léopold (seen here in old age) insisted that his interest in the Congo was purely philanthropic, but his critics saw the venture as a brutal quest for profit. In an unusually vitriolic outburst, Mark Twain wrote that 'in fourteen years, Léopold has deliberately destroyed more lives than have suffered death in all the battlefields of this planet for the past thousand years.' As if this was not indictment enough, Joseph Conrad's novel *Heart of Darkness* was based on his horrifying experiences of the Congo in 1890.

Léopold II was convinced that Belgium needed a colony to achieve wealth and recognition. He had expressed this belief as early as 1860, while he was still the Duke of Brabant, sending a slab of marble to a government minister inscribed *Il faut à la Belgique une colonie*. During the 'Scramble for Africa' of the 1880's, Léopold claimed the

331

Congo as his own private empire. It was almost the last territory available, and Léopold had little idea of the worth of this vast tract of unexplored land, eighty times the size of Belgium. He hired the British explorer, Henry Morton Stanley (seen here in an appropriate uniform), to chart the Congo River from 1874 to 1879, buying up the land from bewildered African chiefs. In Room 4, we can see several relics that Stanley carried with him on his explorations, including a battered old suitcase, which still has a faded label attached to it by his wife Dolly, declaring imperiously, 'This Portmanteau belonged to H. M. Stanley. It was carried across Africa. It must never be removed from my Room and *never* on any account be used.' We can also read a facsimile of a letter sent by Stanley to James Gordon Bennett, the editor of the *New York Herald*, who had financed Stanley's 1871 expedition in search of the Scottish explorer Dr Livingstone. 'Animated only with the desire to do my duty to the *New York Herald*, I halted at nothing, was ever pushing on until my men cried out from sheer fatigue, "Have mercy!"'

The same room contains relics of Livingstone, who died in a remote African village, two years after Stanley tracked him down and uttered the famous remark, 'Dr Livingstone, I presume?' We can inspect the metal travelling case he took on his final journey, a fragment of his fur rug, and a handful of dry leaves gathered by a devoted admirer from the mpundu tree in Chitambo (now in Zambia), where his heart was buried in 1873. Another traveller removed part of the tree's trunk and preserved it like the relic of a medieval saint.

This room also contains several old maps of Africa including Ortelius' *Theatrum orbis terrarum*, published in Antwerp in 1612, yet showing far more detail than the British map published by John Cary in 1821, which marks a large blank area in the centre of Africa as 'Unknown Parts'. Ortelius obviously hazarded a guess at the interior of Africa, whereas Cary was more honest about his ignorance.

The museum has preserved most of its original decor, including Room 14's dramatic murals depicting the landscape of the Congo and a fascinating frieze of thirty-two historic photographs showing scenes such as the swollen Congo river, a boa constrictor in the act of swallowing its outsize prey, and a narrow-gauge steam train labouring up a steep mountainside on the line built by Léopold to link Matadi and Léopoldville, two ports on the Congo separated by the un-navigable Stanley Falls.

Children particularly enjoy the large Zoological Dioramas in Room 12 containing stuffed lions and zebras displayed amid tropical landscapes. They also like to peer at the hidden wildlife in the dioramas of African Mountain Scenery in Room 2. Originally exhibited in the Congo Pavilion at the 1958 Brussels World Fair, these illustrate the different zones of natural vegetation on the slopes of the Ruwenzori massif. Stanley climbed this extinct volcano in 1889, no doubt accompanied by his well-worn suitcase and his exhausted bearers. The first scene shows the base of the volcano covered by dense equatorial forest, with civet-cats skulking in the undergrowth and green parrots peering out from the tangle of creepers. The next zone is mountain forest, home to the sleek-feathered dark blue Lady Ross touraco. Climbing higher in the next scene, we reach the bamboo forest, followed by wooded heath, then a curious landscape of moss-covered rocks and beards of lichen hanging from the branches. Finally, we reach the top, where Stanley must have breathed a sigh of relief as he gazed over an Alpine landscape ruled by white-collared crows. Belgians flocked to see these dioramas at the 1958 World Fair, little realising that the Congo would become an independent state just two years later. After exploring this old and engaging collection, we can pause in the museum café, which occupies a lofty room looking onto the main courtyard. When the sun shines, we can sit out under white parasols drinking Earl Grey tea. Surrounded by tall ferns and African statues, this can feel almost like an outpost of the Belgian Congo.

III. Tervuren town. On leaving the museum, we should walk through the formal gardens, landscaped by the French architect E. Lainé for the 1897 Exhibition. The pond, canal and stat-

ues were Léopold II's attempt to create a Belgian version of Versailles. The King indulged another whim in 1897 by constructing three makeshift Congolese villages on the edge of the lake. Almost three hundred Congolese spent several months living in straw-covered huts, paddling long Congo river canoes on the lake to entertain the visitors. Before the year was out, the damp Belgian climate had claimed seven victims, whose graves we come to later.

On reaching the lake, we turn right along a waterfront walk that was a favourite spot for 18th-century picnics, as we saw in the print on p. 326, which was based on a drawing by Jean Faulte. The artist shows the old Tervuren Castle during the reign of Charles of Lorraine, when the nobles, dressed in the latest French fashions, spent the summer boating on the lake or picnicking on the grass. The gothic hall in the drawing was built in the 13th century by Duke John II of Brabant. It was one of the largest such halls in medieval Europe. The castle lay derelict in the 15th century, but was restored and improved by Archdukes Albert and Isabella to its appearance in the Faulte's view. The great gallery was hung with an impressive collection of baroque paintings, including the six views of the Ommegang commissioned by Isabella in 1615. All this splendour vanished in 1780, leaving just a heap of rubble on the waterfront and, behind, a little chapel we will come to soon.

We now continue around the water's edge, and turn left along a narrow cobbled lane, which leads past the former stables of the ducal castle and enters the town square through a monumental gateway built for the 1897 Exhibition. A church stands on a slight rise to the left. This was begun in the 13th century as a ducal chapel, though little now remains of the original. The building we see now mainly dates from the 14th century, while the north portal was added in the more flamboyant gothic of the 15th century. The most striking feature inside is a rood screen added in the 1520's by two architects from the Keldermans family. Anthony of Burgundy, who died at Agincourt in 1415, lies buried in the church, along with his wife and two sons. Out in the churchyard, a row of identical tombs next to the church mark the graves of the seven Congolese who died during the 1897 Exhibition.

We now go back to the lake and cross the road to a promontory shaded by the heavy foliage of lime trees. This was the site of the great hall we saw in Faulte's view, of which little now remains apart from the overgrown foundations behind the fence and the Sint Hubertuskapel, built in 1617 by the court architect Wenceslas Coeberger. This chapel is dedicated to Hubert, the patron saint of hunting, who is said to have died on this spot in 727.

IV. Tervuren Park. If we have an hour to spare, we can wander through the old ducal estate known as the Warande, which lies to the south of here. Beginning at St Hubert's Chapel, we turn left to reach the woods, then follow the sign marked *Warandewandeling*. A meandering path leads to a crossing, where we follow the path marked by a wooden post daubed with blue paint. This route winds among the trees, most of them beeches planted by the Austrians, but with a few stray oaks surviving from earlier times.

The path soon swings sharply around a deep valley formed during the last ice age, to emerge in a clearing known as the Zevenster, where several avenues converge. The three massive stones in the middle of the clearing are sometimes taken to be prehistoric relics, though they were in fact dragged here on a whim of Léopold II.

We now follow the Duisburgsedreef, which leads down to a hidden pond. Here, we turn left along a straight avenue. On reaching a stretch of road where cars are permitted, we keep straight on, still following the blue posts, then turn left up a gravel track. At the next crossing we turn right, which brings us to a lake fringed with rolling lawns and exotic fir trees. Turning left along the lake, a meandering path leads to a sad abandoned mill that once belonged to the monks of Park Abbey, near Leuven. Pressing on, we come to a bridge on the right, which takes us across the canal where Charles of Lorraine used to sail in his gondola. We now turn left along the waterside to return to the museum.

Brussels Explored Further

Brussels Explored Further

We have seen the main sights now, but more remains to be discovered if our time here allows it. The suburbs of Brussels are dotted with historic buildings, unusual museums and romantic parks. Here are a few ideas to fill any odd moments we have.

I. Small Museums. The **Musée Communal d'Ixelles** at Rue Jean van Volsem 71 is well worth a visit, though it is not the easiest place to find. Founded in 1892, it occupies a 19th-century abattoir built in an unfashionable district of Ixelles. The commune has done its best to put up signs pointing the way, but it is still easy to get lost in the dense 19th-century streets. To make matters worse, the museum has unusual opening hours (see page 379), making it something of a miracle that anyone ever visits the place at all.

Those who do make their way up the hill are rewarded with a drawing of a stork by Dürer, a bronze head by Rodin and an almost complete collection of Toulouse Lautrec posters. The museum also has a large collection of Belgian paintings, including many works by members of Les Vingt bequeathed by Octave Maus. The Ixelles gallery provides an intimate setting for Rik Wouters' *Nel in a Red Hat* of 1905, Magritte's *The Happy Donor* of 1966 and Delvaux's *The Dialogue*, painted in 1974 and showing two nude women in a mysterious classical city. The museum recently obtained a *View of Amsterdam*

painted by Jan Baptist Bonnecroy in 1657. This large view was completed (if the date is correct) about seven years before the *View of Brussels* reproduced on pages 4-5. Bonnecroy stood on the north bank of the IJ to paint a stormy sky with patches of sunlight. Notice the people bathing naked on the near shore.

The small bust titled *Suzon* by Auguste Rodin is the only surviving relic from the period Rodin spent in Ixelles at the outset of his career. His studio was in fact just around the corner from here. We find it by turning right on leaving the museum and then first left along Rue Sans Souci. He worked at No. 111 from 1872, having moved to Brussels the previous year to work on some of the friezes we have already seen on the Bourse. He remained here until 1877, carving caryatids for buildings along the boulevards and statues to decorate the Palace of the Academicians. During a visit to Italy in 1874-5, Rodin fell under the spell of Michelangelo and returned to Brussels to produce his first great work, *The Age of Brass*, a nude modelled on a Belgian soldier called Auguste Neyt. When it was exhibited in Brussels, a critic made the hurtful suggestion that the figure must have been cast from life, not modelled by Rodin. This did nothing to deter collectors such as Dr Max Linde, who ordered a cast of the work to put in his winter garden in Lübeck, then sent Rodin this wistful photograph. Little of Rodin's work remains in Brussels, apart from the architectural sculpture we have already seen. His former studio in the Rue Sans Souci is still occupied by a sculptor. If we look at the entry buzzer, we can see the name Rodin listed beside the top bell, but this is presumably a joke.

The **Museum David and Alice van Buuren** at Avenue Leo Errera 41 has such restricted opening hours that we are unlikely ever to discover its curious charm. Located in a quiet suburban street in Uccle, but reached fairly easily by taking tram 23 or 90 to the Cavell stop, this handsome Art Deco suburban villa was built in 1923 by a wealthy Dutch banker. Open a mere two days a week, it nonetheless attracts a steady stream of art lovers and keen gardeners. The former come here to see a splendid collec-

tion of paintings, though they may be rather saddened to know that the version of Bruegel's *Fall of Icarus* hanging in the house has recently been proved to date from after Bruegel's death (like the one in the Musée d'Art Ancien). The collection also includes works by the First Latem School including five fair-haired Flemish children sitting down to lunch in Gustave van de Woestijne's *Children at Table*, which hangs on the staircase. The garden was landscaped in the 1950's by René Pechère, a specialist in theme gardens based on renaissance gardening books and classical texts. He designed a labyrinth for the Van Buurens inspired by the Song of Songs and an intimate renaissance Garden of the Heart planted with hedges and box trees.

A subdued light fills the **Musée Charlier** at Avenue des Arts 16 in St Josse, a 19th-century mansion designed in 1890 by Victor Horta, but too early to show any signs of his Art Nouveau style. This was the home of Guillaume Charlier, a prolific 19th-century sculptor whose works decorate several buildings in Brussels. The rooms here provide a suitable period setting for

341

Charlier's private collection of paintings by Constantin Meunier, James Ensor and Emile Claus. The museum is sometimes used for concerts and exhibitions.

The suburban house at Rue Esseghem 135 where René and Georgette Magritte lived for twenty-five years has been converted into the **Musée René Magritte**. The rooms have been furnished following the Magritte's rather conventional bourgeois taste and the back garden has replanted in its original style. It is debatable, though, whether Magritte would have approved of the exercise. Georgette would certainly have been horrified. 'I can't bear the thought of all those people walking over my nice carpets,' she said when the idea of a museum was once mooted.

The **Hôtel Wielemans** at Rue Defacqz 14 was built for Léon Wielemans, owner of the Wielemans-Ceuppens brewery, which now lies in ruins near the Gare du Midi. The house was designed by Adrien Blomme in the 1920's in a curious mixture of Art Deco and Moorish. A ship sailed from Seville in 1927 carrying over four thousand Moorish tiles to decorate the house. The building was restored by a bank and is now used for art exhibitions. It is worth paying the entrance charge to look inside at the gleaming tiled patio, the curious antique bedroom with silver walls, and the bathroom covered with abstract Moorish tiles.

II. Laeken. We might have time to squeeze in a tram trip to the northern suburb of Laeken, where a cluster of eccentric buildings stand on the edge of the royal estate. If we take tram 92 to the stop named Araucaria, we can hike up the hill to a small park where an elaborate Chinese pavilion was built in 1900. On the far side of the road, we can see a Japanese pagoda looming above the trees, while a replica of the Neptune Fountain in Bologna stands in the middle of a traffic roundabout nearby.

It hardly needs to be said that these buildings were put up by Léopold II. No other Belgian monarch would have had the imagination, or indeed the money, to erect these Oriental fantasies. Léopold was fired with the idea of creating an avenue lined with exotic buildings after he visited the Paris Universal Exhibition of 1900. The elderly king, like thousands of other visitors, had wandered through a cluster of pavilions known as 'The World Tour.' One of the attractions was a Japanese pagoda in which an invention known as the *Maréorama* offered the illusion of sailing on a steamer from Marseilles to Constantinople. Set on building a pagoda near his palace at Laeken, Léopold employed Alexandre Marcel, the architect of the Paris attraction, to build an exact replica. The sumptuous wooden details were carved in Yokohama to create an authentic appearance.

Léopold bequeathed his pagoda to the Belgian state in 1909, intending it to become a museum. It had been open to the public for some years, but closed owing to a lack of funds. Recently restored as a museum of Japanese art, it is now one of the strangest sights in the city. We reach it through a pedestrian underpass which has wood-lined walls and a bamboo gate designed to evoke the Buddhist notion of a transition from the everyday world to a sacred domain. We

emerge in a little Japanese garden where water trickles from bamboo pipes and an arched bridge crosses a pond stocked with goldfish. We then enter a shadowy interior decorated with carved wood, red lacquer and gilded details.

There is more. Léopold commissioned Marcel in 1901 to build a traditional Chinese tea house (the **Pavillon Chinois**) in the park opposite. Much of the exotic external decoration was carved by Chinese craftsmen (who included Léopold's head among the carved details). Léopold intended the building as an exotic restaurant, but this plan was quietly forgotten after he died in 1909. Nobody was quite sure what to do with the building and it passed from one government department to another. It has now been faithfully restored to display a collection of Chinese porcelain from the Musée du Cinquantenaire.

On leaving the Chinese pavilion, we turn right until we come to a roundabout with a replica of Bologna's Neptune Fountain stranded in the maul of traffic. Like it or not, we have to cross this busy road to enter the **Parc de Laeken** on

the other side. We follow the path to the right, then turn left up a deserted road. This leads to a summit where we find a dilapidated neo-gothic monument built in memory of Léopold I in 1881. From here, we can look down on the 18th-century Palais Royal, where Napoleon signed the fateful order in 1812 that sent his troops into Russia. The Belgian royal family occupy this palace, which is famous for its spectacular greenhouses designed by Alphonse Balat and open to the public for a few weeks in late April and early May.

It is almost pointless to provide directions to our next destination, for the **Atomium** has been looming in the distance since we entered the park. On a foggy day, though, we may require some guidance. We take the curving road that brought us here, then turn left along the broad Avenue du Gros Tilleul. This brings us to a roundabout with a large statue in honour of Adolphe Max, the city mayor who refused to obey German orders during the First World War. We can make a brief detour here up a path on our right lined with clipped trees. This leads to the curiously forgotten Parc d'Osseghem, where we get this odd view of the Atomium from an open-air theatre. It might be worth sitting down here to read about this strange memento of the 1958 World Fair which stands in the middle of a traffic roundabout like a space craft in a boy's comic.

The Atomium is very much a creation of the 1950's, symbolising faith in technological progress. The steel structure represents the nine atoms of an iron molecule magnified one hundred and sixty-five billion times. This odd architectural folly dominates the northern heights of the city, especially at night when tiny lights flit across the spheres to represent the paths of the electrons. Over the years, this futurist folly lost its original shine and turned into a decrepit relic of the atomic age. It is to be restored by 2004, but until then the website, www.atomium.be is probably more appealing than the real thing.

The main building we see from the observation deck of the Atomium is the Art Deco **Palais du Centenaire**, built in 1930 for the centenary

celebrations of the founding of the Belgian state and now used for travel fairs, car shows and the like. We can also see a cluster of brick houses below us built a few years ago in an attempt to recreate the mock Flemish village at the 1958 Fair. Called Joyful Belgium, this feature drew huge crowds, perhaps because it offered an escape from the relentless futurism elsewhere. Older Belgians would, of course, have recognised Joyful Belgium as a copy of earlier mock Flemish towns such as the one at the Universal Exhibition of 1910 pictured on page 38. Indeed this is a tradition that goes back more than a century, to Léopold's Exhibition of 1897 in the Cinquantenaire Park.

Our vantage point allows us a glimpse of the **Mini Europe** theme park below, which contains several hundred small-scale replicas of famous European buildings. This is, in a way, a realisation of Léopold's dream of recreating the World Tour he had seen at the Paris Exhibition, though he would have wanted the buildings to be exact replicas rather than one twenty-fifth of their true size. We can wander along winding paths that take us past the Sacré-Coeur in Paris and the Leaning Tower of Pisa, each building reproduced in fastidious detail. Not all of the details, I should add, are accurate. If we bend down to look at the miniature gothic inscription on the façade of Sienna's town hall, we may be disappinted to read: 'Made by Solarhome, Eindhoven, 1988.' Nor is our children's sense of geography much improved by seeing the miniature port of Barcelona next to a smouldering model of Vesuvius. Yet Mini Europe does occasionally mirror events in the real world: the fall of the Berlin Wall was soon followed by a little ceremony here in which a miniature model of the Wall was knocked down by a tiny crane. And each new country that joins the European Union is eventually represented by a miniature building in this park.

There are other odd buildings in this quarter, such as the Taverne Nadelo on the Avenue de l'Atomium (which occupies a futuristic building left over from the 1958 Fair), the twenty-three screen Kinepolis cinema complex, the Océade swimming pool, the King Baudouin football stadium, and a planetarium. Once we have seen enough, we can catch the metro back to the centre.

III. The Erasmus House.

Our next trip takes us west to Anderlecht, a former village which was swallowed up by Brussels in the 19th century. Anderlecht has an interesting late gothic church and a small Béguinage, but the main reason for coming here is to look around the Maison d'Erasme at Rue du Chapitre 31. We can reach the house (which is closed on Tuesdays and Fridays) by taking the metro to Saint Guidon. On leaving the station, we should look for the white spire of Saint Guidon and head in that general direction. After passing the brasserie In de Stad Brugge (not bad for lunch) we go straight ahead down Rue du Chapitre.

An old stone arch leads to a brick house in a garden. This was once the chapter house of the Saint Guidon church. Erasmus stayed here for five months in the summer of 1521 as the guest of his friend Pieter Wychman, a canon in Saint Guidon. The house grew into something of a

347

shrine to Erasmus, prompted by a visit here in 1691 by William III, Stadholder of the Netherlands and King of England, accompanied by the elderly Dutch diplomat Constantijn Huyghens. The Erasmus house was eventually bought by the local council in 1930 and opened as a museum.

Most of the building dates from 1515, as we can tell from the four iron numerals attached to a wall, though we enter by an older 15th-century building. Lovingly restored in the style of the Flemish renaissance, the house has leaded glass windows that shed a dusty golden light. Its rooms are furnished in renaissance style with heavy oak chests, gilded leather walls and paintings in the disturbing style of the Antwerp Mannerists. An *Adoration of the Magi* painted in about 1485 by Hieronymus Bosch (No. 236 in the collection) was moved here from Saint Guidon church.

The museum has an extensive collection of portraits of Erasmus (all copies), several curious portraits by 19th-century romantics, and some wonderful 20th-century ephemera such as banknotes, theatre posters and caricatures of Erasmus. His portrait even appears on a L.N.E.R. poster advertising railway excursions to Cambridge, where Erasmus spent several miserable months teaching theology and Greek. More surprising still, we can see the figure of Erasmus at the far right of a painting of *The Judgement of Solomon* by Frans Francken the Younger (No. 258).

Erasmus relished having his portrait painted by the great artists of his day, and was clearly piqued when Albrecht Dürer abandoned a portrait begun in 1520. 'I would like to have my portrait painted by Dürer,' he wrote to Willibald Pirckheimer in 1525, 'for who would not wish to be painted by such a great artist. He began by making a charcoal sketch in Brussels, but he claims to have lost it long ago.' Dürer and Erasmus met several times in Brussels and Antwerp in 1520 and 1521, but their opposing attitudes to the vexing question of Luther appear to have soured the relationship. Dürer's diary entry of 17 May 1521 included a hysterical outburst against Erasmus: 'O Erasmus of Rotterdam, where do you wish to stand?' he asked. 'Hark, ye knight of Christ, ride off with Christ our Lord at your side, defend the truth, grasp the martyr's palm.' Erasmus, quite sensibly, remained more sceptical about the claims of Luther, writing in a letter to Ulrich von Hutten, 'If Christ were to grant me the strength, then I would elect to be a martyr, but I would not want to be a martyr for Luther.'

Despite their differences, Dürer eventually produced this woodcut portrait of Erasmus in 1526, apparently using the sketch which he once claimed to have lost. The portrait (No. 123 in the collection) now hangs in the room known as Erasmus' Study, which is nothing less than a precise reconstruction of the room that Dürer drew. Dürer shows Erasmus sitting at his desk in the dead of winter, wearing three coats, one on top of the other, and a hat pulled down over his ears. It is so cold that Erasmus is holding the ink bottle in his left hand to prevent the ink from freezing. Dürer seems to have had some misgivings about this portrait, for he included an apologetic inscription in Greek: 'His works provide a better impression.' He also added –

this time in Latin – the untruthful assertion: 'Painted from nature'. Erasmus, too, was unimpressed with the final result, commenting laconically: 'Resemblance: none.' In a letter to Pirckheimer, he grumbled, 'It is hardly surprising that the portrait is not a better likeness, since I am not the same person that I was five years ago.'

We must not leave without exploring the garden, which used to contain nothing more than some fragments of local architecture, but was recently redesigned by René Pechère in a mediaeval style inspired by Flemish paintings such as Bouts' *Judgement of Emperor Otto* (reproduced on pages 132 and 133). If we stand in the far corner, we obtain a splendid view of the spire of Saint Guidon, our next destination.

On our way to the church, we might take a brief detour to look at the Béguinage, which we can visit free with our ticket from the Erasmus House. The tiny houses contain an enjoyable folklore collection, including religious relics, old bicycles, historic maps of Anderlecht and fragments of sculpture. We will also see some 19th

century photographs of the church which show the tower without the graceful white spire. Though designed in the 15th century by Jan van Ruysbroeck (the architect of the town hall spire on Grand'Place), it was not built until 1898.

Let us take a look inside, entering by a porch built in about 1350 and now looking somewhat dilapidated (though soon to be restored). The church is a vast, chilly Brabant gothic structure with faded murals, oil paintings, medieval tombs and carved reliefs. It is surprising to see Belgian First World War soldiers among the figures in several of the Stations of the Cross.

The chapel of Saint Guidon near the entrance was built by Matthijs Keldermans in late gothic style. It contains paintings of the *Life of Saint Guidon*, an obscure local pilgrim whose grave was the scene of various miracles, the last of which happened in 1112 when a cripple was healed. Saint Guidon is recognised locally as the patron saint of horses and cattle. The shrine we see here is a 19th-century work.

The one other thing to do in Anderlecht (apart from watching the famous local football team) is to walk down Rue Porselein (on our right on leaving the church). Several houses in this ancient lane have been given painted façades covered with poems. The view looking back down the street to the church spire is quite inspiring.

IV. Saint Boniface district. There is more interesting Art Nouveau in the district near the Eglise Saint Boniface. We begin at the Porte de Namur metro station and walk down the Chaussée d'Ixelles, then turn left down Rue Francart and right into Rue Saint Boniface. This street leads to the crumbling Eglise Saint Boniface, but before looking at the church, we should stop to admire the Art Nouveau house at No. 22, on the right side of the street. We can see Blérot's signature and the date 1900 carved on the stone to the left of the door. The date appears again in the sgraffito panel with twin girls above the door. The familiar flamboyant signature can also be spotted on two houses on the left side of the street, at Nos. 17 and 19. The first of these has kept its Art Nouveau door, which now forms

the entrance to Comptoir Florian, an elegant little coffee shop which serves coffee from Tuesday to Saturday, 11-5.

Blérot bought ten building plots in this neighbourhood to create a small Art Nouveau district that has survived almost intact. The corner shops at No. 15 and 20 are clearly Blérot's work, with their bay windows and Art Nouveau touches. If we turn right along Rue Solvay, we find three more of his houses at Nos. 12-16, each with its idiosyncratic details (such as the oriel windows on No. 12). In the opposite direction along Rue Solvay, we can spot another Blérot house at No. 22, dated 1900 and now in need of restoration. We have to look closely to find Blérot's signature on the house opposite, at No. 19, as it is hidden under the cornice, to the left of the sgraffito flower.

Continuing down Rue Saint Boniface, which leads to an appealing little square where the bust of Count Charles Woeste, with his striking Van Dyck beard, stands on a plinth surrounded by an adoring mother and two girls. The monument unfortunately fails to tell us anything about

Woeste, a conservative Catholic politician from Aalst who helped Léopold II in his Congo adventures. Woeste was a loud opponent of women's suffrage, which makes one wonder if the figure of the adoring woman is appropriate.

The Eglise Saint Boniface was built in 1847 by Joseph Dumont. It was the first neo-gothic church in Brussels, though this distinction has obviously not helped to save it from neglect. It contains beautiful confessionals, and Pre-Raphaelite-looking murals in the right transept painted in 1909 by Ernest Wanfe. We turn left on leaving the church to return to Chaussée d'Ixelles, where a bronze bust of Ernest Solvay stands on the far side of the road, looking much as he did in the photograph on page 88. His son Armand commissioned Horta to build the Art Nouveau mansion we saw on walk 8, but the father was more traditional in his architectural tastes.

Having explored the neighbourhood, we can sit on the terrace of L'Ultime Atome at 14 Rue Saint Boniface to admire the Blérot buildings opposite. Or we might succumb to the charms of Au Flan Breton tea room at 54 Chaussée d'Ixelles. It is very cramped downstairs, though this does not deter its regular customers. You will see women laden with shopping bags and the inevitable small dog squeezing through the narrowest gap to seize the last chair. The cakes are worth any amount of discomfort. The upstairs room is more spacious though less lively.

V. Art in the Metro. The enlightened Brussels public transport authority has commissioned dozens of Belgian artists to create works for its underground network, so that a trip on the metro is often enlivened by a chance encounter with modern art. The Bourse underground tram station has a large mural by Paul Delvaux titled *Our Old Brussels Trams* which shows several historic trams outside the old Woluwé depot (now a museum of public transport). Commuters are occasionally amused by Marc Mendelson's whimsical Pop Art mural titled *Happy Metro to You* at Parc station, though Roger Somville's 1976 mural *Our Times* at Hankar station is more likely to irritate people.

Travelling on line 1A out to Heysel, we can see eerie bronze figures by Paul van Hoeydonck suspended above the tracks at Comte de Flandre station. The strange spotlit statues we see as the train pulls out of Stuyvenbergh station were created by Yves Bosquet in memory of Queen Elisabeth, who lived in the nearby Château de Stuyvenbergh. Taking line 1B west to Bizet, we can step out at Aumale to look at several large photographs by Jean-Paul Laenen showing the neighbourhood during the construction of the metro. Arriving at Bizet, we will see a sculpture celebrating the French composer.

Line 1B heads east past a series of unusual stations, beginning with Vandervelde where Paul de Gobert decorated the entire station with a huge panorama showing the former view from the Groenenberg, a summit near the metro station, looking north along the Woluwé valley. The next station is Alma, where Lucien Kroll created a weird organic architecture composed of undulating walls and giant toadstools. This architecture blends perfectly with the nearby campus of the Université Catholique de Louvain-la-Neuve where Kroll built interesting organic architecture in the 1970's, including a student's residence inspired by the hill towns of Tuscany. Two stops further is Stockel, where an entire wall is decorated with figures from Tintin cartoons.

The transport authority is now renewing some of its older stations. The station at Maelbeek has been attractively redesigned by a team of architects working alongside a Belgian cartoonist. Anyone interested in knowing more can pick up a folder published by the transport authority which lists works of art in the network.

VI. Forest walks. One of the unexpected pleasures in Brussels is to step off a city tram and wander down a cobbled lane into the forest. Some parts of the forest can get crowded on a Sunday, but the more remote areas remain silent apart for the distant hoot of an owl. Trees first sank their roots into the clay-rich hills south of Brussels at the end of the ice age. The deep channels that run through the woods were scoured by glaciers as they moved slowly towards the Ardennes. Most of the ground has never been tilled, and so has remained virtually untouched for ten thousand years. The same cannot be said of the trees, which were originally a healthy mixture of beech, maple, ash, elm and rowan berry, but, following the way of ancient forests, are now almost all beech, and the forest is at its best in autumn.

Monks settled in the woods in the middle ages, building the monasteries at Groenendaal and Rouge-Cloître. Hidden away in a wooded hollow, the Abbaye du Rouge-Cloître was founded in the 14th century by Augustinian monks, and took its name from the reddish tint of its walls. The abbey church has gone and the walls are no longer red, but the priory, chapter house, farm and mill have survived. After a nervous breakdown, the great Flemish artist Hugo van der Goes spent the last five years of his life as a lay monk in the abbey. Tormented by a sense of failure, he attempted suicide in 1480 and died the following year.

The forest changed its appearance under the Austrian Hapsburgs when straight *drèves*, or drives, were created, and large areas of heathland planted with beech. The new style of forest management was the result of a dispute in the 1770's between the Forest Master, Count de Beughem de Capelle, and the Under Master of the Forest, Jean Charles Théodore de l'Escaille. The Count – a frail old man by then – hoped that his son would succeed him as Forest Master, but L'Escaille wanted the job for himself. The Austrians resolved the dispute in a not very satisfactory manner by putting Joachim Zinner in charge of reforestation. We may recall that Zinner was the Austrian landscape gardener who partly planned the layout of the Parc de Bruxelles. He proposed planting beeches along the *drèves* to create the appearance of a cathedral nave. Naturally, the formal courtly gardener soon came into conflict with the fiery-tempered L'Escaille, who favoured a natural planting, with a mixture of trees of different ages. As we can see the moment we enter the forest, the Austrian governors backed Zinner's plan, though the great storms of recent years have shown the wisdom of L'Escaille's more traditional approach.

It is something of a miracle that these woods still survive at all. Had it not been for the artist René Stevens and the burgomaster Charles Buls, the woods might now be paved over and dotted with suburban villas. Buls and Stevens led a group of forest lovers who in 1909 set up the League of Friends of the Forêt de Soignes. They managed to halt the destruction of the forest, though it took them fifty years of campaigning to persuade the Belgian government to classify the ancient forest, or what was left of it, as a protected nature reserve.

The Forêt de Soignes was once the domain of aristocrats and wood-cutters, but the 19th-century brought railway and tram stations. Many parts of the forest can now be reached from Brussels by public transport. The Abbaye de Rouge-Cloître is not far from the Hermann-Debroux metro station, while tram 44 gets us close to Tervuren Arboretum and Park. But the simplest route is to take tram 94 from Place Royale or Place Louise, getting off at the Coccinelles halt. Once across the road, we can follow the cobbled Drève du Comte to reach

the shady forest. Continuing down a sunken path, we come to a misty pond known as the Etang des Enfants Noyés, which has nothing to do with drowned children (*enfants noyés*) but is simply a careless translation of an old Dutch name.

Having cleared up that confusion, we turn left up a tarred road which curves gently around the hillside. On reaching a crossroads in the woods, we cross the Chemin des Deux Montagnes and plunge down into a valley. At the bottom of the path, we turn left along a sandy footpath called the Sentier du Vuilbeek which runs beside a small stream. After following this for about twenty minutes, we find ourselves back on the Chemin des Deux Montagnes. Turning right here, we go under the railway line and down a steep road, passing a locked gate that once led into the Parc Tournay-Solvay. At the bottom of the hill, we pass a house with a faded inscription. This was once a fashionable 19th-century *laiterie* where people stopped to drink a glass of milk on the terrace. We turn right here and follow the edge of the lake to reach the former village of Boitsfort. After crossing the Chaussée de la Hulpe we continue down Rue Middelbourg to reach the centre of Boitsfort. Here, we can end up in a café before catching tram 94 from the terminus across the road.

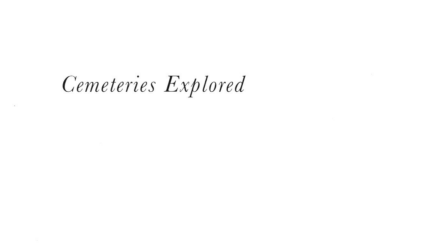

Cemeteries Explored

Cemeteries Explored

We might find it interesting to explore a few of the cemeteries in Brussels in search of familiar names of people we have met on our walks. The funeral monuments are often buildings in miniature, so we find examples of Flemish gothic, renaissance, neoclassical and even art nouveau. Most cemeteries tend to have a main avenue where former burgomasters and generals are commemorated by impressive tombs, while lesser mortals are relegated to side alleys. Some of the older cemeteries are enlivened by statues of mournful angels and weeping girls, such as the figure on page 366. As well as the four described here, the wistful old cemetery in Uccle (see page 300) is worth a visit. As a rule, cemeteries are open from about 8 am to 5 pm.

I. Laeken Cemetery. Not many people find the way to Laeken Cemetery, which stands in a forgotten corner of northern Brussels, next to the imposing, though woefully dilapidated, Eglise Notre-Dame de Laeken. The cemetery was begun during the period of Austrian rule at the end of the 18th century, but its most striking tombs were erected in the 19th century. King Léopold I built the Church of Notre Dame de Laeken in memory of his wife. The flamboyant neo-gothic church was designed by the young architect Joseph Poelaert, and consecrated in 1872, though it remained unfinished until 1949. The tombs of the former Belgian kings are now in the crypt, though the public rarely gets admitted.

We will need a good map to find this cemetery. The easiest approach is to take the metro to Bockstael station, named after a burgomaster buried in the cemetery. We then walk down Rue Léopold I, a drab back street flanked by railway cuttings, brick walls and scrapyards. Just when we are beginning to doubt that this could possibly lead to a royal cemetery, we see the monumental double gates next to the Salu workshop.

Enthusiasts of Laeken Cemetery like to compare it to Père Lachaise in Paris, where maps are sold at the gate to guide visitors to the tombs of the famous. But Laeken is uncharted, so we are left to wander at random, coming by chance upon ruinous gothic chapels with rusting wrought iron filials, miniature oriental mosques and even the occasional menhir hewn from solid rock. If we go down the main avenue, we pass several neo-gothic tombs with dusty stained glass windows. Many of these tombs, and others in the cemetery, were carved from 1872 onwards by the monumental sculptor Ernest Salu and his successors. Ernest Salu

finally designed his own tomb, which we find to the right of the main avenue, near a spot where five alleys meet. A white bust of the sculptor, with a neat beard framing his face, stands on top of a pedestal entwined with ivy.

A short avenue runs to the right just beyond the Salu tomb. This brings us to one of the grandest tombs in the cemetery, built in honour of Emile Bockstael, the burgomaster who turned Laeken from a Flemish village into a royal suburb. A marble bust of the elderly burgomaster sits under a large neoclassical arch carved in the Salu workshop. With his long, thick beard clipped like a shovel, Bockstael bears an uncanny resemblance to King Léopold II in his prime.

Joseph Poelaert is commemorated by a neoclassical tomb to the right of Bockstael. He died in 1879 while toiling to complete the Palais de Justice. The bust of Poelaert on the tomb has weathered badly, yet it is still possible to see signs of grief and despair in his drooping moustache, deeply-etched wrinkles and lank strands of hair. Just behind the Poelaert tomb, a black classical capital with a lyre on top catches our eye. Designed by Charles-Auguste Fraikin, it commemorates André van Hasselt, a 19th-century literary figure who died in 1874.

If we continue down the alley behind Poelaert then turn left, we come to a splendid tomb crowned by a group of three female figures representing Education. This was carved in 1864 by Albert Carrier-Belleuse, a prolific French sculptor who was living in Paris at this time. He came to Brussels in 1870 to work on the stock exchange, bringing his student Rodin with him. The statue here commemorates three women of the Ghémar family – Henriette, Sophie and Rosalie.

The architect Léon Suys, who drew up the plans for the Senne project, lies buried in the family tomb, which we find by returning down the alley we have just walked up until we come to a group of tombs in a circle. Suys himself designed the neo-baroque tomb, and it bears a vague resemblance to the large arches on his Bourse building of 1868-73. The figure in the medallion is his father Tilman, who built the Palace of the Academy, near the royal palace,

and planned the Léopold Quarter.

If we continue straight ahead and turn left along the next alley, we should find the tomb of Jef Dillen, a 19th-century art collector, near the disused eastern entrance. We can hardly miss the tomb, as it is surmounted by a version of Rodin's *Le Penseur* of 1904. If we look around the back, we can see the signature A. Rodin and the name of the Paris foundry that produced this copy. Rodin's own tomb in Meudon is surmounted by another version of *The Thinker*.

A weeping willow shades the splendid tomb of Maria Félicita Garcia, who lies buried near the remains of a 13th-century church. If we peer through the double bronze doors, we can perhaps make out the white statue carved by Guillaume Geefs, showing Maria singing the lead role in Bellini's *Norma*. Four lines by Alphonse de Lamartine are inscribed on the tomb, praising her beauty, genius and love. 'Weep, Earth! And you, Heaven, receive her,' the epitaph declares.

Maria was a famous Spanish opera singer who first sang in Naples in 1813 at the tender age of

five. Her voice, described by one critic as 'like the costliest gold', thrilled audiences at Covent Garden and La Scala for over a decade. Her life was almost as tempestuous as the Italian operas she sang. After a brief marriage to François Malibran in 1830, she remarried the Belgian violinist Charles de Bériot in 1836. A few days after the wedding, Maria (or La Malibran as she was fondly called) was thrown by a horse while riding in a London park. Struggling to conceal her injuries, she went on to sing in Drury Lane that evening. A few weeks later, while performing in Manchester, she collapsed on stage and died nine days later, aged twenty-eight. Her husband brought her body back to Brussels, burying her in this splendid domed tomb.

The Atelier Salu stands next to the cemetery entrance, looking, as this old photograph shows, much as it did when Ernest Salu worked there. Peering through the grimy windows, we can see inside a room that looks very much like a 19th-century artist's studio, with its white marble statues, potted ferns and gilt-framed mirrors.

This is an intriguing place, the more so because of a notice on the window, put up many years ago, announcing the imminent birth of The Museum of Funeral Art. When you ring the bell, the noise echoes through the empty hallway, and no one comes, suggesting that the Museum of Funeral Art may have quietly died. Yet there are still plans to open it one day, allowing us to wander around the dusty sculpture workshop where many of the tombs we have just seen were carved.

II. Brussels Cemetery. Brussels Cemetery, to the east of the old town, is a deeply romantic place, especially in the spring when the avenues are lined with pink cherry blossom trees. As we wander down the empty alleys, we sometimes notice statues like the one on page 366, showing a young woman grieving over a tomb. This is the city's biggest cemetery, where we find the tombs of 19th-century Congo explorers, soldiers who perished in various European wars and the occasional forgotten musician. We can reach the cemetery from Place de Brouckère on bus 66, or from Rond Point Schuman on bus 67, both of which terminate near the cemetery gate. A map next to the entrance indicates some of the important features, such as the Rond Point des Bourgmestres, where several mayors of Brussels are buried. Here, we find Jules Anspach, who created the grand boulevards, Charles Buls, whose efforts saved many of the city's historic buildings, and Adolphe Max, deported after he refused to obey the Germans in the First World War.

The most impressive monument lies in a quiet corner of the cemetery, at the the end of an avenue thick with pink cherry blossom in the spring. If we turn right down Avenue 8, we will find the huge Waterloo Monument unveiled by the elderly Queen Victoria in 1890. The bronze figure of Britannia stands above a mausoleum built to commemorate dead officers, who are described as 'emblems of Britannia's grief and pride'. Looking at the figure of Britannia, she seem to be more overcome with grief than pride, as she holds her helmet in one hand and her trident in the other. Fallen flags, plumed helmets, broken swords and tangled harnesses are strewn at her feet, while three sleepy British lions stand guard at the corners. Major General Sir Alexander Gordon is one of the officers buried here. Badly wounded during the battle, he was taken to the inn where Wellington had established his headquarters in Waterloo village. Gordon died in the night in a bed we will have seen if we visited the Wellington Museum.

The victims of other wars are also buried in Brussels Cemetery. A monument on the Rond-Point des Allemands commemorates German soldiers who died in Belgian hospitals during the Franco-Prussian War of 1870. On Avenue 9, a curious memorial erected by the French Circle of Brussels recalls the French soldiers, mostly in their twenties, who died in Belgium in 1870. Designed in a severe Egyptian style, the monument features a bronze sphinx crouched beneath an obelisk.

A plot near the back of the cemetery, signed *Pelouse 10*, is tended by the gardeners of the Commonwealth War Graves Commission. It contains the tombs of Second World War airmen shot down over Belgium. Another plot has the graves of Germans who died in Brussels in the First World War. The sombre grey tombstones are each carved with several names, many listed as volunteers or reservists. Elsewhere, a hedge conceals a plot containing the graves of eighteen Belgians shot by the Germans in the First World War. An Art Deco relief shows a man baring his chest to the firing squad as women hold garlands.

The Demi Rond-Point Bischoffsheim is named after a German banker whose monument stands on this crescent. We also find this tomb of Alexandre Delcommune, looking very jaunty in an explorer's felt hat. Delcommune, who came from Namur, spent twenty years mapping the remote regions of the Belgian Congo on behalf of Léopold II. On one of his expeditions to Katanga in 1890, he was to have been taken upriver on a steamboat commanded by Joseph Conrad. But Conrad fell out with Alexandre's irascible brother Camille, the station manager in Kinshasa. After a wretched journey on a derelict steamer, Conrad returned to London in disgust.

One of the distinguished people on the

Rond-Point des Bourgmestres was not a burgomaster. He was not even Belgian. A tall obelisk commemorates the French painter Jacques-Louis David, whose painting of Marat murdered in his bath we may have already seen in the Musées des Beaux-Arts. David had sided with the Revoutionaries in 1789, voting for the execution of Louis XVI. After the final defeat of his hero, Napoleon, he exiled himself in Brussels, living with his wife in a grand town house that is still standing (but only just) at Rue Léopold 5. David was obviously considered an important artist when he died in 1825, earning himself a place next to the burgomasters. The French government occasionally requests the return of David's bones, but the Belgian authorites inevitably give some wily reason for refusing.

Not far from here, we find a cluster of British graves to the left of the main alley on the enclosure *Pelouse 17*. One of the tombs belongs to Evan Jenkins, the Anglican minister in Brussels who invited Charlotte and Emily Brontë to Sunday lunches. He was originally buried in the Protestant cemetery, but the tomb was moved here when the old cemetery closed.

We have to search along *Chemin 25* for the tomb of Paulette Verdoodt, a Belgian singer buried under a curious tomb decorated with a sphinx. A bronze relief and a mounted sepia photograph are all we have to remind us of this beautiful singer who once enchanted audiences with her voice. Perhaps the inscription in hieroglyphics would tell us more.

III. Ixelles Cemetery. The cemetery in Ixelles, not far from the university, is a wonderful romantic graveyard where we find artists, musicians and generals buried. The tombs reflect the range of architectural styles popular in 19th-century Ixelles, including splendid examples of neoclassical, gothic, romanesque, art nouveau and even oriental styles. Some tombs have weeping maidens offering consolation to the dead, but my favourite statue is this bronze figure about to snip a thread with his scissors.

We can take bus 71 to the Cimetière d'Ixelles. The cemetery is located in a lively student quarter, surrounded by cafés, restaurants and florists.

Before going inside, we might stop for a coffee at the Pain Quotidien opposite the gates at Chaussée de Boondael 479, where students sit sipping coffee and discussing comic strips. We enter the cemetery through an impressive neoclassical gate, then head down a leafy avenue shaded by yews and pines. On reaching a roundabout, we turn down Avenue 3. The names of the avenues are marked on Ixelles street signs, which gives the cemetery a curious residential air. Like the *commune*, the cemetery has its grand boulevards and roundabouts, its quiet lanes and crowded neighbourhoods.

It even has its own history. If we continue down Avenue 1, past the man snipping a thread, we come to a tomb on the left inscribed with the words *Marguerite à bientôt*. At noon on 30 September 1891, an event occurred here that shocked all of Brussels. Georges Boulanger, a French general who had fled here after an aborted coup, entered the cemetery accompanied by his secretary and another friend. The party walked straight ahead down Avenue 3 until they reached this tomb, where Marguerite de Bonnemain, the general's thirty-six year old mistress, had been buried ten weeks earlier. After asking his two friends to leave him for a moment, the broken-hearted general sat down behind Marguerite's tomb, took out his army pistol and shot himself in the head. His own tomb, next to Marguerite's, is inscribed *Georges*, followed by a phrase from his suicide note: 'Marguerite, how could I have lived two and a half months without you?'

If we now turn left, we can walk up Avenue 17 to look for Victor Horta's sober tomb (on the left near a second roundabout). Yet we are more likely to notice the grandiose military tombs assembled around the roundabout, commemorating officers and soldiers who died in the First World War. The largest tomb is that of Charles Foulon, a young doctor killed by a shell in 1917 while he was dressing wounds in the trenches. We can see reliefs of battle scenes on the outside of the monument, and a stained glass window with a portrait of Foulon inside the chapel.

If we go back along Avenue 1, we pass the tomb of Charles de Coster who found fame as the author of *La Légende d'Uilenspiegel*. The tomb is decorated with a statue of Till Eulenspiegel, the Flemish folk hero who wandered through 16th-century Flanders seeking to avenge the death of his father, burnt at the stake as a heretic.

If we turn right into Pelouse S, we may be able to find the rugged red sandstone tomb of the sculptor Constantin Meunier and his wife. Back at the main roundabout, we can walk down Avenue 5 to look at the tomb of Antoine Wiertz, a modest stone slab commemorating the artist who thought of himself as a second Rubens. The Solvay family are buried not far away, in Pelouse W, under an Art Nouveau tomb designed by Victor Horta. Once we are back at the round-about again, we should turn down Avenue 1 to look at the strange white tombstone on the left which marks the grave of the surrealist Marcel Broodthaers, who died in Cologne in 1976 on his fifty-second birthday. The tomb is inscribed with an elegant calligraphy reminiscent of Broodthaers' mock museum labels. 'O melancholy jagged castle of eagles,' the inscription reads. The back of the tombstone is decorated

with enigmatic symbols that look like Eygptian hieroglyphics. The wine bottle dated 1924 makes sense – Broodthaers was born in 1924 – and the pipe was a favourite motif, but what are we to make of the tortoise, mathematical symbols, book and bird? Or the motto, in a mixture of Dutch and French – *Chez le droguiste op den hoek* (at the chemist on the corner). In death, as in life, Broodthaers leaves us baffled.

IV. The Enclos des Fusillés. A cobbled lane near the Belgian broadcasting tower leads to the hidden Tir National, a former firing range where Edith Cavell was executed in 1915. The British nurse, then forty-nine years old, had been arrested by the Germans on August 5, accused of helping Allied soldiers to escape to the Netherlands. She pleaded guilty and was taken to Saint Gilles prison, a curious English gothic building, to await execution. Despite protests from Britain and America, Cavell was driven to this deserted spot at dawn on October 12. She was forced to watch Philippe Baucq, a Belgian architect, die in a hail of bullets, before

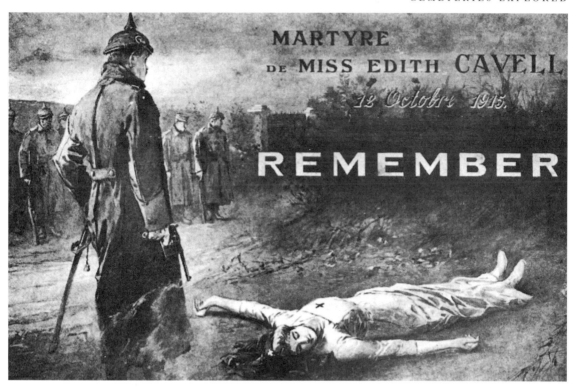

being led to the wooden execution post. Prim to the last, she asked for some pins to tie her dress tightly around her ankles. She was struck by four bullets, though a false story was spread that the firing squad had fired over her head, causing her to faint with shock, and forcing the officer in charge to shoot her in the head. No such thing ever happened, but it made excellent propaganda for the Allies.

The Germans had committed atrocities from the moment they invaded Belgium. They shot six villagers and set fire to Battice on 4 August 1914, torched the historic town of Leuven on 25 August and used poison gas for the first time in warfare on 22 April 1915. But the volley of shots fired at dawn on 12 October touched a raw nerve among the Allies. Young British and French soldiers rushed to enlist after reading newspaper accounts of the execution or seeing posters such as the one on page 371, printed in France, which helped to popularise the false story of the German officer who shot her with his revolver.

Edith Cavell's body was taken back to London in 1919 for a state funeral. An impressive monument was erected near the National Gallery, and a hospital in Uccle was named in her honour.

The Enclos des Fusillés is not an easy place to find. The enclosed cemetery lies hidden behind a hedge off the Rue Colonel Bourg, about ten minutes on foot from the Diamant metro station. The strangely silent enclosure contains three hundred and forty-two concrete crosses in memory of soldiers and civilians shot by the Germans in 1914-18 and 1940-45. Edith Cavell is commemorated by cross number 4. Cross number 11 is dedicated to Gabrielle Petit, a Belgian woman shot at dawn on 1 April 1916. 'I'll show them that a Belgian woman knows how to die,' she declared before her execution.

Appendices

Brussels for Children

Any suggestion of a trip to Brussels may meet with opposition from children, but you must tell them about the wonderful parks, the two children's museums, the puppet theatres, the dinosaur museum and, if all else fails, the Italian ice cream shops (such as Il Gelato at Rue Vanderkindere 168). But begin with the parks. The most convenient is the Parc de Bruxelles, a large formal park in the Upper Town where your children can rub along with half a dozen different nationalities while you sit in the shade reading *Villette*. Should the playground fail to appeal, you might encourage them to hunt in the park for the 18th-century statue of a dog, which should keep them occupied for half a hour.

Then there is the Bois de la Cambre, where they can go roller skating and buy an Italian ice cream at the Il Gelato stand (near the children's playground). If we take tram 93 or 94 from outside the Parc de Bruxelles, we can get off at the Legrand stop near the entrance to the Bois. Or we can take tram 91 or 92 to reach the Parc de Wolvendael (getting off at the Square des Héros stop). The old-fashioned playground at the top of the hill makes a small charge for children (and expects adults to buy a drink), but it keeps them amused with its swing boats, wooden pirate ship and screaming miniature racing cars.

It is worth pointing out that Brussels has not one, but two children's museums. The Musée des Enfants at Rue du Bourgmestre 15 puts on fascinating temporary exhibitions that allow children to touch objects, daub paint on paper and generally run riot for an afternoon. The quaint Musée du Jouet at Rue de l'Association 24 occupies a cavernous town house which is slowly filling up with a nostalgic collection of rusted train sets, battered dolls and dented pedal cars. Nor can any conscientious parent miss the opportunity offered for dinosaur spotting. The Musée de l'Institut Royal des Sciences Naturelles may sound dull (Belgian museums always do), but it owns a spectacular collection of dinosaurs, both genuine skeletons and growling mechanical models. It also has whale skeletons, mock prehistoric caves and (I will leave you guessing on this one) an intriguing staircase.

A half-hour metro ride gets you to Bruparck, where you can take your children to the Atomium, more for the long metal escalators than the dullish exhibition. After that, they can be edified by a visit to Mini Europe, a theme park crammed with scale models of famous Europe buildings reproduced in astonishing detail. There are also cafés, a playground and an old-fashioned fairground carousel.

I have not mentioned the Centre Belge des Bandes Dessinées, as I half suspect that this comic book museum is really intended for nostalgic adults rather than lively children. It does, though, have a well-stocked library where children can sprawl on cushions reading Lucky Luke in French, so perhaps I have misjudged it. The museum is certainly worth a visit for its Art Nouveau interior, not to mention the well-

stocked souvenir shop. Children are allowed to touch some of the objects and enter stage sets based on famous cartoons. The occasional yelp tends to be tolerated by the guards.

Young children might be persuaded to look at the paintings in the Musées des Beaux-Arts, particularly if the visit can be turned into an adventure. They might enjoy a tour, for example, that concentrated on paintings depicting children. There are plenty of examples, such as the girl reading a book upside down in the Metsys altarpiece in Room 22, the sad 16th-century painting of a girl holding a dead bird in Room 25, and the baby whose mother is wiping his bottom in Jacob Jordaens' earthy *The King Drinks* in Room 57. It would be wonderful if we could offer our children Pieter Bruegel the Elder's *Children's Games*, but that delightful painting was carted off to Vienna when the Austrian Hapsburgs ruled the region. We are left only with the children fighting in the mud in Pieter Brueghel the Younger's *Flemish Fair* on p. 375.

Tourist Information

I. Brussels. The city tourist office is in the gothic town hall on Grand'Place, tel. 02.513.89.40. The Belgian tourist office at Rue Marché-aux-Herbes 61 is often less crowded, and gives information on Tervuren, Waterloo, Bruges and other Belgian destinations.

II. Waterloo. The Waterloo tourist office is next to the Wellington Museum, at Chaussée de Bruxelles 218, tel. 02.354.99.10. It has much to offer the battlefield pilgrim. A trip to Waterloo was somewhat easier in the 19th century than it is nowadays (unless you have a car). A local bus (the W) leaves regularly from Place Rouppe in Brussels, stopping in Waterloo and at the Waterloo-Gordon crossroads on the edge of the battlefield. The return journey is more complicated. A coach tour is simpler, and is likely to include a visit to Gaasbeek Castle, a handsome renaissance château with beautiful gardens; but this means that time at the battle-field is strictly limited. A more satisfactory option, probably, is to rent a car for the day, driving out to Waterloo town on the Chaussée de Waterloo and then taking the N5 in the direction of Charleroi to reach the battlefield.

III. Tervuren. The Tervuren tourist office can be called on 02.769.20.81. Tervuren can be conveniently reached by taking tram 44 from Montgomery metro station.

IV. Before you leave. The Belgian tourist office in London is now two separate organisations. The Brussels-Flanders office (tel. 020 7458 0044) provides information on Brussels and Flanders Region, while the Brussels-Ardennes office (te. 020 7458 2888) covers Brussels (again) and Wallonia. Both are at 31 Pepper Street, London E14 9RW. The Belgian tourist office in New York, as yet undivided, is at 780 Third Avenue, Suite 1501, New York N.Y. 10017 (tel 212 758 81 30).

V. Getting there and getting around. Brussels is now served by an excellent network of high-speed trains that stop at Gare du Midi. Eurostar trains run from London Waterloo to Brussels in 2 hours 40 minutes. Thalys trains travel to Brussels from the Gare du Nord in Paris in 1 hour 25 minutes. Slower Thalys services also run from Amsterdam in 2 hours 39 minutes and from Cologne in 2 hours 32 minutes. On arrival at the Gare du Midi, the simplest way to reach the centre is by changing onto a train travelling in the direction of Gare Centrale. You can also take one of the underground trams (Nos. 3, 55 or 90) to the Bourse station for Grand Place, or to Rogier station if your hotel is on Place Rogier. The Upper Town can be reached by taking the metro three stops to Place Louise. If you arrive at Brussels airport, take the airport train into Brussels. Get off at Gare Centrale for Grand'Place and the centre, or continue to Gare du Midi to change onto the metro for the Upper Town.

The transport ticket system is simple to use. You can buy a ticket for one journey from a bus or tram driver, or a magnetic card valid for ten journeys at metro stations or newsagents displaying a public transport sticker. You must remember to insert the card in one of the orange machines located at the entrance to metro stations or inside the tram or bus. The ticket is valid for an hour's travel on the public transport network, but you must insert it each time you change vehicles. The machine then reads the magnetic strip and stamps the ticket if required. The trip to Tervuren on tram 44 is not covered by the ten-strip ticket. You should buy a single ticket from the driver.

The 19th-century tram network has fortunately survived unscathed despite the unhealthy obsession with the motor car in the 1960's and 1970's. We can still take a tram (No. 93 or 94) down the grand Avenue Louise to get out to the Bois de la Cambre, or travel down Avenue Brugmann (No. 90 or 91) to admire the harmonious 19th-century architecture. A tram will take us to the Japanese Pagoda (No. 92) or the Forêt de Soignes (No. 94), but the most extraordinary tram ride (No. 44) runs through the beech woods to the Africa Museum at Tervuren.

Opening Times of Museums and Churches

Most museums in Brussels are closed on Mondays and on public holidays (January 1, May 1, November 1 and 11, and December 25). All but a few museums charge for entry, but the Musées Royaux des Beaux-Arts and the Musée du Cinquantenaire are open free on the first Wednesday of the month from 1-5.

I. The old town. The national art collection is found in the **Musées Royaux des Beaux-Arts** at Rue de la Régence 3. The Old Masters, such as Bruegel and Rubens, hang in the **Musée d'Art Ancien**, while modern artists such as Magritte and Ensor are found in the **Musée d'Art Moderne**. Both museums are open Tuesday to Sunday 10-5. The Ancient Art and 19th-century rooms are closed 12-1 while the 17th-century and Modern Art collections are closed 1-2. The museum shop and café stay open without a break. The **Musée de la Ville de Bruxelles** on Grand'Place is open Monday to Friday 10-5 (closes one hour earlier October to March), Saturday and Sunday 10-1. The comic book collection in the **Centre Belge de la Bande Dessinnée** at Rue des Sables 20 can be seen Tuesday to Sunday 10-6. The **Musée de la Dynastie** is open Tuesday to Sunday 10-4.

II. The Museum Park. The three major museums located in the Cinquantenaire Park are best reached by taking the metro to Mérode. The **Musée du Cinquantenaire** is open Tuesday to Friday 9.30-5, Saturday and Sunday 10-5. The **Musée Royal de l'Armée** is open Tuesday to Sunday 9-12 and 1-4.30. The vintage car collection in Autoworld is open April to September, daily 10-6, October to March, daily 10-5.

III. Other museums. The **Musée Communale d'Ixelles** at Rue Jean van Volsem 71 is open Tuesday to Friday 1-7, Saturday and Sunday 10-5. The **Musée Horta** at Rue

Américaine 25 is open Tuesday to Sunday 2-5.30 and the nearby **Contretype photograph gallery** in the Hôtel Hannon at Avenue de la Jonction 1 is open Wednesday to Friday 11-6, Saturday and Sunday 1-6, making it feasible to visit both of these Art Nouveau buildings at the same time. The **Musée Constantin Meunier** at Rue de l'Abbaye and **Musée Wiertz** at Rue Vautier 62 are open Tuesday to Sunday 10-12 and 1-5, but close every second weekend. The **Tour Japonaise** and the **Pavillon Chinois** (facing each other on Avenue Van Praet and best reached by taking tram 92 to Araucaria) are open Tuesday to Sunday 10-4.45. The **Maison d'Erasme** at Rue Chapitre 31, and the **Béguinage** are open Saturday, Sunday, Monday, Wednesday and Thursday 10-12, 2-5. One ticket is valid for both museums. The **Musée David et Alice Van Buuren** is open Sunday 1-6 and Monday 2-6, closed 25 December to 1 January. The **Musée Charlier** at Avenue des Arts 16 is open Monday to Thursday 1.30-5, Friday 1.30-4.30. The **Musée Magritte** at Rue Essegem 135 is open Wednesday to Sunday 10-6. A maximum of 20 visitors at any time. **Album** at Rue des Chartroux 25 is open Thursday to Tuesday 1-6. The **Lift Museum** in the Rue de la Source, is open Tuesday and Thursday 2-5.

IV. Churches. The **Cathédrale St Michel et St Gudule** is open 7-6 except during services. The **Eglise Notre-Dame du Sablon** is open 9-6. The **Eglise St Nicolas** is open Monday to Friday 7.30-6.30, Saturday 9-5.30, Sunday 7.30 am-7.30 pm. The **Eglise de la Chapelle** is open daily 1-4, but closed on public holidays. The **Chapelle de Nassau**, inside the Bibliothèque Royale Albert I and now used for exhibitions, is open Monday to Saturday 12-5. The **Eglise St Guidon**, Anderlecht, is open 9-12 and 2.30-6 (closing an hour early in winter). It is closed on Sunday afternoons and public holidays.

VI. Further sights. The **Atomium** on the Boulevard du Centenaire, near Heysel metro station, is open every day of the year, April to

August 9-8, September to March 10-6. The **archaeological site** on Place Royale is open on Wednesday and Saturday 1-5 and Sunday 10-2. Visitors by guided tour only.

VI. Waterloo. The **Musée Wellington** at Chaussée de Bruxelles 147 is open every day, April to October 9.30-6.30, November to March 10.30-5. The **Lion Mound**, the **Visitors' Centre** and the **Panorama**, all on the battle-field south of the town, are open every day, April to October 9.30-6.30, November to March 10.30-4.

VII. Tervuren. The **Africa Museum** is open Tuesday to Sunday, April to mid-October 9-5.30, mid-October to March 10-4.30. The **Congo Pavilion** is used for functions and is not normally open to the public.

Choosing an Hotel

We have to decide between an hotel in the Lower Town (lively and close to Grand'Place) or one in the Upper Town (quieter and convenient for the parks). A few grand hotels have survived such as the Métropole and the Astoria, but most are modern buildings constructed in the past forty years. Hoteliers in Brussels can normally fill their rooms from Monday to Thursday with conference delegates, interpreters, lobbyists and journalists, but many are virtually empty from check-out time on Friday until Sunday evening or even Monday. The larger hotels can also be deserted during July and August, and for a couple of weeks around Christmas, forcing many to cut their prices dramatically. Some of the small family hotels have also begun to offer reductions, making Brussels one of the cheapest cities in Europe for a weekend break.

I. A room in the Lower Town. Hotels in the Lower Town are close to Gare Centrale, Grand' Place and the Musée des Beaux-Arts. You will find excellent restaurants, shopping arcades, bars and cinemas in the neighbourhood.

Amigo, Rue Amigo 1. Tel. 02.547.47.47. The aristocratic air and antique furnishings suggest an old hotel, but the Amigo was in fact opened in 1958 to accommodate visitors to the World Fair. The hotel takes its name from an old prison on this site built by the Spanish governors. The entrance lobby is paved with red bricks and gray stones that blend in with the older buildings nearby from the Spanish period. Bedrooms are spacious and elegant, with carefully-chosen antiques and 19th-century Belgian paintings. Each room is different and regular guests tend to develop a fondness for a particular number. My own choice would be a room on the sixth floor at the front of the hotel, with a balcony looking out on the gothic town hall. (171 rooms)

Crowne Plaza, formerly **Palace**, Rue Gineste 3. Tel. 02.217.62.00. The Palace, built in 1908, was one of the great European hotels of the 1920's, when it was a favourite with film stars such as Orson Welles and Grace Kelly. It fell on hard times in the 1970's and was almost demolished. But times have changed and its urban location is now highly desirable. The building has been restored to its original state and some rooms retain their old furniture, including the bed in Room 150 where Princess Grace spent a night in the 1950's. (360 rooms). Now part of the Six Continents hotel group.

La Madeleine, Rue de la Montagne 20-22. Tel. 02.513 29 73. A cheerful hotel occupying two neo-baroque houses. The location is ideal (near Gare Centrale and Grand'Place), though its rooms are small. Those with a car should park in the nearby Agora underground garage, but be sure to remember the floor number to avoid a harrowing hunt. Brontë readers might be interested to note that the Madeleine is not far from the site of the Hôtel Hollande where Charlotte and Emily spent their first night in Brussels. It is also a few doors down from the site of an hotel where Baudelaire stayed. (55 rooms)

Métropole, Place de Brouckère 31. Tel. 02.217.23.00. This grand hotel on the lower boulevards was built in 1894-5 by Alban Chambon. A splendid relic of the Belle Epoque, it is decorated with brown Tunisian marble, stained glass windows and gilt chandeliers. Little has changed since Sarah Bernhardt and Albert Einstein stayed here in the early years of the century. The splendid iron lift – made by the same company as those in the Eiffel Tower – still carries guests to the upper floors. For all its polished brass and smart doormen, the Métropole has a slight air of declining grandeur. The bedrooms, though undoubtedly large, are furnished in a rather dated 1950's style. (400 rooms)

New Siru, Place Rogier 1. Tel. 02.217.75.80. This Art Deco hotel from the 1930's claims to be the world's first art hotel. The corridors and bedrooms were decorated in 1989 with original works of art by contemporary Belgian artists. You can sleep in a room with four granite rocks suspended above the bed (No. 211) or ask for one with two arrows embedded in the ceiling

(No. 513). Some of the rooms are quite small, but those in the corner tower such as Nos. 208 and 408 are more spacious. The hotel bakes its own bread for breakfast and has an excellent brasserie. (101 rooms)

Noga, Rue du Béguinage 42. Tel. 02.218 67 63. A friendly hotel in a quiet street near the Eglise du Béguinage. The walls are hung with faded photographs, including a curious picture in the entrance hall of three Belgian maids. Rates are lower at the weekend.

Welcome, Rue du Peuplier 5. Tel. 02.219 95 46. Probably the smallest hotel in Brussels, with comfortable bedrooms and an intimate breakfast room filled with flowers. It has friendly owners and a seductive location near the Place Sainte Catherine. (6 rooms)

II. A room in the Upper Town. The Upper Town tends to be quieter than the Lower Town, yet there are still enough excellent restaurants and cafés to detain us here. Most journeys from here involve trams rather than the metro.

De Boeck's, Rue Veydt 40. Tel. 02.537 40 33. A handsome 19th-century mansion with large rooms and high ceilings. A family-run hotel with an old-fashioned reading room. It is located near Avenue Louise in a district dotted with Art Nouveau architecture.

Lloyd George, Avenue Lloyd George 12. Tel. 02.648.30.72. A small and inexpensive hotel located in a Brussels town house facing the romantic Bois de la Cambre. Breakfast is served in an attractive café which also functions as a restaurant. Popular with academics and students, it is ideally located for the Université Libre des Bruxelles, rambles in the woods and Sunday strolls around the Abbaye de la Cambre.

Manos Stéphanie, Chaussée de Charleroi 28. Tel. 02.539.02.50. A comfortable hotel furnished with rococo desks and Italian fabrics. The owners (who also run the nearby Manos Hotel) take immense care on interior design and floral arrangements. Rooms are no more expensive than in many dull business hotels. (48 rooms)

Rembrandt, Rue de la Concorde 42. Tel. 02.512.71.39. A small hotel located in a pink 19th-century corner house near Avenue Louise.

The bedrooms are small, but tastefully decorated with old furniture, paintings and vases of flowers. Worth asking if Room 6 is available when you book.

Les Tourelles, Avenue Winston Churchill 135. Tel. 02.344.02.84. An old-fashioned hotel located in a quaint building with half timbering and turrets that looks as if it belongs in Deauville. It was once a girls' boarding school, and it still has something of the air of Madame Beck's *Pensionnat*. Its creaky wooden staircases and assortment of antique furniture give it a period charm unlike any other Brussels hotel, though some may be vexed by the lack of a lift and the policy of not accepting credit cards. My favourite room is No. 7, a two-room suite facing the romantic garden. (21 rooms)

Food and Beer of Brussels

Where do we begin? We can experience some of the finest cooking in Europe, or settle for a simple local tavern serving steak and *frites* with a glass of beer. Brussels at the last count had more than two thousand restaurants, many of them located in the warren of medieval lanes around Grand'Place and Place Sainte Cathérine. The people of Brussels have been eating well since the middle ages, when the guilds controlled the quality of meat and fish. A love of good food is reflected in the works of Flemish artists from Pieter Bruegel the Elder to James Ensor. Bruegel's scenes of wedding feasts show peasants revelling in the pleasures of country food and strong ale, while this painting by Frans Snijders tempts us with a feast of roast game, ripe fruit and hunks of salmon. A Dutch artist could never have painted such a scene without adding a moral warning, such as a spilt glass to symbolise mortality, or a slice of lemon as a reminder that appearances can be deceptive, but the Flemish tradition admits to no such fears. The message is one of pure and boundless enjoyment.

This pleasure-seeking tradition remains robust in Brussels, so we stand a good chance of eating well during our stay. We can hunt for fresh croissants in a café, sample a Vietnamese snack at a market stall, dive into a cake shop on a rainy afternoon or spend an entire evening in a gastronomic restaurant. Even a battered stand on a market square can be counted on to provide perfect *frites* – fried twice so that they are crisp on the outside and fluffy inside. When the need arises, we can head down to Place Sainte Catherine to eat a portion sitting on a wooden bench under the crumbling exterior of Poelaert's sad church, or go further afield to Chez Marius or Maison Antoine (described below).

The extraordinary beer culture in Belgium is slowly becoming known outside the country. In the past, local beers were hardly drunk outside

the village or town where they were brewed, and the only Belgian beer served abroad was Stella Artois. A few of the more distinctive brews are now being marketed in Britain and America, such as Hoegaarden and Leffe, though there remain hundreds of old-fashioned Belgian ales produced in traditional breweries and sold in the local taverns.

Brussels has its own unique beer known as lambic, which forms the base of Gueuze, Faro, Kriek and Framboise. Lambic, which has a distinctively tart, flat taste, is fermented in large open tanks by microbes found only in the Senne valley. Gueuze is made from lambic that is left to mature in wooden barrels for three years, Kriek is flavoured with Schaerbeek cherries, Framboise has raspberries added, while Faro is a low alcohol brew with sugar added which is sometimes given to Belgian children. The city once had fifty Gueuze breweries, but the only surviving example is the Cantillon brewery at Rue Gheude 56 in Anderlecht. We can visit this wonderfully old-fashioned institution to watch the beer being brewed and bottled using equip-ment installed in the 1930's, then sample a glass of the finished product poured by the genial owner.

There are six hundred other beers in Belgium, and each café will have its own list of speciali-ties. It is no simple matter running a café in Belgium, for you need to keep different glasses for the various beers. The lovely Duvel comes in a large brandy glass, Gordon's sweetish Scotch Ale is served in a thistle-shaped glass and Kwak is poured into a stirrup-cup which has to be supported on a wooden stand.

Where to eat
Amadeus, Rue Veydt 13. Tel. 02.538.34.27. Closed Monday lunch. A former industrial build-ing once occupied by artists' studios, Amadeus has been decorated with enormous flair to create a fashionable restaurant and wine bar. The vast brick-paved interior is decorated with statues and mirrors. The food is not outstanding, but the spare ribs are perfectly acceptable. Worth a visit simply to drink a glass of wine in the dark candlelit bar.

Antoine, Place Jourdan. Antoine has been frying *frites* the way Belgians like them since the 1950's. His stall is on a square near the European Quarter, and so his customers are an interesting mixture of Danish translators, Irish journalists and displaced locals who drive back to their old haunt for the sake of Antoine's *frites*. The ritual is fascinating to observe. Antoine (or one of his assistants) scoops a few *frites* into a paper cone, adds some salt, shouts *bonjour* to a lady trailing a dog in a knitted coat, folds a larger sheet of paper into a cone, shouts to a man coming out of the hardware shop across the street, adds some more *frites* and salt, and so on until the process is complete.

Aux Armes de Bruxelles, Rue des Bouchers 13. Tel. 02.511.55.50. A traditional Brussels restaurant which has been run by the Veulemans family since 1921. The interior is furnished in comfortable brasserie style with wooden partitions and large mirrors. The *waterzooi* is outstanding.

Aux Beaumes de Venise, Rue Darwin 62. Tel. 02.343.82.93. An attractive brasserie off Place Brugmann with bare wooden floors, potted ferns and the merest murmur of background music. The kitchen produces delicious French cooking accompanied by generous helpings of vegetables. A good place to end up after looking at Art Nouveau architecture in St Gilles and Ixelles. Closed Saturday lunch and Sunday. Take tram 91 or 92 to Darwin.

Belgo Belge, Rue de la Paix 22. Tel. 02.511.11.21. A modern brasserie in the fashionable St Boniface quarter, with painted high ceilings and inventive lighting. The cooking is traditional Belgian style but with touches of creativity, such as sausages served with three interpretations of stoemp (mashed potatoes and carrots). The atmosphere is lively and surprisingly noisy. It could almost be London.

Bonsoir Clara, Rue Dansaert 22. Tel. 02.502.09.90. A fashionably bare restaurant with zinc tables crammed into two rooms. Interesting Mediterranean cooking and unusual wines make this one of the most popular new restaurants in the Lower Town.

Chaochow City, Boulevard Anspach 89. Tel.

02.512.82.83. A big, noisy Chinese restaurant near the Bourse where you can eat a dish of the day in the snack bar. The service is so rapid that your food is on the table before you have taken off your coat. You can have a more leisurely meal in the large restaurant at the back, where noisy groups of Chinese come to celebrate weddings.

Comme Chez Soi, Place Rouppe 23. Tel. 02. 512.29.21. Pierre Wynants has turned a former *estaminet* run by his grandfather into a world-famous restaurant. Serious diners book months in advance for the chance to sample Wynants' hot oysters with *chicons* and diced bacon, or his sole in a frothy Riesling sauce. The waiters are trained to follow a serious ritual, which includes returning to your table with a saucepan to offer a second helping. Yet the mood is relaxed and Wynants likes to stroll around the restaurant chatting with his customers as they sip their coffee. The Art Nouveau interior was added as a hommage to Horta.

L'Eperon d'Or, Rue des Eperonniers 8. Tel. 02.513.97.67. An intimate restaurant located in a 16th-century house near Grand'Place. The restaurant has an old-fashioned Belgian charm, and offers local specialities such as veal kidneys in Leffe beer, and tomatoes filled with snails and wild mushrooms.

Fils de Jules, Rue du Page 35. Tel. 02. 534.00.57. A modern Ixelles restaurant with unusual Basque dishes served by the tallest waitresses in town. The author has never tasted anything quite so delicious as the *chipirones* (fried squid).

Gallery Resto-Bar, Rue du Grand Cerf 7. Tel. 02.511.80.35. An airy modern restaurant offering delicious Vietnamese dishes such as dim sum and chicken in coconut. Inexpensive and friendly, it makes an ideal place for a late meal. Close to the cinemas on Avenue Toison d'Or and open every day except Monday until midnight.

Brasserie Horta, Rue des Sables 20. Tel. 02. 217.72.72. Open Tuesday to Sunday 10-6. An airy brasserie on the ground floor of an Art Nouveau department store designed by Horta. Linked to the Belgian Comic Book Museum, it offers traditional Belgian brasserie dishes such as *stoemp* and shrimp croquettes. A good place to take children.

Intermezzo, Rue des Princes 16. Tel. 02. 351.09.37. A crowded Italian cantina next to the Théâtre Royal de la Monnaie. Delicious pasta is served at communal tables. Open Monday to Saturday at lunchtime and on Friday from 7 pm to 10 pm.

Chez Jean, Rue des Chapeliers 6. Tel. 02. 511.98.15. An old-fashioned Brussels restaurant founded by Jean in 1931. The old iron stove belts out heat as motherly waitresses serve enormous steaks drenched in butter accompanied by large bowls of *frites*. Expect a mild rebuke if you fail to eat the lot.

Kasbah, Rue Dansaert 20. Tel. 02.502.40.26. An exotic Moroccan restaurant lit by dozens of antique lanterns. Youngish and stylish customers tuck into enormous plates of couscous and various spicy Moroccan specialities.

't Kelderke, Grand'Place 15. Tel. 02.513.73.44. An authentic Brussels brasserie located in a 17th-century vaulted cellar furnished with long wooden tables. 't Kelderke is famous for Belgian specialities such as *Carbonnades*, mussels, rabbit in Gueuze and hearty winter *stoemp*. Run by an amiable Belgian with a large moustache known to his many fans as Jef Stoemp.

I Latini, Place Sainte Catherine 2. Tel. 02.502.50.30. A bustling Italian trattoria located in a 17th-century building with ochre walls, Tuscan murals and thick pink table cloths. Charmed by the Italian brothers who run I Latini, you begin to imagine yourself somewhere in the back streets of Sienna. The hours slip by pleasantly as you dine on home-made pasta, *fritto mista* and tiramisu, rounded off perhaps with a tot of the brothers' best grappa.

Malte, Rue Berckmans 30. Tel. 02.539.10.15. Open every day from early morning until after midnight, this old Saint Gilles town house is furnished with lumpy sofas, metal chairs and improvised lamps made of wire and paper. Tattered French novels lie scattered around, walls are decorated with framed pages from old manuscripts and the staircase is lit by flickering candles. The menus include literary quotations and the table mats are decorated with faded photographs of Venice. Perhaps the food is not the best in town, but the prices are reasonable and the atmosphere on a good night is scintillating, especially on summer evenings when you can eat in a walled garden lit with strings of lights.

La Manufacture, Rue Notre-Dame du Sommeil 12. Tel. 02.502.25.25. Closed Sunday. A stylish restaurant located in an old street with an evocative name. Once a leather factory, the restaurant retains an industrial feel with its clanging metal staircases and iron columns. The French brasserie cooking is imaginative and inexpensive, and the wine list outstanding.

Les Perles de Pluies, Rue Châtelain 25. Tel. 02.649.67.23. An elegant Thai restaurant located in a handsome town house in Ixelles. The staff wear brightly-coloured Thai costumes and the rooms are decorated in the style of a Buddhist temple. It takes time to read through the menu, which describes in great detail the various styles of Thai cooking. The soup with coconut milk and lemon grass is excellent, and the staff could

not be more friendly.

Plattesteen, Rue du Marché-au-Charbon 41. Tel. 02.512.82.03. Closed on Sunday. A well-preserved old Brussels brasserie with its original mirrors, wood-panelling and neon signs. It has recently become popular with fashionable local artists and designers who clearly prefer the nostalgic patina of age to the bare minimalism of new restaurants. The perfect place for a steak or roast chicken, served with a basket of bread and a beer.

La Quincaillerie, Rue du Page 45. Tel. 02. 533.98.33. A fashionable restaurant located in a former ironware shop in Ixelles. The original wooden drawers where screws and bolts were once stored have been preserved to create a striking interior. Tables occupy alcoves, corridors and a warren of little rooms. Frantic and slightly chaotic, it nonetheless remains as popular as ever.

Rosticceria Fiorentina, Rue Archimède 43. Tel. 02.734.92.36. The real article. An old-fashioned Italian restaurant with starched white table cloths where Italians employed by the

Commission have been eating for more than thirty-five years. Run by a mother and daughter, it comforts homesick Italians with its minestrone soup, veal escalopes and osso buco. Friendly and lively at lunchtime, but rather quiet in the evenings.

Brasserie de la Roue d'Or, Rue des Chapeliers 26. Tel. 02.514.25.54. A beautiful Brussels brasserie lavishly decorated with polished wood, large mirrors and eccentric murals inspired by Magritte. Popular with local politicians, artists celebrating the sale of a painting and the occasional student whose mother has instructed him to eat a good beefsteak at least once a week. Belgians wallow in the authentic brasserie details such as baskets of bread, tubs of Cerebos salt at each table and the constant clatter of plates. The menu is strong in French and Belgian brasserie specialities such as *waterzooi*, kidneys

and lamb stew. The kitchen is open from noon until late.

Thoumieux, Rue Américaine 124. Tel. 02.538.99.09. A handsome Parisian-style brasserie near the Place du Châtelain with crisp white tablecloths and wooden partitions. The kitchen specialises in the rich cooking of the French provinces, including herring with potatoes and grilled lamb. The little touches of old France are irresistible, such as the large jar of pickled gherkins that comes with the cassoulet.

Vincent, Rue des Dominicains 8-10. Tel. 02.511.23.03. A traditional Brussels restaurant entered through the kitchen. One wall is decorated with an enormous tile picture showing two Flemish fishermen battling against a stormy sea. Vincent specialises in traditional Belgian dishes such as steaks drenched in melted butter.

Entertainment

Do not despair. Brussels is not as dull as people say. We need only pick up Wednesday's copy of *Le Soir* or read the What's On section of *The Bulletin* to find out the diversity of entertainment on offer. We will find opera, plays in half a dozen languages, modern Flemish ballet, excellent temporary exhibitions, a choice of fifty or so different films (almost all screened in the original language), guided tours of Art Nouveau architecture, Sunday concerts in the park, puppet theatres and perhaps even a circus or two.

Yet it is often difficult to track down the events. There is no notion of a theatre district in Brussels or a quarter where everyone tends to gather at night. The Grand'Place and Place Louise have a certain nocturnal energy, but other venues are scattered throughout the nineteen *communes*. A modern play might be staged in an abandoned warehouse in the canal district, or in a suburban cultural centre at the end of a long bus ride. Your taxi driver might spend twenty minutes trying to find an obscure location where a play in English is being performed. This is part of the problem in Brussels, though some people positively relish the challenge of seeking out elusive venues.

I. Bars. We have already discovered the nostalgic charm of Cirio and Mort Subite, yet there are other secret bars near Grand'Place that are worth hunting out. In searching for La Bécasse, it may help to know that the name means a woodcock, and that the narrow lane where it is located (at Rue de Tabora 11) is indicated by a copper woodcock set in the pavement. We can sit here at a heavy oak table drinking the local Gueuze out of a solid stone pitcher. Another ancient lane nearby leads to Au Bon Vieux Temps at Sint Niklaassteeg 4, a snug 17th-century Flemish tavern where locals gather to vent their spleen at the government's latest outrage. One of the weirdest bars in Brussels, if not the world, is Le Cerceuil at Rue des Harengs 10 where customers swig beer from fake skulls. The equally curious Le Greenwich at Rue des Chartreux 7 is occupied by chess players who ponder every move with the utmost gravity. Another oddity is La Fleur en Papier Doré at Rue des Alexiens 55, a dark 17th-century tavern crammed with dried flowers, faded certificates and old photographs of solemn Belgian couples. The café was for obvious reasons a favourite meeting place of Brussels Surrealists in the 1920's.

II. Theatres. Most plays in Brussels are performed in French at the Théâtre National or the Théâtre du Parc. Dutch speakers in Brussels have their own splendid 19th-century theatre, the Vlaamse Schouwburg, built in flamboyant Flemish Renaissance style but now suffering from the decline in the Flemish population. British theatre companies sometimes perform classical or modern works in this wonderful setting.

A narrow cobbled lane leads to the Toone Theatre, where puppet plays are staged in local Brussels dialect. The people of Brussels have a curious affection for puppet theatres that dates back to the 17th century. A genial cloth-capped puppet master keeps alive this old tradition in the city's last surviving puppet theatre. Many of the plays performed here were written in the 19th century by Michel de Ghelderode, whose puppet-filled study is preserved in the National Library. De Ghelderode was ambivalent about spending time in the company of Toone's painted wooden puppets with their fierce Spanish faces: 'There is something disturbing about a puppet. Every time I find myself alone among a crowd of puppets hanging on their hooks, I feel a spasm of fear, a sense of unease.'

III. Festivals. The Belgians are fond of festivals, as we know from Bruegels' paintings and Ensor's scenes of revelry such as *The Intrigue*, seen on p. 154. Hardly a week goes by without a local market in which streets are closed off and the smell of grilled sausages fills the air. We might also stumble upon one of the many medieval fêtes when sturdy citizens pull on leather breeches and lace-up bodices to recreate the spirit of Bruegel's Brussels. The official calendar begins with Carnival, though this is more of a small town festival, celebrated with great enthusiasm in southern towns such as Binche and Malmédy. The high point of the Brussels year is the Ommegang parade in late June or early July, when locals and aristocrats strut through the Grand' Place in a flamboyant reconstruction of a 1549 procession. The circus season arrives in late autumn, when two or even three circuses put on shows, usually on Place Flagey or next to the Boitsfort Hippodrome.

IV. Cinemas. Cinema has been immensely popular in Brussels since the day in 1896 when Louis and Auguste Lumière demonstrated their new *cinématographe* in the Galeries Saint Hubert. The city had dozens of cinemas in the 1920's, most of which have been demolished, though the Pathé Cinema designed in 1913 by Paul Hamesse has been rescued from ruin. The construction in 1989 of the twenty-six-screen Kinepolis complex on the edge of town forced several old cinemas to close, but others have survived by radically improving their picture quality and seating. We can catch an astonishing range of films in Brussels, almost always in the original language with French and Dutch subtitles. The most attractive cinema is the two-screen Arenberg in the Galerie Saint Hubert, not far from the plaque commemorating the Lumière brothers' visit to Brussels. The UGC De Brouckère is a stylishly converted old theatre in the Lower Town where mainstream films are shown, while Vendôme in the Upper Town tends to feature interesting foreign films. The Cinema Museum has a loyal following among young film enthusiasts who cannot resist watching The Blue Angel for the tenth time or a Chaplin silent film with live piano accompaniment.

Even if it is raining solidly, we can amuse ourselves flicking through the twenty-four or so television channels in our hotel room, perhaps settling down to watch an old episode of *Pride and Prejudice* on a Flemish channel or conceivably becoming mesmerised by the appallingly tacky game shows on Italian television. Whatever we do, we won't be bored.

Books on Brussels and Waterloo

I. Books on Brussels. Travel books on Brussels, at least in English, are rather thin on the ground. The best of the guidebooks is Antony Mason's *Brussels, Bruges, Ghent and Antwerp* (London, Cadogan, 1995), full of information, anecdotes and addresses. The *Blue Guide to Belgium and Luxembourg* (London, A&C Black, 2000) is good on art and architecture, but lacks the detailed coverage of cafés and restaurants that a Brussels visitor may require.

We can deepen our appreciation of Flemish art by buying Erwin Panofsky's two-volume *Early Netherlandish Painting* (New York, Harper & Row, 2 volumes, 1971) or Max J. Friedlaender's *From Van Eyck to Bruegel: Early Netherlandish Painting* (New York, Phaidon, 1969). Those with an interest in Magritte can choose from several books, including the *Catalogue Raisonné* by David Sylvester (Fonds Mercator, 1992). Rodin's formative years in Belgium are covered in the fascinating exhibition catalogue *Vers l'Age d'Airain:*

Rodin en Belgique (Musée Rodin, Paris, 1997). The guide to *The Royal Museums of Fine Arts of Belgium* (Brussels, Alice Editions, 1996) is an intelligently written and beautifully illustrated guide to this exceptional collection, with useful biographies of Belgian artists and clear discussions of art trends.

The secrets of the Belgian kitchen are revealed in Ruth Van Waerebeek's *Everyone Eats Well in Belgium Cookbook* (New York, Workman, 1996). This handsome chef's cookbook contains distracting anecdotes on the rituals of Belgian family lunch and the best addresses to buy Belgian chocolates. Anyone with an interest in the beers of Belgium can be guided through the brews by Michael Jackson, who has been diligently hunting out elusive Belgian ales for decades. Jackson guides the reader through hundreds of local brews in his *Great Beers of Belgium* (MMC, 1998).

I need hardly mention Charlotte Brontë's *Villette*, which is *the* Brussels novel. Her earlier, unsuccessful effort *The Professor* is also an enjoyable read. There is, regrettably, no guide to Charlotte Brontë's Brussels, but those with an interest in her stay in the city will find a good account in Elizabeth Gaskell's classic *Life of Charlotte Brontë* (Oxford University Press, 1996) or in one of several excellent recent biographies, the best being Lyndall Gordon's *Charlotte Brontë, a Passionate Life* (Vintage, 1995) and Juliet Barker's *The Brontës* (Weidenfeld and Nicolson, 1995). Those looking for lighter reading for the Eurostar might enjoy Nicolas Freeling's *You Who Know* (Warner Futura, 1994), a satisfyingly complex thriller involving Brussels Eurocrats, the IRA and a nicely sketched European background.

II. Books on Waterloo. An entire library could be filled with books on the Battle of Waterloo, fought ten miles south of Brussels in 1815. The one-day battle which claimed some forty thousand lives seized the imagination of all Europe. To novelists, it provided an irresistible backdrop, with enough heroism and tragedy to satisfy the most demanding of romantic readers. In 1816, when the fields were still littered with boots, buttons and bullets, Byron was taken on a tour by Major Lockhart Gordon. On returning to his lodgings at Rue Ducale 51, opposite the park, he sat down and drafted several stanzas to incorporate into *Childe Harold's Pilgrimage*. The poem *The Eve of Waterloo* captured the nervous excitement in Brussels on the night before the battle, in lines British schoolchildren once knew by heart.

We can dip into Thackeray's *Vanity Fair* to find a vivid description of Brussels at the time of the battle, though nothing of the battle. 'Our place is with the non-combatants,' Thackeray had the honesty to confess. Victor Hugo might have said the same, since he was only thirteen when the battle was fought, but he chose to include a gripping account of the battle in *Les Misérables*, part of which he wrote while staying at the Hôtel des Colonnes (demolished in 1962) in the village of Mont St Jean. Stendhal's *Charterhouse of Parma* also includes a Waterloo episode which captures the confusion of the battle.

Travel writers also rushed to the Low Countries immediately after the battle. Robert Hills' *Sketches in Flanders and Holland* is a fascinating book of observations and sketches done a few weeks after the Napoleonic wars ended. Southey set off soon after, while wounded soldiers were still being treated in Brussels. His *Journal of a Tour of the Netherlands in the Autumn of 1815* describes a walk across the battlefield and a night spent in an inn with bullet holes in the roof. A few months later, Henry Smithers made a similar tour, putting his impressions down in *Observations made during a residence in Brussels and several Tours through the Netherlands*, though his account lacks the immediacy of Southey and Hills.

For those who want to tramp across the battlefield, guidebook in hand, David Howarth is the ideal companion. His *Waterloo* (Pitcairn Pictorials, 1990) is an excellent little guide that surveys the battlefield from five different viewpoints, but not, quite rightly, from the top of the Lion Mound, which was not built at the time. His *A Near Run Thing* (Windrush Press, 1997) provides a longer account of the battle.

III. Where to find books. Brussels has more English bookshops than the average British town and each one has its merits. Waterstone's at Boulevard Adolphe Max 71-75 is the oldest and largest. Well stocked with books and magazines, it is often impossibly crowded with browsers on Saturday afternoons. The Sterling Bookshop at Rue du Fossé-aux-Loups 38 is a smaller, more manageable shop with a good children's section. The Strathmore Bookshop at Rue Saint Lambert 110 offers suburban readers a good selection of English books, while The Reading Room at Avenue Georges Henri 503 is a helpful little bookshop with a good choice of contemporary fiction. For second-hand art books, we should visit the exceptional Posada at Rue de la Madeleine 29. We might also find the odd book of interest in the Book Market at No. 47 in the same street. The vast Slegde bookshop at Rue des Grands Carmes 17 has some serious academic books reduced to a fraction of their original price, along with a large collection of second-hand British and American novels.

Acknowledgements

I would like to thank the staff at the Musée de l'Armée archives, the Bibliothèque Royale Albert Ier and the Musées des Beaux-Arts for their help in locating illustrations. I am also grateful to Ann Dinsdale of the Brontë Society for her efforts in finding a photograph of the Pensionnat Heger and Burgomaster Yves de Jonghe d'Artdoye for granting permission to photograph funerary memorials in Ixelles cemetery.

Several colleagues on *The Bulletin* have been invaluable sources of information on Brussels, in particular Cleveland Moffeett, Brigid Grauman, P. L. Smith and Lisa Johnson. Finally, I would like to thank Alexander Fyjis-Walker for taking up my suggestion of a guidebook on Brussels and for providing numerous insights and improvements.

Brussels, Spring 2003

List of illustrations

CREDITS

Index

Streets (including rues, avenues, chaussées, places, portes, squares, parvis, impasses, ruelles, chemins) are listed by name, and where this is a person, by surname (eg. Rue Felix Delhasse is under D).

Houses, palaces, hôtels particuliers etc. (including houses called 'Maison') are listed under their name, as are commercial hotels that are of historical interest only.

The following are listed under general headings: bars and cafés (some of which are both); beers; churches and other religious buildings; restaurants; foods, including cuisines and particular dishes; *galeries*; hotels; museums and galleries; monuments; parks; theatres and cinemas; railway stations; metro stops; tram stops; wars. Painters known as 'the Master of' are under Master.

Figures in **bold** refer to a principal entry. Figures in *italic* refer to illustrations.

PALLAS GUIDES

Amsterdam for Pleasure
Derek Blyth

Ideally you would take Derek Blyth with you to Amsterdam,
but *Amsterdam Explored* is almost as good
The Times

One quickly develops enormous respect for his knowledge
The Low Countries Yearbook

Superbly informative
RA Magazine

Excellent
Daily Mail

Derek Blyth guides us expertly
TLS

316 pp including 16 pp colour, 50 b/w illustrations, maps, practical information. Second edition ISBN 1 873429 47 9 £14.99

PALLAS GUIDES

Flemish Cities Explored
Bruges, Ghent, Antwerp, Mechelen, Leuven and Ostend
Derek Blyth

The best of all cultural travel guides *The Times*

The essential companion
Sunday Correspondent

No one should travel to Bruges without a copy
Val Hennessey, Daily Mail

An ideal travelling companion for the serious art lover
Geographical

A pocket-sized friend
The Lady

320 pp including 50 plates, and 7 maps, practical information. Fourth revised edition   ISBN 1 873429 30 4   £12.95

PALLAS GUIDES

Venice for Pleasure
J. G. Links

Not only the best guide-book to that city ever written, but the best
guide-book to *any* city ever written
Bernard Levin, The Times

One of the most delightful and original guides ever
Jan Morris

The world's best guide book *William Boyd, The Spectator*

One of those miraculous books that gets passed by hand,
pressed urgently on friends
Sean French, New Statesman

If there is a cult guide book, this is it *The Good Book Guide*

J. G. Links' little charmer *The Lady*

311 pp including 55 illustrations, 36 pages colour plates, and 5 maps   Seventh revised edition ISBN 1 873429 40 1   £14.99

PALLAS GUIDES

Other books on Venice

The Stones of Venice
John Ruskin

One of the greatest works of architectural history, replete with passion and learning. Edited and abridged by J. G. Links, and extensively illustrated with Ruskin's own drawings.
272 pp illustrated with diagrams and sketches, introduction, index ISBN 1 873429 45 2   £12.99

Effie in Venice
Edited by Mary Lutyens

The letters home of Effie, Ruskin's vivacious and energetic young wife, and a wonderful picture of Venice in the mid-nineteenth century. Illustrated.
352 pp including 16 pp plates Bibliography, notes, index ISBN 1 873429 33 9   £12.99

Timeless Venice
Mark Robinson and Hilary Sadler

A pathbreaking exploration of Venice via de' Barbari's monumental map of 1500. CD-ROM and book.
CD-ROM and 80 pp book Bibliography, notes, index ISBN 1 873429 98 3   £19.99

PALLAS GUIDES

Madrid for Pleasure
Michael Jacobs

One of the best current foreign writers on Spain
Time Out

Jacobs is an engaging, wonderfully informative and ever-surprising companion. His eye is clear, except on mornings after, his style is sceptical and one feels throughout that what he writes is true
Jan Morris

He has a gift for finding exotic corners in a familiar city and of resuscitating the forgotten with colourful intensity *Paul Preston, TLS*

The George Borrow of the High Speed Train era
ABC Madrid

A zestful, beautifully fluent text *Lookout*

Without peer *The Bookseller*

286 pp including 64 pages colour, 50 b/w illustrations, 7 maps   Third revised edition ISBN 1 873429 24 X   £14.99

PALLAS GUIDES

Other books by Michael Jacobs

Andalucía
A Pallas Guide

The best one-volume introduction to the region *Rough Guide*
Take no other *Cosmopolitan*
464 pp including colour plates, illustrations and maps. Practical information and full index ISBN 1 873429 43 6   £15.95

The Road to Santiago
A Pallas Passion Guide

Packed with historical as well as architectural goodness *The Guardian*
280 pp including 90 pp plates, maps and diagrams   Practical information, full index ISBN 1 873429 42 8   £12.95

In the Glow of the Phantom Palace
A Pallas Edition

It justifies travel writing. *Felipe Fernández Armesto, TLS*
224 pp including illustrations and maps. ISBN 1 873429 36 3   £12.99

This is a Pallas for Pleasure guide book, published by Pallas Athene.
To find out more about other books in this series,
and about our other books, please or write to us at
59 Linden Gardens, London W2 4HJ
or visit
WWW.PALLASATHENE.CO.UK

Series editor: Alexander Fyjis-Walker
Series design consultant: James Sutton
Editorial assistants: Jenny Wilson, Ava Li, Della Tsiftsopolou
Maps by Ted Hammond

Special thanks go to Polly Vaughan Hudson for a lot of walking, and to
Eleanor Rogers, without whom the walking would not have been possible; and particularly,
as always, to Derek, most understanding and patient of authors

Set in Monotype Baskerville

Printed in China for
Pallas Athene
59 Linden Gardens
London W2 4HJ

British Library Cataloguing
in Publication Data
A catalogue record for this book
is available from the British Library

ISBN I 873429 I4 2

First published 2003